THE
PLANT
HUNTERS

THE
PLANT
HUNTERS

B. J. Healey

Charles Scribner's Sons New York

Library of Congress Cataloging in Publication Data

Healey, B. J.
    The plant hunters.
    Includes bibliographical references and index.
    1. Plant collectors—Biography. 2. Plant intro-
duction—History. I. Title.
QK26.H37   581'.092'2 [B]   74-32295
ISBN 0-684-14214-7

1 3 5 7 9 11 13 15 17 19 C/C 20 18 16 14 12 10 8 6 4 2

Printed in the United States of America

With grateful thanks to the many people who have so generously given me their time and assistance; Miss Mea Allan, author of *The Trades-cants; Their Plants, Gardens, and Museum, 1570–1662*, for permission to quote her reconstruction of John Tradescant's Mediterranean voyage; Professor Sergei Konovalov, University of Oxford, for permission to quote from his transcription of Tradescant's Russian Journal; Mr. Charles Niles, Department of Special Collections, Boston University Library, for historical and bibliographical information; Mr. David Philcox, M.Sc., of the Royal Botanic Gardens, Kew, for information and advice; the librarians and staffs of the Ashmolean Museum, Oxford, the British Museum Department of Natural History, the Lindley Library of the Royal Horticultural Society, and the library of the Wellcome Institute of the History of Medicine; my old friend J. S. Vinden for advice and information; and not least my wife for her patient typing and checking.

Contents

vii

THE
PLANT
HUNTERS

(1)

Adam, King Cyrus,
John Parkinson and Others

We have it on respectable authority that God Almighty first planted a garden, and if we are to believe the Gravedigger in Hamlet "There is no ancient gentlemen but gardeners, ditchers and grave makers; they hold up Adam's profession." Gardeners, we know, are gentlemen and there is no good reason why ditchers and gravediggers should not be too; but whether Adam was the first one is rather more open to doubt. According to the Talmud he only remained in the Garden of Eden for twelve hours—the sixth hour he slept and Eve was created, the seventh he married the woman, the tenth he fell, and the twelfth hour he was cast out—while it is at least possible that the Eden story was grafted on to a still older legend of the Garden of the Hesperides.

There was a seventeenth-century Swedish professor who proved, to his own if nobody else's satisfaction, that Adam's garden was situated in Sweden; while that of the Hesperides, or The Daughters of Evening, lay somewhere to the west of Greece in the Atlas Mountains. Here the nymphs Hesperis, Aegle, and Erytheia tended the tree of golden apples which had been presented by Gaea, the Earth Goddess, to their mother Hera when she married Zeus; and, as the Tree in Eden was bound up with a serpent, so this was guarded by the ever wakeful hundred-headed dragon Ladon. The similarities and the symbolism of the apple—or perhaps more correctly the forbidden fruit since some later scholars have suggested that the Apples of the Hesperides were more probably oranges[1]— are obvious in both stories, while the terms "Eden" and "Paradise" are curious and interesting examples of how fresh meanings become attached to words over the ages. The first in its original form meant simply delight or happiness; and the Greek *paradeisos*, which we now generally take for "Heaven," then signified

---

[1] In this connection it is interesting to note that in his monumental work *Paradisi in Sole Paradisus Terrestris*, of 1629, John Parkinson describes and illustrates the orange along with apples and actually calls it *Malus aranilia*.

1

only the parks and pleasure grounds of the Persian kings, the great gardeners of their age.

Except that these legends suggest the immense antiquity and symbolic importance of gardening we know nothing factual about its beginnings. All we can say is that when the nomadic families paused in their wanderings and took to the cultivation of land and the deliberate collection of plants and seed they were bringing in the first faint dawn of civilization; and, so far from Adam, it seems more likely that long before the early societies of the Eastern Mediterranean, in which the spirits of the earth and fertility were almost exclusively regarded as female, the primal gardeners and plant collectors were women. The men would have been busy with the hunt or with fighting—and perhaps equally busy bragging about it—and it was most probably these incredibly remote ancestresses of all gardeners who made the first tentative discoveries that the grain of certain grasses was both edible and satisfying, that the leaves of other plants had pleasant flavors; and, much later still, that many more possessed healing and medicinal powers.

This is, of course, an extreme generalization. The process must have been sporadic, in its early stages almost entirely accidental, and in some ages tied up with primitive magic and religion, traces of which still exist clinging to some plants. We do not know. Archaeologists can tell us that after the simple digging stick the spade and hoe came into use some time between 7,000 and 4,000 B.C. and that the first plow was probably invented before 2,000, but there is little they can tell us about the plants themselves. We have to wait for the appearance of permanent records, both written and pictorial, before we get on to more solid ground.

Then we find, for instance, that an Egyptian papyrus dated eighteen centuries before Christ mentions colchicums and squills as being used in medicine. Others record that the ancient Pharaohs grew anemones, narcissi, and lilies, while flax was a staple crop; and in 1495 B.C. Queen Hatshepsut organized an expedition from Thebes to Punt—probably present day Somalia—to bring back myrrh trees. Sixteen hundred years before Christ again we find iris, crocus, and the Madonna lily clearly recognizable in the incomparable wall paintings of the early Cretan civilization; and there is little doubt that at the same time gardening and the systematic collection of plants were at an advanced stage in the far away countries of the East.

Plant hunting is as ancient as gardening itself; and, often under the patronage of kings, churchmen, and learned societies, the plant hunters have been all sorts and conditions of men. Priests and soldiers, explorers, sailors, scientists, and gardeners; adventurers and sometimes eccentrics, wealthy and far otherwise—Sir Joseph Banks who equipped a great expedition at a personal cost of £10,000; John Bartram, a Quaker farmer of Philadelphia, who left his farm in charge of a hired hand in order to learn Latin, study botany, and go off himself; F. N. Meyer, a Dutchman, who collected for the United States government and went everywhere on foot, on one incredible journey alone covering more than 1,800 miles; and many more. Their letters, diaries and books are some of the best records of exploration and adventure we have; their discoveries and introductions, from Oriental and American lilies to colorful Asiatic primulas, the fabulous blue poppies of the Himalayas, and countless others, are familiar to every gardener, but the men themselves are almost unknown.[2]

That is what this book is about. Plants, and men, and even books themselves; sometimes their peculiarities and occasionally the mysteries surrounding them. A frankly gossipy and discursive account designed for that unsung and dispraised season of the gardener's year when you can afford to let the garden look after itself for a few months, the winter. When darkness and the weather conspire to give you all the excuse you need for lazy reading and a conscienceless release from the direful necessity of actually going out and doing something; when you can afford to let your mind wander over an alpine meadow sheeted with crocus, a Tibetan valley sky blue with meconopsis, or a rhododendron forest in the Himalayan foothills. I have a great deal of sympathy with the armchair gardener as being one myself by nature and inclination, so it is the armchair gardener to whom this book is addressed; and of course any others who might care to read it.

[2] Their discoveries can often be recognized by the second word of a plant's specific name—*Farreri, Davidii, Douglasii*—this ending in *i* or *ii* where a man is concerned, and *ae* or *iae* for a woman. Sometimes, too, the discoverers are commemorated by their names being given to an entire genus: as *Tradescantia, Clarkia, Lewisia*, etc. See B. J. Healey, *A Gardener's Guide to Plant Names* (New York: Scribners, 1972).

Let us start by taking a brief look at ancient history . . .

Babylon now is no more than an obscure halt on a railway line in Iraq; an end foretold in the Bible where we read, "And a mighty angel took up a stone like a great millstone and cast it into the sea, saying, Thus with violence shall that great city be thrown down, and shall be found no more at all." All that is left of the Hanging Gardens are the ruins of the terraces on which they are supposed to have been set, but in their day they were one of the Seven Wonders of the Ancient World. They are said to have been built and planted by Nebuchadrezzar for his wife's pleasure some time about 570 B.C.; or according to another and probably incorrect account created by the Persian King Cyrus—who conquered Nebuchadrezzar—to satisfy a favorite courtesan who was pining for the hill tops and trees and flowers of her native Persia. They are later by a thousand years than the gardens and parks depicted in the wall paintings of Ancient Crete but in them, and through King Cyrus, we have at least a very early hint of trees and plants being collected and planted by design purely for pleasure.

Although there have been many attempts at pictorial reconstruction nobody really knows what the Gardens looked like but Sir Thomas Browne—the respected physician of Norwich, as learned as he was rambling, who wrote *The Religio Medici* and a number of other papers between that in 1635 and his death in 1682—clearly points to Cyrus as one of the earliest recorded collectors. In *The Garden of Cyrus*[3], where the old doctor examines very nearly everything under the sun from the formation of the Roman battalions to whether Noah planted the first vineyards, and describes very acutely the anatomy of birds and insects and the germination of seeds, he says:

> The *Persian* Gallants who destroyed this Monarchy maintained their Botanicall bravery. Unto whom we owe the very name of Paradise: wherewith we meet not in Scripture before the time of *Solomon*, and conceived originally *Persian*. The word for that disputed garden, expressing in the Hebrew no more than a field enclosed . . .

[3] Its full title is *The Garden of Cyrus; or the Quincunciall, Lozenge, or Network Plantations of the Ancients, Artificially, Naturally, Mystically Considered.* 1658.

Cyrus the Elder brought up in woods and mountains, when time and power enabled, pursued the dictate of his education and brought the treasures of the field into rule and circumscription. So nobly beautifying the Hanging Gardens of *Babylon* that he was also thought to be the authour thereof . . . A person of high spirit and honour, naturally a King . . . Not only a Lord of Gardens, but a manuall planter thereof: disposing his trees like his armies in regular ordination. So that while old *Laertes* hath found a name in Homer for pruning hedges, and clearing away thorns and briars; while King Attalus lives for his poysonous plantations of Aconites, Henbane, Hellebore and plants hardly admitted within the walls of Paradise; While many of the ancients do poorly live in the single names of Vegetables; All stories do look upon *Cyrus* as the splendid and regular planter.

Laertes, who renounced the throne of Ithaca to cultivate his plot—which seems to have been fairly neglected—is one of the gardeners mentioned in the *Odyssey* along with Alcinous who appears to have enjoyed something like four acres on what is now the island of Corfu. Attalus must have been one of the much later Attalid dynasty who held Pergamum in Northwest Asia Minor during the third and second centuries B.C. and which, in spite of those "plants hardly admitted within the walls of Paradise," was a great and spectacular city; an important center of literary studies with a library which was said to rival that of Alexandria, and where the use of parchment for writing was first developed on a large scale.[4]

The good old doctor seems to have made a curious mistake there, all the more strange as being one of the most learned men of his day and a physician himself. Pergamum lay about fifty miles from Izmir in what is now Anatolian Turkey; the remains of a temple of Aesculapius still stand here and since that is a Latinized form of the Greek Asclepius, god of medicine, it seems fairly certain that Sir Thomas Browne's "poysonous plantations" were in fact a physic or medical garden, with plants collected and cultivated by the order of King Attalus. Medicine was already highly advanced and temples dedicated to Asclepius in one form or another—son of Apollo, who ages before had been taught the

---

[4] Our word "parchment" is ultimately derived from "Pergamum."

healing and curative powers of certain plants by Chiron the Centaur—
were to be found all over the Graeco-Roman world. They were, in a
sense, the district hospitals and the priests who tended these gardens
were the doctors of their day.

We really begin to discover something about plants themselves, and
about the actual practice of gardening at the time when Alexander the
Great was busily conquering the known world in the third century B.C.
Then Theophrastus (371–287 B.C.), who has since been called the
"Father of Botany" and who was a pupil, friend, and successor to
Aristotle, among many other works wrote the first systematic studies in
Historia Plantarum, An Enquiry into Plants, and *De Causis Plantarum*,
The Growth of Plants; and it appears that he used a great deal of
information, almost certainly including specimens, brought back from
Alexander's campaigns by the learned men who travelled with the
Macedonian armies. We learn also from his will that he had in Athens
what might now be called a botanic garden. A very charming will it is,
too; for when he died at the fine old age of eighty-six he left this garden
to his friends for their pleasure and study, appointed a custodian to look
after it, and directed that his slaves should be given their freedom after
a reasonable period of faithful and satisfactory service.

Among many other subjects Theophrastus describes the original form
of carnation, *Dianthus caryophyllus*, crocuses, anemones, gladioli, grape
hyacinths, narcissi, ranunculi, scillas, etc. It is interesting to note, by the
way, that bulbs figure largely in these early lists since most of them
come from areas associated with hot dry summers[5]—typically the
Mediterranean regions—and because the bulb itself is so easily and
safely transportable; a formation which might have been expressly
designed by nature to withstand the slow and arduous journeys of those
days. But to come back to Theophrastus, he describes also several
varieties of rose; distinguishing the different flower formations, from five
to twelve, twenty, or a hundred petals, details their habit of growth and
gives instructions for pruning. Rather curiously these were all white or
pink; apparently red and yellow roses had not yet appeared.

[5] Generally in the northern hemisphere between latitudes 30° to 50°, which, besides
the Mediterranean, includes large tracts of the United States and south and southeastern
Russia. Some also have come from South America and South Africa, but the Himalayas,
China, and Japan have provided few except lilies.

During the next three or four hundred years several lesser works appeared and plants were still being collected. Some, including the mulberry and peach, were probably brought by way of Persia along the great Silk Road from the ancient horticulture of China which had been developing separately for centuries and was only to be fully explored by the plant hunters of our own more recent centuries. By early Christian times the Romans were carrying actual gardening far beyond anything attempted by the Greeks. There are innumerable descriptions of Roman gardens, including that of Pliny the Younger in Tuscany. This is said to have been almost an extension of the villa itself, reached through a terrace and portico adorned by statuary, with much box pruned into decorative shapes, a marble summer house, a fountain, sitting out places, and plane trees for shade. In short very like many of the great Italian gardens today.

Which brings us naturally to Pliny the Elder. There is no record that Gaius Plinius Secundus was a collector himself; among all his other multifarious activities he could scarcely have found the time. But just as someone has said that it is impossible to discuss the universe without sooner or later bringing in the name of God so, on a rather smaller scale, it appears to be difficult to write about plants and plant collecting without introducing Pliny the Naturalist. He was a man of insatiable curiosity and tireless industry, and the thirty-seven books of his *Historia Naturalis*—although a Roman book might be little more than what we should call a long chapter today—are an extraordinary hotch-potch of rather dry cataloguing, acute observation and comment, information about the art, science and manners of his period, and some surprisingly credulous but nevertheless entertaining anecdotes.

It was, in its way, the first encyclopedia; containing sections on the physics of the universe, the geography of Europe, Asia, and Africa, the physiology of man, eight books on botany and descriptions of plants with eight more on their medicinal properties, others on metallurgy and minerals, and for good measure a digression on the methods and history of art. But for the gardener its comparatively small interest lies in its information on Roman gardening including the smell of good ground, in showing how greatly the number and variety of plants had increased since the time of Theophrastus, in listing the red rose for the first time—one wonders whether that had reached Rome by way of Persia from the East—and in describing the healing qualities of plants, as for instance that "greene Onions applied with vinegre to the place bitten with a mad dog . . . in three days cureth the hurt without danger . . ."

The *Natural History* is hardly a work one can read continuously, but wherever you dip into it you are almost certain to come across some curious passage, like Pliny's story of the dolphin which "loved wondrous well a certain boy a poore mans son" and used to carry him on its back every day to school in Puteoli but which, when the boy died of some illness, itself pined away "untill for very griefe & sorrow he also was found dead upon the shore." Or his praise of elephants in that they "embrace goodness, honestie, prudence, and equitie (rare qualities I may tel you to be found in men)." And his comment on radishes, as they "breed wind wonderful much . . . A base and homely meat therefore it is, and not for a gentleman's table . . ." [6]

All this of course has nothing whatever to do with plant hunting, but having started on Pliny we must do him justice. He was a good, sturdy, old-fashioned Roman with an intense dislike of the Greeks, and after a lifetime of service to Rome and hard work—in which besides the *Historia Naturalis* he contrived to dash off twenty more books on the German wars, thirty-one on the "Recent History of Rome," and others, which are lost, on military science, oratory, and grammar—he died in the great eruption of Vesuvius when Pompeii and Herculaneum were destroyed in 79 A.D. His nephew, Pliny the Younger, in a letter to Tacitus, describes how his uncle, Pliny the Elder, then being in command of a Roman fleet stationed at Misenum perceived a column of smoke rising above the mountains and at once detached a light, fast ship to take him round to investigate. Standing close in, under the hail of stones and ash which was then burying Pompeii, for several hours he dictated his observations to his secretaries. Not content with this however the next day he went ashore, having a pillow tied over his head for protection, and there in the darkness and terror, amid the violent concussions with the hail of ash falling thicker than ever, he was asphixiated by the poisonous gasses rolling down from the volcano. He

[6] From Philemon Holland's translation. 1601.

was then only fifty-five or six; he died of pure scientific curiosity, and somehow that pillow tied above his head gives it the final touch of grotesque improbability.

About the same time, and during the reign of Nero, another profoundly learned man with a truly magnificent name, Pedanios Dioscorides (or Dioscurides), was writing a *Materia Medica*, or herbal; in only five books this time. As a Greek physician who served as a doctor on campaign with the Roman Army he must have had a great deal of experience, and he described the medicinal properties of now some six hundred plants. This work was the first of its kind in Europe, and was to become easily the most important, being translated from the original Greek into nearly all of the Mediterranean languages, and surviving for more than twelve centuries as the chief source of pharmaceutical knowledge.

It was the work on which most later herbals from the eleventh to the sixteenth century were to be based, and in the sense that much of the learning from these very popular books actually passed into and augmented the general country love of herbal cures its influence may have extended even for several hundred years more. It is perfectly possible that our own great-grandmothers were using recipes and simples ultimately traceable to Dioscorides. There were even beautifully illustrated versions, and one miniature from the early thirteenth-century Arabic translation can still be seen, in the Freer Gallery of Art, Washington, which depicts a man shouting in horror on being bitten by a mad dog. Its careful detail shows the animal's lolling tongue which was supposed to be an infallible sign of the dreaded rabies.

But after Dioscorides and then the decline of the Roman Empire came the long night of the Dark Ages. No doubt in the Far East horticulture was still developing, and in Persia much of the classical tradition survived for a time, but in Europe knowledge, learning, and the love of plants prudently retired to the safety of the monasteries until the first stirrings of the Renaissance, though even there much of it was lost, forgotten, or became ossified.

Since we are now well into a second Dark Age it is difficult to imagine the tremendous surge of vitality, optimism, and curiosity which

came with the Renaissance, or was the Renaissance, in Europe. Stirring
first about the beginning of the twelfth century, it took over men's
minds and spirits in much the same way that civilization seems to have
appeared relatively suddenly in Egypt, Mesopotamia, and the Indus
Valley about the year three thousand B.C. Nobody has ever quite
satisfactorily explained how or why it happened, but for the first time
man saw himself as the measure of all things, created in God's image.
The earth was good and given to him for his own; it was, in a way, the
rediscovery of Eden. It was sometimes a brutal age, often harsh and
cruel, but it suffered none of the fashionable, pessimistic preoccupations
of our own day, and men were again looking and moving outward,
adventuring both intellectually and physically, expecting wonders and
finding them.

We have a fair amount of information about mediaeval plants from
the new herbals which were appearing and gardens are again depicted
in painting—in a small panel by a Master of the Upper Rhine in the
Städelsches Kunstinstitut, Frankfort-on-Main, for instance, there is an
appealingly innocent picture of the Garden of Paradise which shows
eighteen different kinds of flower in bloom at the same time—and in the
exquisite miniature illustrations to the various Books of Hours and
Calendars which were then being produced. But gardens are still very
much the private pleasure of princes and nobles, who are shown richly
dressed and sitting about singing and playing musical instruments and
making love, while only occasionally can you see a gardener himself at
work in much more sober clothes.

These were mostly on the Continent. No similar pictures of gardens
in Britain exist, and it is generally thought that they were not nearly so
advanced as those in Germany, France, and Italy. The new style seems
to have spread to England roughly at the time of Henry VIII's meeting
with Francis I at the Field of the Cloth of Gold in 1520, and Cardinal
Wolsey laid out the first English pleasure garden on a magnificent scale
at Hampton Court, which later the King himself appropriated. It was a
dangerous amusement in those days to set yourself up in a state greater
than your master's. Nevertheless the Tudor nobility took up the fashion;
great gardens began to be planned, and garden design, the craft of

horticulture, and the science of botany started to develop at a phenomenal rate. For centuries the house—or monastery—had surrounded the garden to keep it safe; now the garden surrounded the house. It was the Tudor gentry who, from this, first gave the impetus to systematic plant hunting by sending out their own gardeners.

By the early sixteenth century, European sailors and soldiers were bringing fresh and strange plants from the exciting new countries of eastern North America, South America, and Mexico; and far to the east they were discovering other civilizations that had already developed their own horticulture.

It would be tedious to list all of the introductions in their correct order, even if it were possible to trace many of them now, but there were bulbs in plenty—*Fritillaria imperialis*, the crown imperial, irises, martagon lilies, Persian ranunculus, and tulips—and of course the tomato, then called the "love apple." Of this John Parkinson, whom we shall meet later, says in 1629 "They grow naturally in the hot Countries of Barbary and Ethiopia; yet some report them to be brought from Peru, a province of the West Indies. Wee only have them for curiosity in our gardens, and for the amorous aspect or beauty of the fruit." On which it is interesting to notice that decorative tomatoes are again appearing on seedsmen's lists: red and yellow striped, cherry tomatoes which bear small fruits in long sprays, and others.

Our ever popular though incorrectly named African and French marigolds are both supposed to have been brought back by the Spanish armies from the West, though here again Parkinson reports, "They grow naturally in Africa, and especially in the parts about Tunis and where old Carthage stood, from whence long agoe they were brought into Europe . . . but the kind with hollow leaved flowers, as Fabius Columna setteth it down, is accounted to come from Mexico in America." [7] There is no doubt however that the Spanish did introduce the potato from Peru some time about 1530, and that it was being grown in large quantities as a market crop around Seville by 1570, nor that a Spanish physician sent by Philip II of Spain to Mexico brought

[7] The species have now become inextricably hybridized, but this would probably be *Tagetes lucida.*

An outdoor scene with a mad dog biting a man; an illustration from a richly decorated 12th century Arabic translation of Dioscorides' *De Materia Medica*. Courtesy of the Smithsonian Institution, Freer Gallery of Art, Washington, D.C.

Opposite: The title page to John Parkinson's *Paradisi in Sole Paradisus Terrestris*. From the original in the Wellcome Library, by courtesy of the Trustees, The Wellcome Institute for the History of Medicine, London.

PARADISI IN SOLE
Paradisus Terrestris.
or
A Garden of all sorts of pleasant ffowers which our
English ayre will permitt to be noursed vp:
with
A Kitchen garden of all manner of herbes, rootes, & fruites,
for meate or sause vsed with vs:
and
An Orchard of all sorte of fruitbearing Trees
and shrubbes fit for our Land
together
With the right ordering planting & preseruing
of them and their vses & vertues
Collected by John Parkinson
Apothecary of London
1629

Qui veut parangonner l'artifice a Nature,
Et nos Parcs à l'Eden: indiscret il mesure.

Le pas de l'elephant par le pas du ciron,
Et de l'Aigle le vol par cil du moucheron.

back with him one of the most gorgeous of all exotic beauties—which grew wild there and was said to have almost magical medicinal properties—what is now called *Tigridia pavonia*.[8]

One of the most extraordinary facets of plant collecting—and speculative mania—was the great tulip madness that swept Holland in 1634. The tulip had been introduced from Turkey, where it was first noticed and described by Augenius Busbequis, ambassador of the Emperor Ferdinand II in the second half of the sixteenth century; by 1559 it was recorded as growing in Germany, was first illustrated by the Swiss botanist Gessner in 1561, and Carolus Clusius, professor of Botany at Leyden, was cultivating it in 1571. By the early sixteen hundreds the Haarlem growers had already built up a flourishing trade and were offering new and apparently rare colors. The blooms were extremely fashionable and extremely costly, especially the so-called broken or bizarre types, and it was probably these which touched off the craze. People started to gamble in the bulbs.

Sometimes it was the hope that a yet unflowered bulb would throw up an even more valuable variety, or more often an innocent belief that existing varieties would retain their rarity and value as they increased; but insane prices were paid for single bulbs. There are records of a miller who traded his mill for one, and more of a man who sold a working brewery for another. One bulb of the much prized "Semper Augustus" realized five thousand florins with a carriage and pair thrown in; and one of "Viceroy" was bartered for two loads of wheat, four of rye, four oxen, eight pigs, twelve sheep, two hogsheads of wine, four barrels of beer and two of butter, one thousand pounds of cheese, a bed, a suit of clothes, and a silver beaker.

[8] It is surprising that *Tigridia pavonia* is not seen more often in gardens. Eye-catching alike in the curious three-petalled shape of its large flowers and their splendid coloring—sometimes white but more often deep yellow to orange and pinkish crimson to mauve, with blotched and spotted central segments—it is no more difficult to grow than gladiolus, and though individual blooms will only last for one day, each spathe usually carries six or more which open in succession. It is more than worth its garden space, and will flourish in any warm and sunny spot where it can be given plenty of moisture while growing. In favored localities it will actually overwinter in the ground but normally it should be lifted after flowering and stored in dry peat or sand. A small corm, and usually on offer by most good bulbsmen, it needs planting in clumps of twenty-five or more to obtain the best effect.

Clubs or "Collegiums" sprang up in most of the main cities and sales were conducted by complex rules, generally at an inn or tavern, with purchaser and vendor, often an excited audience and an arbitrator to see fair play; the final price agreed on always included a supplement for wine money. At the height of the craze, bulbs were sold by weight like precious metals—the standard being the "azen" which was less than a grain—or it was possible even to speculate on margins, like playing the stock market. You would make an engagement for a bulb against planting time; if by then its value had risen the dealer would pay you the difference above your original offer, if it had fallen you paid him—and in either case he retained the bulb. Such deals were said to have often involved entirely non-existent bulbs, and the chances of fraud were only too obvious.

One of the oddest chapters in the history of gardening, the bulb craze lasted for just about three years, and when the market finally collapsed in 1637 it left a trail of disaster: bankruptcy, thousands of small speculators ruined, a government unable to control the financial repercussions, and general disillusionment. With their good sound common sense the Dutch order the tulip industry better now. They produce upwards of four billion bulbs annually and their bulb markets and tulip fields are among Holland's main tourist attractions.

I am always cautious about quoting figures, since by looking somewhere else you can often find a different set, but these following may be taken as a fair guide. In his own day Dioscorides listed about 600 plants. By the time of Charlemagne (742–814) from perhaps rather dubious monastic records, the number of plants generally in cultivation appears to have fallen as low as 40. Over the next seven centuries to 1441 the number rose only to 97, as listed in an early manuscript work in English on gardening. John Gerard's well-known *Herball* which was published in 1597, and which incidentally he lifted more or less wholesale from the slightly earlier Belgian botanical writer Rembert Dodaens—though to be sure he did add many of his own observations, illustrations and descriptions of new plants in Britain—describes a great many more.[9] Then in 1629, with his *Paradisi in Sole Paradisus Terrestris*,

[9] There had been numerous herbals published in England—the *Grete Herball* in 1526,

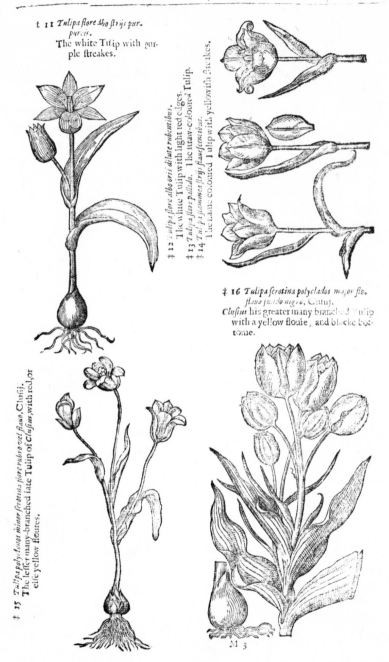

‡ 11 *Tulipa flore albo ftrijs purpureis.*
The white Tulip with purple ftreakes.

‡ 12 *Tulipa flore albo oris dilute rubentibus.*
The white Tulip with light red edges.
‡ 13 *Tulipa flore pallido.* The ftraw-coloured Tulip.
‡ 14 *Tulip. filamentis ftrijs flaue femitris.*
The ftraw coloured Tulip with yellowifh ftreakes.

‡ 16 *Tulipa ferotina polyclados major flo. flauo patido nigro,* Clufij.
Clufius his greater many branched Tulip
with a yellow floure, and blacke bottome.

‡ 15 *Tulipa polyclonos minor ferotina flore rubro vel flauo,* Clufij.
The leffer many-branched late Tulip of *Clufius,* with red, or elfe yellow floures.

M 3

An illustration from John Gerard's *Herbal.* From the original in
the Wellcome Library, by courtesy of the Trustees, The Wellcome Institute for the History of Medicine, London.

An illustration from a 15th century manuscript herbal; a mandrake uprooted by a dog. From the original in the Wellcome Library, by courtesy of the Trustees, The Wellcome Institute for the History of Medicine, London.

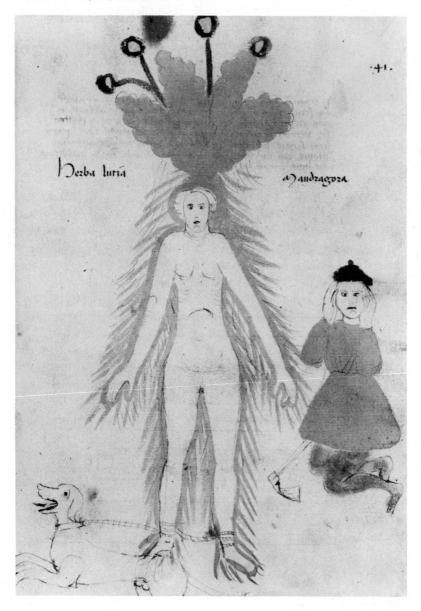

John Parkinson gives us a full 1,000. Nothing could better illustrate the sudden explosion of interest and discovery. In nearly seven centuries only from 40 to 97; and then in slightly less than two hundred years more from 97 to 1,000.

The *Paradisus* has been described as the most lovable of all gardening books and it was certainly the first of them in our modern sense, giving advice on how to grow the rare and unusual plants then coming into Britain, and laying emphasis as never before on flowers to be admired for beauty rather than cultivated only for their use in medicine. It is a large book of 612 quarto pages with 110 full-page woodcut illustrations, and one of the most attractive title pages in existence. The main title is a seventeenth-century pun on Parkinson's own name, "A Park in the Sun," and it goes on, "Or A Garden of all sorts of pleasant flowers which our English ayre will permit to be noursed up: with A kitchen garden of all manner of herbs, roots & fruits for meate or sauce used with us, and An Orchard of all sorts of fruit bearing Trees and Shrubs fit for our land together With the right orderinge planting & preserving of them and their uses & vertues. Collected by John Parkinson, Apothecary of London."

Naturally enough the first block is a view of the Garden of Eden with trees and flowers and birds, a stream running through the whole, and no sign of the serpent yet, although Adam has already discovered the sartorial value of a well-placed leaf. He appears to be busy pruning, while Eve is picking strawberries; the apple tree is well in the center rather curiously along with what one takes to be date and banana palms, a cactus which is probably prickly pear, and a flourishing pineapple. A rose and a vine climb gaily over two of the trees and there is also a cyclamen of the *europaeum* type, a reflexed Turk's cap lily, a carnation or gillyflower—which was introduced by the monks from Normandy about the year 1100—what is plainly pot marigold, *Calendula officinalis,* several unidentifiable composites, the now rather uncommon form of autumn crocus with checkered flowers, *Colchicum variegatum,* and two distinct forms of tulip, including one of the broken color variety.

---

based on the French *Grand Herbier;* William Turner's *New Herball* in 1551; the Latin works of Matthias de L'Obel (after whom lobelia is named) and others—but Gerard's became easily the most popular.

It is a very pleasant garden indeed, and the book itself is a masterpiece of concise and accurate plant descriptions which have rarely been bettered, together with factual information of where they come from. Of *Canna indica*, for instance—our popular Indian shot or Canna lilies—Parkinson says, "These plants grow naturally in the West Indies, from whence they were sent into Spain and Portugal, where Clusius sayeth he saw them planted by the houses sides, flowring in the winter, which might be in those warme Countryes. We preserve them with great care in our gardens for the beautiful aspect of their flowers." There is a note also which clearly demonstrates the confusion of names at that period, before Linnaeus came along with his binomial system to classify everything from a buttercup to a sea-cow. "They are called of some *Canna Indica*, and *Arundo Indica*, of others *Cannacorus*, and of some *Flos Cancri*, because the colour of the flowers, as well as the forme of the buds, are so like a Sea Crabs cle, or claw."

There is a fine scorn of superstition too in his notes on the mandrake—*Mandragora officinarum*—a plant which at that time was still supposed to be possessed of all sorts of magical properties and evil powers.[10] He writes:

> [T]he roote is long and thicke . . . consisting many times but of one long roote, and sometimes divided into two branches a little below the head . . . as myself have often seene, by the transplanting of many, as also by breaking and cutting off many parts of the rootes, but never found harm of so doing, as many idle tales have been set down in writing, and delivered also by report, of much danger to happen to such as should dig them up or break them; neyther have I ever seene any forme of man-like or woman-like parts in the rootes of any. . . . But many cunning counterfeit rootes have bin shaped to such formes, and publickly exposed to the view of all that would see them, and have been tolerated by the chiefe Magistrates of the Citie, notwithstanding that they have been informed

[10] Among other qualities it was supposed to be an infallible love potion, to induce fecundity in women and, according to some tales, to confer the power of foretelling the future. Its root was said to be shaped like a human being since it was engendered under the earth from the seed of some dead person put to death for murder, and it shrieked when taken from the ground. The act of pulling it up was invariably fatal, so a dog was used to drag it out, always at midnight, with one's ears stopped against its screams, and only after the prescribed spells and incantations. The unfortunate dog always died.

that such practices were meere deceit, and unsufferable. . . . this you may
be bold to rest upon and assure your selves, that such formes as have bin
publickly exposed to be seene, were never so formed by nature, but only
by the art and cunning of knaves and deceivers, and let this be your
Galeatum against all such vaine, idle and ridiculous toyes of mens
inventions.

In short, Parkinson was among the first gardeners of the new age.
Born in 1567, probably in Nottinghamshire, he travelled to London as a
young man and there founded a garden in Long Acre close by Covent
Garden, almost certainly a physic garden to start with. It was said to
have been well stocked with rarities, was much admired, much talked
about, and much visited by other gardeners; of whom John Tradescant,
with his own plantation at Lambeth and a traveller and specific plant
hunter himself, must certainly have been one. Parkinson was famous
and highly respected, had been Royal Apothecary to King James I until
that king died in 1625, and in 1640 published a second important work,
Theatrum Botanicum, now describing over three thousand plants, with
2,600 illustrations—including one of Tradescant's many discoveries, the
"Turkie-purple Primrose" which we shall come back to later with John
Tradescant. He died, as the saying is, full of years and honors in 1650 at
the age of eighty-three, and the genus *Parkinsonia*, two species of trees
from tropical America, is today named after him.

For the wider background, in the year John Parkinson died, Oliver
Cromwell invaded Scotland against Charles II who had just landed
there, and Parliament was already growing restive under Cromwell's
near-military dictatorship. Nevertheless, tea imported from China was
being drunk for the first time in England and the first coffee shop, with
coffee from Arabia, was opened in Oxford. In America, the first volume
of early American poetry had appeared entitled *The Tenth Muse Lately
Sprung up in America*, by Anne Bradstreet. By this year too the ancient
civilizations and mysterious islands of the East had been rediscovered,
the Dutch navigator Abel Tasman had sailed round part of the coastline
of what was to become Australia, and vast empty areas elsewhere were
waiting to be explored. Above all lay the great new lands to the west,

with distances and treasures still only remotely guessed at, which were to exert an irresistibly magnetic pull on the European mind for centuries to come, and the earliest of the adventurer plant hunters already had their own connections with America.

(2)

John Tradescant and
the Turkie Purple Primrose

In the early seventeenth century London was a collection of villages
and great establishments; as it still is today if you know where to look
among the depredations of the improvers and social planners. To the
east lay the City, huddled within its wall and extending westward as far
as the old Fleet River; and then on the bend of the Thames came the
houses of the nobility—Essex, Arundel, Somerset, the Savoy Palace, and
Durham—until turning south you reached Westminster and the seat of
government. North-westward, beyond the Strand, was Covent Garden
—or at that time Convent Garden—and the market, nursery, and
apothecaries' gardens: John Parkinson's at Long Acre, Ralph Tuggy's
where pinks and other flowers were grown, John Gerard's at Holborn,
and toward Whitehall that of Edward Morgan, who specialized in the
primula family.

They would all be contemporaries and intimates of John Tradescant;
Parkinson wrote of him as "my very loving good friend" and refers often
to his discoveries in the *Paradisus* and *Theatrum Botanicum*. Tradescant, a simple man of yeoman stock, not only lived to become the
greatest gardener of his day but also introduced to Britain the greatest
number of new, strange, and exotic trees and plants yet seen; exotic, as
the tulip still was then, in the true meaning of the word as coming from
abroad or, as Tradescant himself described it "from forren parts." He
was to found a remarkable garden of his own at South Lambeth near
Lambeth Palace, the official residence of the Archbishop of Canterbury;
he amassed a unique collection of rare and strange objects and
curiosities from all over the world which, by a series of somewhat
mysterious circumstances, eventually became the nucleus of the
Ashmolean Museum at Oxford; and, as I shall suggest later, he or some
of his circle of friends may have made what would be among the earliest
deliberate experiments in hybridization—experiments which perhaps

resulted in the forebears of all of our modern strains of garden polyanthuses.

Except that he married an Elizabeth Day at Meopham, in Kent, in 1607 we know very little for certain about John Tradescant's early life. It is thought that he was born between 1570 and 1575—which would make him a few years younger than John Parkinson—and in her scholarly and deeply researched study of the Tradescant family Mea Allan suggests that he learned the gardener's craft from his father who, being described as a yeoman of London, would be a husbandman owning freehold land, and probably a market gardener himself.[1] It seems more than likely. That John was a gardener of uncommon skill and ability is attested by the posts he occupied at a comparatively early age, by the scope of his duties, and by the wages he received;[2] and this itself would seem to argue a wide knowledge which could only come from family background and practice. Miss Allan traces the Tradescant connections and young John Tradescant's progress and shows that he was probably first employed by William Brooke, Lord Cobham at Cobham Hall, only a short distance from the village in which he was married; one of many gardeners but no mean start in life, for the gardens at Cobham were already included among the greatest in England for their vines, fruiting and ornamental trees, and flowers from the far parts of Europe.

His real career started, however, with Robert Cecil, 1st Earl of Salisbury, at the new Hatfield House in Hertfordshire; it was at the old Hatfield Palace, sitting under her favorite oak tree—the remains of which may still be seen—that Queen Elizabeth I received the horseman who had ridden the seventeen-and-a-half miles from London at breakneck speed to tell her that her sister Queen Mary was dead and

[1] *The Tradescants; Their Plants, Gardens and Museum 1570–1662* (London: Michael Joseph, 1964). The most authoritative work on the family yet written or likely to be written.

[2] In the service of the 1st Earl of Salisbury, Robert Cecil, at Hatfield House between 1609 and 1614, £12 a quarter against the "French Gardener's" £6.5s. Later, in 1630, as Keeper of His Majesty's Gardens, Vines, and Silkworms, to King Charles I, £100 per annum compared with £30 paid to the first gardener of the then new Chelsea Physics Garden in 1673—a salary which, not unnaturally, subsequent gardeners there found woefully inadequate.

that after years of danger she was Queen of England. The Palace of Hatfield had been a royal residence since the time of Henry VIII, when it was "acquired" from the Bishops of Ely on the Reformation, and it came to Robert Cecil in a rather curious way. Cecil was the son of Lord Burghley, Elizabeth's incomparably faithful Secretary of State; their house was Theobalds, a few miles from Hatfield and far more commodious and modern than the palace itself. Cecil, then merely Sir Robert, was sufficiently unwary to invite Queen Elizabeth's successor James I there for a visit; and James so fell in love with the place that he made one of those royal offers which were not lightly refused—that he would give Cecil the old Hatfield Palace in exchange for Theobalds. He was not known as "the wisest fool in Christendom" for nothing.

The exchange had two sequels. The more immediate being indirectly to set John Tradescant off on his travels and to bring into England trees, fruits, and flowers which had never been seen there before; the later that while Theobalds was demolished in the eighteenth century Hatfield still stands as one of the finest Jacobean houses ever built, and the gardens stocked and planted by Tradescant still exist. By 1607 Cecil was employing an army of workmen to tear down most of the old palace, engaging the finest masons, craftsmen, designers, and artists to build and decorate the new house, even buying a quarry in Normandy to provide Caen stone for the main front. In 1609 he took John Tradescant into his service to work on the gardens—there is an inventory still in existence which lists almost everything planted there—and by then Tradescant had a young son, the second John who was to be his only child and who was to work with him in later life and travel to Virginia himself.

Compared with those of later plant hunters, Tradescant's journeys were neither very long nor outstandingly adventurous. It is a truism of plant hunting that as areas of settlement and urbanization extend, the search for new genera and species must move out farther into more and more inaccessible places, but at this time there were quite enough plants that were yet new and strange in England to be found relatively close at hand. The European countries, particularly the Netherlands and France, were still considered to be, and were, in advance of England in the crafts of propagation and nursery gardening, and

Tradescant's first journey was literally a shopping expedition on behalf of Robert Cecil. He set off on that in the autumn of 1611; then in 1618 he went with Sir Dudley Digges on an embassy to Russia—which in his diary he calls "A Viag of Ambusad"—travelled round the Mediterranean probably as far as Constantinople in 1621, attended George Villiers, Duke of Buckingham, at the proxy marriage of Henrietta Maria of France to King Charles I in Paris, 1625, and finally served with Buckingham again in the foolish and ill-fated 1627 assault on the French coastal city of La Rochelle. There is no record that he ever visited Virginia, though as a shareholder in the Virginia Company, formed in 1617, he must have held a land grant there and later received imports of many Virginian plants in England.

John Tradescant's accounts of purchases made for Cecil in continental Europe are extraordinarily interesting as showing not only what plants and trees were available in the European nurseries then, but their relative prices. It is quite clear that he was already in a position of considerable trust and Cecil appears to have allowed him a free hand to pick up whatever he found of interest; he followed these instructions as liberally as they were given. Setting out in September 1611 with £6 "towards bearing of his charges into Flanders & other parts beyond the seas," he was away for three months and his plant bills amounted in modern terms to nearly £4,000, or about $9,000. It was garden buying on a scale almost as grand as the building of Hatfield itself and payment was covered by bills of exchange arranged through the Chamberlain of the Exchequer, Sir Walter Cope, who was himself then planting a new garden at what is now Holland House in Kensington, London, and also had an interest in the journey.

Tradescant travelled from Flushing (Vlissingen) all through the Netherlands, purchasing at one nursery after another; and though a complete list of several thousand pounds worth of garden stock would be rather considerable, some items at least are worth noting: as "Two pots of gilliflowers 12 sorts in on[e] pot and of Seed gilliflowers plants in on[e] pot" for £1.6s. Gilliflowers were pinks and, even allowing for the fact that they were extremely popular at this period, two dozen plants at £1.6s. against prices ranging from 1s.6d. to 2s.0. for apple, pear, cherry, and mulberry trees seems to be almost fabulously expensive, especially when we consider the relative values of money then and now. The unmistakable inference therefore is that they must have been new varieties, and this again hints at hybridization. Then he paid "For flowers Called anemone, 5s. . . . for the great Red Currants 6 plants 1s." and along with more cherry, quince, medlar, and apple trees he accounts, "for tulipes roots at Harlem at ten shillings the hundred 800, £4 . . . for on[e] dussin of great blake curants 1s. . . . for on[e] vine Caled biggare, nothing . . ." That entry, the "vine Caled biggare, nothing" is amusing too. Was it thrown in for make weight, or does it suggest there was some hard, tough bargaining between the shrewd English gardener and the equally sharp Dutch nurserymen?

Tulips were still almost unknown in England, and as long as eighteen years later in the *Paradisus* Parkinson counted them among the "outlandish flowers," meaning literally foreign. As an apothecary he must have tried to find a medicinal or culinary use for the bulbs, for he reports that he himself had tried them preserved in sugar and adds ". . . the roots are nourishing . . . for divers have had them sent by their friends from beyond sea, and . . . have used them to be onions in their pottage or broth, and have never found any cause of mislike, or any sense of evil quality . . ." In fact tulip bulbs were eaten as food by the Dutch during the Second World War when for a time they were near enough to starvation, and it was even said that people suffering from various forms of gastric ulcers actually found them to be beneficial.

To come back to John Tradescant's travels, he went on to Brussels where he purchased more tulips, cherry, pear, and walnut trees, and "on[e] apricoke tree called the Whit apricoke, 6s. . . . on[e] Chery tree Called the Archeduks cherye, 12s. . . ." These again were expensive, the cherry extremely so, and of them the white apricot has now become very rare though the Archduke's Cherry remains well known to this day. Apparently in the years following its introduction to England it was in great demand if not always in exactly honest supply, for Parkinson, again in the *Paradisus*, complains "Scarce one in twenty of our nurserymen do sell it right, but give one for another, it is an inherent qualitie almost hereditarie with most of them to sell any man an ordinary fruit for whatsoever rare fruit he shall ask for, so little are they to be trusted." In that respect at least we seem to have improved a little these days; you can usually be fairly certain of getting what you ask for now.

For flower gardeners probably the most interesting of Tradescant's finds on this particular trip are contained in one more account, "The debble Epatega the martygon pompone blanche the martygon pompony orang Coller and the Irys Calsedonye and the Irys Susyana £2." Once more these were expensive and there can be no doubt that they must have been a sensation when they flowered in England. The martagons were of course the reflexed Turk's cap type of lilies, and the hepatica would probably be a double variety of what is now described as *Hepatica media* or *H. transsylvanica* from eastern Europe. Iris Calsedonye I confess I cannot identify, but if Tradescant's name for it means anything—presumably the ancient Chalcedon, now part of Turkey and Bulgaria on the south western coast of the Black Sea—it might have been *I. sintenisii*, which grows wild in that area. *Iris susiana* or the Mourning Iris is still with us today and over the last twenty years or so has been used a great deal with others of the oncocyclus division, particularly among American hybridists, for crossing into our magnificent modern varieties of the complex hybrid tall bearded irises.[3]

Finally packing his precious purchases in hampers he dispatched them to Hatfield from Brussels and then set off for Paris, a journey that took him eight and a half days. Here, furnished with letters of introduction to the British ambassador, he met and struck up a lifelong friendship with Jean Robin—Royal Herbalist to Henry IV and Louis XIII—René Morin, who was to become one of the greatest French

---

[3] For those like myself who have a sneaking fondness for the unusual and even slightly bizarre *I. susiana* is irresistible. William Dykes, the greatest authority on irises and author of the massive work *On the Genus Iris*, once described it rather unkindly as looking like newspaper on which the print has run, but it does have a strange beauty of its own. A large flower of almost globular form, and normally only one to the stem, it is grayish white, heavily veined, and stippled with brown-purple. It is said to be the least difficult of the oncocyclus irises—and that is entirely relative since none of them is easy—but if you can give it a hot position where it will receive adequate though well-drained moisture in the growing season and then quietly bake for the rest of the year it will repay your efforts; and it will certainly attract attention.

nurserymen of his day and a famous collector of insects, butterflies, and
natural curiosities, and other gardeners; it may have been Morin who
inspired Tradescant to start making his own collection of rare and
strange objects. From Robin, among other items, he collected, "8 pots
of orang trees of on[e] years growthe grafted at 10s the peece . . .
ollyander [oleander] trees 6 at halfe a crowne the peece . . . myrtyll
trees 7 at halfe a crowne the peece . . . two fyg trees in an other basket
called the whit fygs withe many other Rare shrubs given me by Master
Robyns 4s," and so on. René Morin contributed, "Pears, plums and
cheryes 60–70 plants cost £6.9s. . . . also of vynes Called muscat two
bundals of plants 4s . . . on[e] pot of gilliflwers cost nothing . . ." etc.
Again that "pot of gilliflowers cost nothing" makes one wonder what
was so special about the two at £1.6s from Holland; especially since
along with many more fruit trees he bought another two in Rouen—
"for on[e] pot of the dubble whit stok gilliflowers and on[e] pot of other
gilliflowers 3s."

The whole vast consignment was at last shipped from Rouen in
December; and when it reached England it required two wherries to
transport it up the River Lea to Hatfield.

Tradescant returned to find his master a sick man, wanting only to
see Hatfield House completed. He never did. Cecil was ill on and off all
through that winter, rallied a little early in 1612 and determined to try
the Bath waters; but in Bath he was troubled by rumors of Parliamentary plotting against him and attempted to return to London. It was the
longest of all journeys for he died on the way. His son William became
the 2nd Earl of Salisbury. And William Cecil was an enthusiast; he
loved gardens, he loved beautiful houses, had Hatfield yet to finish and
furnish, and apparently he loved lavish spending. Entertaining, building, repairing, replanting the gardens at Cranborne and Salisbury House
in the Strand—for which he sent Tradescant to France again to buy
hundreds of roses—his money flowed like the River Thames. Whether
the source actually did start to run dry or whether John Tradescant as a
shrewd and businesslike man himself began to see the red light is
uncertain but Mea Allan has established that he left Cecil's employment
some time between September 1614 and midsummer 1615 and turned

to farming as a sideline. We next hear of him as a gardener with Sir Edward Wotton at St. Augustine's Palace in Canterbury, another palace which King James I had granted to the Cecils and which the 2nd Earl sold to Wotton on the death of his father.

In England, 1617, Virginia was much on men's minds; not only those of merchants and politicians, but sailors, adventurers, and poets. A fabulous land of permanently beneficent climate, where grew the most noble forests and trees man had ever seen, with all manner of exquisite fruits waiting only to be plucked, gold to be had merely for the trouble of bending to pick it up, and even, according to some, beautiful and kindly Indian maids.[4] It was some time before the true stories began to filter back—the appalling voyage, Indians who were sometimes rather less than kindly, hardship due to total inexperience, and sometimes starvation—and in the meantime the Virginia Company's offer of fifty acres of land to every "adventurer" who took one £12.10s. share and every "planter" who actually travelled out there was irresistible. Working for Sir Edward Wotton, John Tradescant must have been fairly prosperous for he became a shareholder himself, and a landowner in Virginia.

It seems more than likely that lured by the tales of strange and beautiful trees and fruits he might have contemplated travelling out there himself one day, but if so more immediate adventures were calling him. About this time Sir Dudley Digges, diplomat and judge, who was also interested in Virginia, and a member of the East India Company and the Muscovy Company, was building himself a splendid new house at the Manor of Chilham and he called in Tradescant to plant the grounds. (Presumably borrowing John from Sir Edward Wotton, for we find John returning to St. Augustine's Palace after the Russian journey.) The two men seem very quickly to have achieved something much more than a mere master and servant relationship—first class gardeners were important people, while clearly Tradescant had the gift of inspiring friendship and trust—and when James I sent Digges on the embassy to Moscow it was very natural to both of them that John should go with him.

[4] One verse of Michael Drayton's ode "To the Virginian Voyage" is fairly typical: "And cheerefully at sea,/ Success you still intice,/ To get the Pearle and Gold,/ And ours to hold, Virginia,/ Earth's only Paradise."

The politics of that curious mission were complex and they do not matter very much now. Briefly, England had mediated in a quarrel between Sweden and Russia and subsequently the Czar granted a Charter of Trade Privileges and sent two ambassadors to London, together with princely gifts of furs and jewels, to continue the negotiations. What Czar Michael really wanted, however, was financial and political assistance against a Polish claimant to the Russian throne, and what the English were after was a secure overland trade route to Persia and India. Somewhat reluctantly the East India and Muscovy Companies were persuaded to enter a joint stock loan of £30,000 each, and Sir Dudley Digges was sent back with the two Russian ambassadors and a retinue of forty-one other persons to settle the matter.

In the event the mission was a failure. Landing at Archangel, Digges travelled less than fifty miles south before he received information that the Poles were already outside Moscow and turned back. However, he sent on seventeen members of his party with a temporary loan for the Czar, but when eventually they reached Moscow they were not the important personages the Czar expected, and they were kept waiting for two months before they were at last granted an audience; in Russia nothing changes very much. His Majesty was more than annoyed to discover that instead of the £60,000 he had been promised these envoys were only offering him a beggarly £12,000 and he sent angry messengers out after Sir Dudley to ask him why. But when they reached Archangel, Digges had already left, and the politics of the affair must have been further complicated by the fact that he, perhaps rather carelessly, had fired a parting salute with loaded cannon, a courtesy which left the Russians "gaping and in great perplexity."

Apart from the long voyage out and home Tradescant was only in Russia for three weeks, but he made good use of his time throughout, not least in keeping his journal "A Viag of Ambusad by the Right Honnorabl Sr Dudlie Diggs in the year 1618 . . ." and a record of "Things by me observed," in Russia.[5]

They left London on June 3, in two ships—the two Russian

[5] This manuscript is now in the Bodleian Library, Oxford. The following extracts are taken from Professor Sergei Konovalov's transcription in the Oxford Slavonic Papers, vol. II, 1951.

ambassadors in one and Sir Dudley Digges and his party in the other—and reached Archangel on July 16 after what must have been an uncommonly bad voyage even for the North Sea. After describing the departure and beating north against contrary winds Tradescant goes on: "my lord himself for 4 dais very sick. . . . Sunday being the 14 day we had sight of toune 7 leags to the Southe of Newcastell. Munday and Tewesday we beate up and down to recover Newcastell but could not . . ." However on Wednesday my lord caused the boat to be hoisted out and Tradescant and one other got ashore to buy provisions, ". . . wheare I bought ii salmons for 5s the cuple, and some for 4s the cuple, which at London would have bin worth 2 li 10s the cuple. Also we went to suppe at the best ordinary in the toune with many dishes; our win being payd for came but to 8d the peece, whiche in London, I think, 2s the peece would have hardly mached it. . . . On Thursday [18 June] we returned to the shippe with sume 17 lis worthe of provission . . ."

They set off once more, but by Friday ". . . the wind scantted to the Nor West, wheare we lay Northeast away withe a leeward way, the wind increasing and changing mor Northe; the Satterday the wind began to rise, on Sunday to encreas, being full in our teethe. Munday and Tewsday still the storm continewing till Thursday morning. . . . In which 4 dayes my Lord Imbassittor was extreem sick, in so much that all they in the ship mad question of his life, partli by sea sickness and partly by over muche coller. . . . on Thursday his lordship after the calme reseved sume meat, whiche in 4 dayes before he hade refused. On the Friday morning being the 26 of June he had a litill sleepe, the Great God be blessed for it . . ." Apparently Sir Dudley continued to improve sufficiently to observe the courtesies, for "On Saynt Peetter's day, on the morning, my Lord sent the Russian Imbassator fresh vyttals, on[e] quarter of mutton, half a littill porker, & 3 live pullets, ther Lent being but then ended; also at New Castell my Lord sent hime two small salmons and 9 gallons of Canary Sack; the curtiseys hathe passed a[s] yet witheout requitall . . ."

When they at last arrived in Archangel he notes "That night came abord of our ship a boat of Sammoyets, a misserable people, of small growth. In my judgement is that people whom the fixtion is fayned of that should have no heads,[6] for they have short necks, and commonly wear ther clothes over head and shoulders. . . . the men and women be hardli known on[e] from the other, because they all wear clothes like mene, and be all clad in skins of beasts. . . . They be extrem beggars, not to be denied." But plant hunting was his main interest and, "On Munday I had on[e] of the Emperor's boats to cari me from iland to iland to see what things grewe upon them, whear I found single rosses, wondros sweet . . . wheare I observed the basnes of the people . . ." who apparently ate cakes that were ". . . sower cream and otmeal pastill very poorli mad, which to them was a great bankit."

It is in "Things by me observed" that he makes his observations on Russian life and agriculture; unfortunately too long to quote much here though some of his comments are too good to miss. Of their drinks, ". . . they be meads made of hony and watter, and also beere; but ther Ruse beere is wonderful base of an ill tast, but ther best meade is excelent drinke, mad of the hony which is the best honny of the world . . ." And of their cattle, "For the mutton and beefe it was bothe small and lean. . . . Ther pidggs they spend wonderfull small . . . ther bacon tastes muche after oylle, because of the muche fishe ther hogs eate . . ."

The plants and trees he found included pine, spruce, fir and larch, which last there is little doubt that he introduced to England, several species of rose and ". . . currants, whit, red and black, far greatter than ever I have seen growing in this cuntrie." There was also angelica, lysimachia, a blue geranium or cranesbill, and the attractive fringed pink, *Dianthus superbus*.[7] He also brought back a "Duke of Muscovy's vest wrought with gold upon the breast and arms; shooes to walk on snow without sinking, The Gorara or Colymbus bird" and other rare and strange objects to add to the collection which was later to be displayed at his house in Lambeth.

[6] Is this Shakespeare's "Men whose heads Do grow beneath their shoulders" in *Othello*?
[7] This is in fact widely distributed, occurring as far afield as Japan and Korea. It has since become one of the many parents of our hybrid pinks, but the seed of the true species may still sometimes be obtained, and it makes an easy and attractive subject for the rock garden. The flowers are beautifully cut and fringed, of a deep pink color with a pale green center.

He sailed from Archangel with his plants and curiosities on August 6—three weeks before Sir Dudley Digges himself—and after another stormy voyage reached home on September 22 when ". . . We landed at Saynt Katharins near London, whear, God be thanked, we ended our viage, having no on[e] man sick, God be thanked."

Returning to Canterbury, Tradescant went back to Sir Edward Wotton and the garden at St. Augustine's, where he was achieving fame growing melons, a technique which he had already developed at Hatfield House. In Canterbury also the following year, 1619, his son John, then aged eleven, was admitted to King's School in the autumn term. But the elder Tradescant still was not to remain settled for long. In that same year it was decided to send out a fleet against Algeria and the Barbary pirates of the Mediterranean, many of whom, incidentally, were English themselves. Again the politics of the affair were confused, but to Tradescant it looked like another fine adventurous trip, almost certainly with fresh fruits and flowers to be discovered. By now, too, he had influential connections—notably with the captains of the Virginia Company—and, though he did not sail with the main force, in February 1621 we find him arriving at Alicante aboard the pinnace *Mercury* under the command of one Phineas Pett. John Tradescant had got himself his adventure in the Mediterranean, though it is doubtful whether he ever so much as saw a Barbary pirate, since Captain Pett himself did not rendezvous with the main force.

Tradescant does not appear to have kept a record of that voyage—or if he did and if it still exists it remains waiting to be discovered—and we are indebted again to Miss Mea Allan for a scholarly reconstruction of his movements during the next several months. She finds no record of Tradescant being at work at St. Augustine's during the following summer, establishes that Phineas Pett and the *Mercury* did not return to England until September, and suggests that for reasons of his own he sailed eastward along the Mediterranean coast to Constantinople, probably as an armed escort to merchantmen. Then working from Tradescant's own garden list at Lambeth, in 1634, she selects the plants which by their names or otherwise are known to have a Mediterranean origin, and next proceeds to eliminate those which can be shown by the best available authorities to have been introduced earlier than 1621. What she has left is, in her own words, "a list of plants which follow from country to country and port to port a tour of the Mediterranean and the Greek Islands along the route a ship would take."

An interesting list it is, for after several acquisitions in Spain and southern France, Tradescant seems to have headed for Italy, where he collected *Hesperis italica*, now *H. matronalis*, and *Crocus neapolitanus*, probably now *C. biflorus*, and then on to Crete where he picked up a few more treasures including a white lupin. Chios in the Greek Islands yielded "Colchicum ex insula Chios," *Colchicum variegatum*—the checkered autumn crocus which eight years later Parkinson illustrated on the title page of his *Paradisus*—and in Constantinople he found *Flos constantinopolitanus*, the well-known *Lychnis chalcedonica* or Jerusalem Cross, with its heads of startling red flowers, and *Gladiolus byzantinus*, which is still offered by bulbsmen under that name.[8] According to Miss Allan's list he collected at least forty-four new plants, including two varieties of narcissus from North Africa together with "the Barbarie Apricocke 2 sorts," three varieties of plum and the Roman peach. We have further evidence of his itinerary in "Barbary Spurres pointed sharp like a Bodkin. . . . A Damascus knife perfum'd in the casting. . . . Divers sorts of Egges from Turkie; one given for a Dragons Egge . . ." etc. It seems to have been a profitable journey.

So the autumn of 1621 sees him back at Canterbury, though he remained there for only two more years, when young John left King's School and Tradescant himself entered the service of the brilliant and successful Duke of Buckingham, George Villiers—favorite of the court, and who was said to have received more honors and occupied more high offices in ten years or so than any other Englishman before or since. John Tradescant's appointment may be seen as the measure of his own success, and the gardens of Buckingham's mansion, Newhall near

[8] The *gladiolus* species have been almost entirely superseded by their massive garden hybrids, but if you like the color—which is a rather violent purplish magenta—*G. byzantinus* is a good plant for an otherwise dull spot in the garden. It is quite hardy in reasonably mild areas and does not need lifting and storing for the winter. Given a sunny position and planted in autumn it may be left to mind its own business for years, and will often spread and naturalize into large clumps. When it can be obtained, *G. atroviolaceus* is a rather similar type in variable dark to violet purple and probably quite as hardy.

Chelmsford, were another of his great opportunities. There he created avenues and vistas, arbors and the then fashionable "knot" gardens, in which intricate beds and patterns were laid out in low hedges and filled with the most brilliantly colored flowers, which still more increased his fame.

Once again he seems rapidly to have become something more than a gardener in the household, for when Buckingham went to Paris to attend the marriage by proxy of King Charles I to Henrietta Maria of France—James had died suddenly earlier that year, 1625—Tradescant travelled with the party. Wedding celebrations, of however unexampled magnificence, have little to do with plant hunting but there is one picturesque incident which seems to indicate how high in royal favor John Tradescant was to become. Among the fifteen-year-old Queen's many gifts and surprises was a great pie said to have been baked for her by the Duchess of Buckingham; and when its crust was opened there appeared a tiny boy, the famous dwarf Jeffrey. The Queen was enchanted and adopted the small creature immediately. Years later, in the list of Tradescant's cabinet of curiosities and rarities we find the items "Little Jeffrey's Boots" and "Little Jeffrey's Masking-suit."

That he already had considerable influence with Buckingham is clear from a letter addressed by him to Edward Nicholas, then Secretary to the Admiralty, also in 1625. "Noble Sir, I have Bin Commanded By My Lord to Let Yr Worshippe Understand that It is H Grace's Plesure that you should In His Name Deall withe All Marchants from All Places But Espetially the Virgine & Bermewde & NewfoundLand Men that . . . they will take Care to furnishe His Grace Withe All manner of Beasts & fowells and Birdes Alyve or If not Withe Heads Horns Beaks Claws skins fethers slipes or seedes Plants trees or shrubs . . ." It followed with further instructions to captains sailing to Turkey and the coast of Africa, and details as to what kind of rarities were required, including "All sorts of the fruts Dried As ther tree . . . flowers laid betwin paper leaves In A Book Dried. . . . All sorts of shining stones. . . . Any thing that is strang . . ." So merchant ships and Navy—terms that were not always quite distinct in those days—were now to be pressed into the service of collecting.

In the same year John gave up his house in Meopham, Kent, and moved to London where besides Newhall Buckingham had three other residences and gardens to be looked after. The Tradescants settled in Lambeth, almost certainly with the Duke's help and patronage, in a pleasant and roomy house with its own acres of land. It was here that Tradescant housed his now large collection of rarities and where he was to plant his famous garden; it was to be known as "The Ark" and in later years to become famous throughout Europe. No visit to London was complete without a visit to John Tradescant's house and garden, and seventeenth-century literature and diaries were full of references to it.[9]

But by 1627 a fresh adventure was calling Tradescant; this in the shape of the foolish, costly, and for Buckingham ultimately fatal attempt to capture La Rochelle, the French city and fortress on the Atlantic coast. For many years since the bloody massacre of St. Bartholomew's Day on August 24, 1572, Rochelle had been the center of Protestant resistance in France, not particularly dangerous to Louis XIII but a nuisance which he was now determined to remove. Buckingham on the other hand saw its relief by the English as essential to the grand design of an alliance of Protestant states against Spain and the Holy Roman Empire, and it says much for his power over Charles that he was able to persuade the King into an expedition which might have embittered his already unhappy marriage still further, made a dangerous enemy of his brother-in-law Louis, and started another war with France.

John Tradescant went along as a soldier—most likely as a gentleman volunteer, for Buckingham would scarcely have commanded the presence of his Director of Gardens—in an army led by Buckingham but which had been scraped together anyhow, even by press gangs—an army ill fed, ill clothed, almost without arms and more than half mutinous. There is no point in telling the whole tragic story but the entire affair was a disaster from start to finish; the local support Buckingham expected did not materialize, ships failed to rendezvous on time, and in the trenches "men died apace." Of the seven thousand who assembled on the Isle de Ré from July 1627 onward less than three thousand ultimately returned to England in November.

[9] By 1749 however it was described by a Mr. William Watson—afterward Sir William Watson, M.D.—as being totally neglected, the house belonging to it empty and ruinous and the garden covered with weeds. The house was finally sold and demolished in 1880.

But John Tradescant brought back *Papaver rhoeas*, the scarlet corn poppy which is the ultimate parent of all our showy modern strains of Shirley poppy,[10] the "Sea Stocke Gilloflower," *Matthiola sinuata* (or *M. incana*) from which our popular sweetly scented garden stocks are descended, and "Seriphium" or *Artemisia maritima*. He at least got something out of the disaster, but in the end it cost him his greatest patron so far, and Buckingham himself his life.

Buckingham's death is another curious story, which started with the defeat of the Isle de Ré and had its sequel nearly a year later in Portsmouth. That October, with the army in disorderly retreat, Buckingham was accosted on the battlefield by an unknown subaltern who demanded that he should be given command of a company since their captain had just been shot dead. It was hardly the most propitious moment to ask for promotion and the Duke brushed him aside. The subaltern was John Felton. In the following months Buckingham forgot him; he had, after all, more important things to think about: his dangerous unpopularity throughout England—in July 1628 Charles I prorogued Parliament when it demanded Buckingham's surrender—his own political maneuvering, and his determination to persuade the King into another assault on La Rochelle.

In the face of growing opposition another army was assembled, and in August 1628 Buckingham arrived in Portsmouth to lead the new expedition. He was staying at a house close to the harbor, surrounded by his officers and gentlemen, where that morning, breakfast being announced, one of them drew the curtains across a doorway aside to let him pass through and he was immediately stabbed in the chest. He cried, "The villain hath killed me," and pulled out the knife himself; but

[10] The corn poppy grows as freely in English fields as it does in French and is generally thought to be indigenous to both countries, but Tradescant would hardly have taken the trouble to collect the seeds of a quite commonplace plant. So is it possible that he introduced *Papaver rhoeas* to Britain, and that it subsequently escaped from cultivation as a number of other apparently wild flowers have done. What is even more interesting is that in the same list a *Papaver rhoeas fl. lutea rodice perpetua* is mentioned. Yet there is no such thing as a perennial yellow *Papaver rhoeas* and it seems possible that here he might have collected the Welsh poppy, *Meconopsis cambrica*, which grows abundantly all down the west coasts of Great Britain and Europe, and is the only species known which grows outside of the far Asian, Himalayan, and Chinese regions.

he was already dying. John Felton was discovered waiting calmly in another room. Just as calmly he announced "I am he you seek" and in his hat they found a paper on which was written a few lines of the House of Commons declaration denouncing Buckingham as an enemy of the kingdom. So the favorite of two kings, the most striking and ambitious figure ever to cross the stage of English history, was assassinated by an unhinged boy with a knife he had purchased from a cutler for one shilling.

For the next two years John Tradescant retired to cultivate his own garden at Lambeth surrounded by his circle of gardening friends and family: his wife Elizabeth, his son John—who was now a gardener himself—John's wife, Jane, and their first child Frances.

Fresh honors were awaiting him however. The King's grief on Buckingham's assassination was said to be extravagant, but really that politically fortunate event removed a dangerous embarrassment. And it incidentally led to John Tradescant's final and greatest appointment as Keeper of His Majesty's Gardens, Vines, and Silkworms, at Oatlands, near Weybridge, in 1630. Buckingham had represented a continual source of friction and jealousy between Charles and Henrietta Maria and it was clearly as a gesture of reconciliation that the King set out to refurbish the old palace and gardens for her. It was a vast place, originally built by Henry VIII and later destroyed by Cromwell, which had been granted to Henrietta for her sole use and pleasure as part of the marriage settlement. For John Tradescant, instructed to replant the grounds in every manner pleasing, it meant a handsome salary and a magnificent opportunity. There is no doubt that he availed himself of it magnificently; to such effect that he remained there until his death in 1637 when, the year after, the younger John also was appointed "Keeper . . . in place of his father, deceased."

John Tradescant must have lived mostly at Oatlands during those years since Lambeth was nearly twenty miles away—too far for commuting in those days—but he still contrived to add to his ever growing collection of plants, trees, and curiosities through ambassadors, sea captains, and merchants. The garden collection itself was becoming so vast that in 1634 he caused a special little book to be printed about it for the benefit of the increasing number of visitors who were coming from all over Britain and many parts of Europe.[11] This listed no less than 768 plants, shrubs, and trees, including 48 varieties of apple, 45 of pear, 33 plums, 12 cherry, and 12 peaches, together with quinces, nectarines and vines.

Some of these came from Virginia, and more were yet to come. The elder Tradescant held land there against the sum of two shares at £12.10s. each in the Virginia Company and imported plants through his connections among the company's captains, and young John visited the colony three times—in 1637, 1642, and 1654—to bring back many more; indeed probably the greater number of our Virginian garden plants are due to the second John. The Tradescant total from America amounts to more than 90 new plants, not forgetting those that still bear their family name; blue, pink, and white flowered perennial *Tradescantia Virginiana*—spiderwort, devil-in-the pulpit, Moses-in-the-bulrushes, etc.—and the ubiquitous trailing house plant *T. fluminensis*, or Wandering Jew. A full list would be merely statistical, but among only a few are the ever popular scarlet runner, or string bean, *Phaseolus coccineus*, our Michaelmas daisies, *Aster novae angliae*, and *A. novii belgii*, one of the most graceful of all lilies *Lilium canadense*, the evening primrose or *Oenothera biennis*,[12] which has now naturalized itself throughout many parts of Britain, and probably the showiest introduction of all, *Lobelia cardinalis*.[13]

By the end of his life the first John Tradescant was an almost

[11] *Plantarum in Horto*. Only one copy is at present known to exist, in the library of Magdalen College, Oxford.

[12] All of the evening primrose species come from America and of these *Oenothera missouriensis* is an excellent plant for any dry, sunny bank. It is of trailing or prostrate growth and carries immense, brilliant yellow flowers for months on end through the summer.

[13] Described by Parkinson, this is another plant that deserves to be better known today. Except for the shape of the much larger blooms it is entirely unlike the eternal dwarf blue lobelias, being perennial, growing up to three feet, and carrying erect spikes of scarlet flowers. It is naturally a waterside plant and so needs moisture, and except in the mildest winter areas it should be lifted and stored in a frame or greenhouse before the frosts come. The named variety "Queen Victoria," with glistening bronze purple foliage, is still the finest, but there are now several hybrids in white and shades of blue to purple. Of these "Blue Peter" is one of the best and hardiest.

legendary figure. Young John was away in Virginia then, and he returned to take up his father's appointment as Royal Gardener at Oatlands in 1638, and also in that autumn to marry again—this time to a Hester Pooks, his first wife Jane Hurte having died three years before, leaving him with two children, Frances and another John. But the storm clouds were already growing. The historic British quarrel between Crown and Parliament was rising to its climax after the long chain of blunders and misjudgments throughout the whole of his reign, which culminated in the King's attempt to arrest the parliamentary leaders in 1642 and the outbreak of the civil war. By that time England was in revolution, but most ordinary people still went about their lives in much the same way as usual, no doubt cursing both sides impartially.

Except that the second John was in Virginia again for part of 1642 we know very little of his movements during the seven long years of the civil war. No doubt for a time he continued to supervise the gardens at Oatlands—where on one occasion later Henrietta Maria, warned that the palace was likely to be attacked, armed herself and all her staff and spent the nights patrolling the park—but mostly he seems to have occupied himself with family and parish affairs and with the Tradescant garden and collection at Lambeth. Battle followed battle until the final defeat at Preston; then came the Rump Parliament with the King himself a prisoner, the trial from which Charles emerged with rather more dignity than his judges, and that final scene on the scaffold outside the Banqueting Chamber in Whitehall on January 30, 1649. As one observer put it, "There was no sound from the people, only a great sigh"; and one wonders whether John Tradescant was there among them.

There is little more to add, except the rather devious means by which the now famous Tradescant Cabinet of Curiosities became the Ashmolean Museum, and the question of the Turkie purple primrose. The first is almost nothing to do with plant hunting, except that no story of the Tradescants is complete without it, and the second is merely an interesting speculation.

Cromwell destroyed Oatlands—together with many other palaces and churches—and all of the Tradescants' work there. John, perhaps wisely, retired to the peaceful seclusion of Lambeth where he was visited several times in 1650 by the strange and complex person of Elias Ashmole, solicitor, astrologer, botanist, collector, and amateur of witch trials. What Ashmole's original intentions were is uncertain, but there is very little doubt that he soon started to turn covetous eyes on what was now the finest museum collection in Europe; it occupied two entire rooms at The Ark and overflowed into the rest of the house. John, apparently by no means such a shrewd man as old John Tradescant in spite of his far better classical education as a King's Scholar, seems to have been completely taken in, although his wife Hester disliked and distrusted Ashmole intensely. Subsequently, Ashmole introduced a Dr. Wharton also and eventually suggested that he and Wharton should compile and publish at their own expense a complete catalogue of the Tradescant collection, both of plants and curiosities.

The work progressed slowly at first. In 1652 John's only son died at the tragically early age of nineteen, Ashmole was embroiled in law suits and bitter domestic troubles with his wife, and in 1654 John Tradescant again set off for Virginia. The catalogue finally appeared in 1656, under the title *Musaeum Tradescantianum* with engravings of the two Tradescants, father and son, by Wenceslaus Hollar, and it was an immediate success. The first printed museum catalogue ever to appear, it contained a complete list of all the rarities both Tradescants had collected since about 1612 and, more important still to students of plants and seventeenth-century gardening, all the plants they had grown at Lambeth.

Ashmole certainly had considerable influence over John, and in the years which followed he used all of it to gain ultimate possession of the Tradescant property. John had originally intended to leave the collection to "the Prince"—later Charles II—but even by 1659 there was still no certainty that the monarchy would ever be restored, and Ashmole eventually induced Tradescant to sign a Deed of Gift awarding it to him after Tradescant's own death and Hester's. Hester however then persuaded John to burn this document; and he seems to have imagined that that was the end of the business, for in 1661 he made a will leaving all his possessions to Hester and directing that on her own death she should bestow his Cabinet of Rarities either on the University of Cambridge or Oxford, whichever she thought fit.

John died early in 1662—in fact two years after the Restoration—and within a month Elias Ashmole brought an action in Chancery against Hester claiming that the Tradescant collection had been freely made over to him by a duly signed and attested Deed of Gift, which deed Hester had then conspired to destroy. It was a complex hearing, but Hester's dislike of Ashmole must have been all too obvious, while he urged that he had compiled the catalogue, *Musaeum Tradescantianum*, and that there was no doubt of John Tradescant's intention; he picked his counsel well and, being a lawyer himself, he knew the procedure. The end was almost inevitable. By order of the court the Tradescant collection was made over to him on Hester's death, and she was enjoined not to sell, remove, or interfere with any part of it during the remainder of her lifetime.

She lived for another sixteen years, still fighting Ashmole although she must have known by now that it was a battle which could end only one way. They were years of continual harassment on both sides and eventually Ashmole bought a house next door to The Ark, presumably to keep an eye on what now, legally, was certainly his property. Then in 1677 he wrote to the University of Oxford offering a free gift of his own collection of coins, etc., together with the Tradescant museum on condition that the university should build a suitable place to preserve them. His offer was accepted; so, just as the Tradescants had wanted, in the end their Cabinet of Rarities went to Oxford, though as the Ashmolean not as the Tradescant museum.[14] It seems to have been a great deal of trouble merely for the sake of a name; and Hester Tradescant herself was found drowned in a pool in the garden of The Ark on the morning of April 3, 1678.

We now come to the interesting question of Tradescant's Turkie

[14] The Ashmolean today is not the original museum built to the designs of Sir Christopher Wren. That is now a Museum of the History of Science, though still known as the Old Ashmolean. The more recent building now called the Ashmolean Museum is an extension of the University Galleries.

purple primrose, which in the *Theatrum Botanicum* of 1640 John Parkinson describes as *Primula veris Turcica Tradescanti flore purpurea*, having flowers of a ". . . violet purple colour, the bottom of them yellow circles . . ." and ". . . another sort little differing from it in anything save in the colour of the flower, which in this is crimson, as in the other purple . . ." In short, the question of whether the Tradescants or some one or more of their circle of gardening friends were already experimenting in hybridization.

It is not an easy one to answer. Natural hybrids have been occurring ever since plants bearing flowers with sexual characteristics evolved,[15] but exactly when artificial hybridization—the deliberate crossing of two species with the intention of combining some characteristics of both in the offspring—really started may never be known. The Abbé Gregor Johann Mendel published his first paper on the subject in 1865, but he was then systematizing the laws of inherited characteristics. John Bartram, the botanist and plant hunter of Philadelphia we shall meet later, is generally credited with some of the earliest experiments in America in 1739, and in England Thomas Fairchild crossed a Sweet William on to a Carnation at an unknown date slightly earlier than that. I suggest, though very cautiously, that the Tradescants and their friends were trying cross-fertilization earlier still; and that the process might also have been known to the Netherlands nurserymen the elder Tradescant visited.

The evidence is admittedly slight but, I think, suggestive. It is difficult, for instance, to believe that the observations of Charles L'Ecluse (Carolus Clusius) on tulip seedlings were unknown to such skillful men; that ". . . when, finally, any early flowering tulips germinate from scattered seed buried in the earth, very few of them retain completely the colour of the mother plants . . ." It is still more difficult to understand a man as shrewd as old John Tradescant paying the large sum of £1.6s. for those two pots of gilliflowers in 1611 unless he was quite certain there was something very new and special about them. Then again we have his known skill with the new and exotic fruit,

---

[15] The two famous apples Cox's orange pippin and Bramley seedling are quite recent natural hybrids, and the common London plane tree is the result of an accidental cross between an American plane and another species from the East.

melons, for which he became famous at St. Augustine's Palace. Every gardener who has ever tried to grow them under glass or in pits—which was Tradescant's method—knows that to be successful you must fertilize the clearly recognizable female flowers with an anther taken from the male.[16] Once more it is difficult to credit that such gardeners as these did not know what they were doing, and from this to cross-fertilization is a very short step.

What was this Turkie purple primrose? Tradescant himself merely lists a *Primula veris angustifolia flore rubro*, a primrose with narrow leaves and red flowers; and Parkinson, who was always very precise, says it came from Turkey. This would seem to make it *Primula acaulis rubra*; and this according to Reginald Farrer "is that beautiful single primrose, red, lilac, purple and crimson, which is the prevalent form throughout the Levant of *P. acaulis*"—while *P. acaulis* is a synonym of *Primula vulgaris*, our common primrose. We have therefore an exotic primrose from the eastern end of the Mediterranean which would naturally hybridize freely and easily with our native species and with *Primula veris*, the oxlip. As it seems it did.

To see how much, let us move to 1665 when John Rea, a nurseryman of Worcestershire, published his *Ceres, Flora, and Pomona*, not such a voluminous work as Parkinson's *Theatrum Botanicum* but useful as showing developments over the last twenty-five years, while his introduction to the chapter on the Primula family as it was then known has its own particular charm. He says, "*Primroses* and *cowslips* are *English* flowers, and well known to every milk maid, being the common ornaments of meadows and pastures, yet there are some varieties of them entertained in our gardens, out of which we will cull the best, and leave the rest to those that delight in such common toys. We have now other kinds of Primroses and Cowslips, that bear diversities of red flowers, more esteemed than those of our own country." He goes on, "The red primrose is of a newer date, more beauty, and greater variety than the former. . . . the greatest difference is in the colours of the flowers, there being almost twenty diversities of red . . . from bloud red to pale Pink colour, some are of a blewish rose colour, sader [sadder]

---

[16] This process was perfectly well known as far back as Babylonian times. As early as 2000 B.C. the male flowers of date palms were an important article of commerce.

and paler, some brick colour, some clove colour, others of the colour of
an old buff coat, and some hair colour; all of which varieties have been
raised from seeds. . . ." [17] Later he continues, "The red Cowslip or
Oxlip is also of several sorts, all of them bearing many flowers on one
stalk, in fashion like those of the field, but of several red colours, some
bigger like oxlips, others smaller like cowslips . . ."

John Tradescant's Turkie purple primrose was not the least of his
gifts to us, and there is very little doubt that our modern strains of
garden polyanthus are a direct link with that fine old Jacobean gardener
and adventurer.

In 1925 the Garden Clubs of Virginia subscribed to provide a
memorial window to John Tradescant in the Old Ashmolean Museum,
Oxford. It was unveiled the following year by Lord Fairfax, himself a
descendant of one of the early Virginians, and portrays a shield carrying
a bend with three fleurs de lys surrounded by a wreath of *Tradescantia
virginiana*. The inscription reads "*Quos arbusta juvent hunc Virgi-
nienses Auspice quo nostris sua frons innascitur hortis*"; The Virginians,
whose pleasure is in planting, celebrate this man by whose auspices
their native leafage decks our gardens.

[17] Note the resemblance in this color range to some of the magnificent strains—"Grand
Canyon," "Desert Sunsets," etc., in Mrs. Florence Bellis's Barnhaven polyanthus raised
from 1935 onward, in some of the modern New Zealand strains and others.

(3)
A Quaker Farmer
of Philadelphia

If the Tradescants were the best known and most successful gardener plant hunters of their century there were others who, although perhaps not so famous, were to make journeys to places farther afield in the years that followed. Trade routes were being extended faster than ever, scientific interest was growing, and the great botanic gardens were being laid out; the earliest of them as long ago as 1545 at Padua in Italy, to be followed by those at Pisa, Leyden, Montpelier, Breslau, Heidelberg, and others, the first in Britain founded by the Earl of Danby at Oxford in 1621, and the Chelsea Physic Garden founded by the Society of Apothecaries of London in 1673. The emphasis was passing from the great, patterned pleasure parks of the landed gentry, and moving toward the deliberate collection of trees and plants which European man had never set eyes upon before.

Botanists set out not only to collect but to observe plants growing in the wild, to make careful drawings of them—skill as an artist, indeed, was as essential as scientific knowledge—and to dry and preserve them as herbarium specimens, still according to those old instructions of John Tradescant, "laid betwin paper leaves in a book." Apart from seeds and bulbs, that was usually the only way of bringing them back; travellers were sometimes away for years on end and until the invention of the Wardian case in 1838 (which see later) few plants could be expected to survive the rigors of those journeys.[1] A curious result of this is that plants were often known, classified, and even named, long before they actually appeared in cultivation; so that later plant hunters would not infrequently go out to search for a plant which was known scientifically although living specimens had never been seen.[2]

[1] Stories of plants being brought back in hats are by no means uncommon. One of the first cedar trees to be seen in Europe is said to have survived the journey from Syria so, and only by sharing its collector's meager ration of one half pint of water daily.

[2] The well-known blue poppy, *Meconopsis betonicifolia*, and the much less known and strange pocket-handkerchief tree, *Davidia involucrata*, are two interesting examples.

As early as 1637—the year of the elder Tradescant's death—William Piso and two young Germans, Georg Marcgrav and Heinrich Cralitz, were exploring the wild and unknown Pernambuco area of Brazil under the command of the Dutch Count of Nassau-Seigen. There is little record of their travels—the Count, in fact, was primarily campaigning against the Portuguese—but some idea of their hardships may be gathered from the fact that Cralitz died within a few months. That expedition lasted seven years before Marcgrav died also, and it was largely due to his efforts that when Nassau-Seigen and Piso finally returned to Holland in 1644 they took with them a collection sufficient to provide material for twelve volumes on natural history, three of them being devoted entirely to plants.

By 1653 another German, Georg Eberhard Rumpf, an official with the Dutch East India Company, was studying the flora of the island of Amboina in what was then the Dutch East Indies. Rumpf is almost forgotten now, although he has been described as the German Pliny, but he surely must have been one of the most courageous, determined, and dedicated workers in the long history of botany; and few men can ever have met so much ill luck. In 1670 he went blind as a result of seventeen years of overwork in the inadequate light of candles and lamps in the then primitive conditions of the East Indies. Only four years later, he lost his wife and one of his daughters in an earthquake. Yet still he worked on and after another twelve years he finished a manuscript representing the total study of a lifetime. This he sent off to Holland to be printed; and the Dutch ship carrying it was attacked and sunk by the French.

With the help of his surviving daughters he set out to rewrite the entire work; and then in 1687 a disastrous fire swept through the Dutch settlement in Amboina and all of the botanical drawings made before he went blind were destroyed. Yet still undeterred he redrafted the whole massive book and had three volumes of it ready for publication by 1690. This time it was safely received by the Dutch East India Company; but the good and penny-wise directors of that august body were unwilling to incur the expense of publication, and after years more of delay and frustration Rumpf died in 1702 without knowing whether his life's work would ever come out. The twelve volumes were eventually edited and published by the Dutch botanist, Johannes Burmann, in 1741. By that time Linnaeus had somehow acquired the credit for the first descriptions of many of Rumpf's plants, but even then the *Herbarium Amboinense* was still considered one of the most remarkable works of its time. It contained descriptions of more than seventeen hundred plants.

The Reverend John Banister was one of the earliest of a long and distinguished line of clerical and missionary plant hunters. Very little is known about him personally except that he was an ardent naturalist—described by one of his friends as "a gentleman pretty curious in these things"—that as a young man he visited the East Indies, and later was sent to Virginia by the then Bishop of London, Henry Compton, whose gardens were and still are at Fulham Palace, London. Banister arrived at Charles Court County, Virginia in 1678 with a brief as we may imagine to look to the spiritual needs of his flock, but also to search no less assiduously for new plants and shrubs. Among his many introductions are *Magnolia virginiana, Echinacea purpurea*, the purple coneflower, *Mertensia virginica*,[3] popularly known as Virginia Bluebells in America and Virginian Cowslip in England. Banister's great contribution, however, was the "Catalogue of Plants observed by me in Virginia," which John Ray published in his *Historia Plantarum* in 1688, and which is still of historical and botanical importance as being the first printed account of the American flora. Unfortunately we know little of Banister's personal adventures or travels save that on one last plant hunting expedition, apparently climbing a steep cliff, it is said that "he fell from the rocks and perished," although another account says that he was accidentally shot.

No record of this period would be complete without the name of Dr. (later Sir) Hans Sloane, who is now generally remembered by Sloane

---

[3] Farrer describes the *Mertensias* as "this glorious race almost all of which are choice delights." *M. virginica* nevertheless still appears to be undeservedly neglected, at least in English gardens. With two-foot sprays of flowers shading from rose pink to blue it is best treated as a wild plant in light shade or woodland, and given only good deep loam will thrive without any other fuss or attention. *Mertensia* is a widely distributed genus and some of the dwarf species—*M. alpina* from Colorado, *M. echioides* of the Himalayas, *M. maritima* from Britain—are among the most beautiful of rock garden subjects. All are tones of blue.

Square and Sloane Street in London. By 1687 he was collecting in Jamaica, where he had travelled as personal physician to the Duke of Albemarle, and though he was only out there a comparatively short time—even that much taken up by demands for his medical services— he brought back upward of eight hundred plant specimens. When he returned to London in 1689 he very quickly became a famous and fashionable physician, and a generous patron of gardeners, plant hunters, and botanists, including John Bartram of Philadelphia. The son of a relatively minor tax official, he lived to be one of the greatest figures of his day, a director of the Chelsea Physic Garden and president of the Royal Society for thirteen years; and like old Tradescant too he was a great collector, particularly of books and manuscripts. Said to have contained fifty thousand items, his collection was finally purchased for the nation, on his death in 1753, at a cost of £20,000 raised by a public lottery; and so, like the Ashmolean, the British Museum came into existence.

The hazards of plant hunting were not always tropical forests, disease, and deadly insects. Engelbert Kaempfer—another German doctor with the Dutch East India Company, whose name is commemorated in the beautiful iris species *Iris kaempferi*—after long travels mostly in Persia arrived in Japan about 1690. As he himself wrote, a "cordial and plentiful supply of European liquors" did much to stimulate easier relations, but even so he and his few companions in the company post on the tiny island of Deshima off Nagasaki, Kyushu, were permanently and jealously guarded by the watchful Japanese. Moreover Europeans were still an exotic novelty in Japan and they were expected to make an annual pilgrimage to the Imperial Court at Tokyo, show themselves to the emperor, pay their respects, and present gifts. In company with local princes and lords, Kaempfer went twice, a trip which took about three months there and back to Deshima, and he complained that he was treated like a circus animal: guarded by day, locked up at night, forced to recite, sing, dance, and mime at the houses of the Japanese nobility on the way, and finally required to put on a kind of royal command performance for the amusement of the emperor's ladies, who remained discreetly hidden behind screens.

In the circumstances accurate field work must have been difficult, but still there were occasions when he managed to escape from his escort, make fleeting botanical observations, and gather plants, though at some risk to himself. In the end he brought back the first known descriptions of hydrangea and ginkgo,[4] bulbs of *Lilium speciosum* and *L. tigrinum*, species of prunus and azalea, many varieties of camellia, and the first tree peonies ever seen in Europe.

Another who seems to have had his troubles is Dr. Samuel Browne, among the most eccentric of the plant hunters and one time ship's doctor, who was appointed surgeon to the British East India Company in Madras in 1688. It was an appointment not without incident, since he was superseded as first surgeon only four years later and in 1693 succeeded in poisoning Mr. James Wheeler, an extremely important local official. Browne's own letter to the Madras governor must be one of the most classically simple statements in history. "Honble Sir: I have murthered Mr. Wheeler by giving him arsnick. Please to execute justice on me the malefactor as I deserve. Your Honour's unfortunate obedient Servant, Sam'll Browne." Browne was committed for trial, when it appeared that his servant had "negligently powdered Pearl in a stone mortar wherein Arsnick had been before beaten . . . ," but acquitted by a grand jury, "who brought in the bill Ignoramus. There was some dissatisfaction at this result."

Two years later he was in trouble again for challenging a Dr. Blackwall to a duel when drunk, and the year after that he was further charged with assaulting a native. "Ananta Terterra doth . . . complain that Dr. Browne broke his face with a pistol, pulled his beard &c . . . which though there is no reason to believe, yet the Dewan's Officers will take occasion to make a demand as customary, and give us trouble

[4] *Ginkgo biloba*, the maidenhair tree, is one of the most curious trees in the world today, having retained its primitive characteristics almost unchanged for several million years. Fossils of ginkgoes appear in the carboniferous layers, and it seems to have reached its greatest development in the Jurassic period, since when it has remained almost unchanged. It is another tree which has died out altogether in the wild and was originally preserved by the Chinese and Japanese who regarded it as sacred. Sometimes reaching up to a hundred feet, it carries small, rather fleshy, bright green fan-shaped leaves which turn golden yellow in autumn, and it appears to be quite unperturbed by town life. Several fine but rather smaller specimens are to be seen growing in parts of London.

by complaining to the Nabob . . ."[5] Apparently largely to avoid trouble with the Nabob, Dr. Browne was committed to custody for causing a breach of the peace, but was discharged after one week on the grounds that his patients required his services.

Nevertheless he appears to have been an enthusiastic botanist and had been corresponding with others of like interest in England since 1690. There is no record of any actual plant collecting as such until 1696, but then between February and July he collected no less than 316 different kinds of plants and dispatched seeds to England which were distributed among some of the most celebrated gardeners and gardens of the day; Oxford Botanic, the Chelsea Physic Garden founded by The Society of Apothecaries of London in 1673, Fulham Palace, and others. But his career of plant collecting was not to last long either; only the next year the British East India decided to abolish his post of second surgeon, and soon afterward he took up fresh work which left little time for botany. He sent all his books of dried herbarium specimens to James Petiver,[6] who afterward wrote in the *Museum Petiverianum,* "I have received near 20 volumes in Folio filled with fair and perfect Specimens of Trees and Herbs, and amongst them some from China, the isle of Ceilon, etc."

One more surgeon of the East India Company who had more than his share of bad luck in the hazards of Eastern travel is the Scotsman James Cunninghame, of whom very little is known. On his first voyage in 1698 his ship was arrested by the Spanish and he and its crew spent some weeks in prison. Released eventually they sailed on for Amoy, on the Chinese coast on the Strait of Formosa where he collected—according to James Petiver again, and apparently within a few months, for he was back in England by 1699—"the Paintings of near eight hundred Plants in their Natural Colours, with their names to all, and Vertues to many of them." In 1700 he made a second voyage, this time to Chusan, stayed there for more than two years, and sent back to England a precise account of the local agriculture including the first known detailed description of the cultivation of tea, up to then a closely guarded secret.

[5] D. G. Crawford, *A History of the Indian Medical Service 1600–1913* (London: Thacker and Co., 1914).

[6] Another famous botanist-gardener and botanical author of his day. Friend of Sir Hans Sloane, demonstrator at the Chelsea Physic Garden, and later Fellow of the Royal Society.

He also complained bitterly of the obstructions "the Chineses" put in his way, writing "Had I the Libertie I could wish for, I might have made greater collections, but the jealousy of these People among whom we live, restrains so much that we have no freedom of rambling . . ." There is a world of meaning between those few lines, but worse was to come.

By 1703, in the face of growing Chinese obstruction the trading station at Chusan was closed down and Cunninghame himself transferred to Pulo Condore—a tiny island lying off the south eastern tip of Indo China—from which the company was seeking now to open up fresh trade with Cochin China. Here in 1705 some of the Macassar employees of the company rebelled, burned down the fort, and murdered all but a few of the Europeans. The Cochin Chinese duly came to their aid, and though at first active enough in slaughtering the Macassars, only a week or so later turned on the rest of the company officials and massacred them too. Badly wounded, Cunninghame was the only survivor and he was carried off and held prisoner for two years, largely on the grounds that the company had sent no gifts to the king of Cochin China. When Cunninghame was at last released, the company made him head of its post at Banjermassin, but even here only ten days after his arrival the station was attacked, once more by incitement of the Chinese, and that too had to be abandoned.

Not surprisingly Cunninghame decided to return home, but he never reached England. He wrote to Sir Hans Sloane and James Petiver from Calcutta early in 1709; after that nothing more is heard of him, and it is presumed that he died at sea. Nevertheless through all of his dangers he sent home more than six hundred specimens of Eastern plants, among them the first camellias ever to be seen in Europe, although Kaempfer had already described them more than ten years before.

About this time too, the French were starting to explore Spanish South America, allowed there by one of the accidents of history and complicated European politics. Charles II of Spain having died childless in 1700, Louis XIV of France, the Sun King,[7] claimed the Spanish

---

[7] Louis XIV created the palace and gardens of Versailles; and probably started the modern fashion of mass bedding out with summer plants. By the time of Louis XV the royal greenhouses—a curious statistic—were said to contain no less than two million flower pots.

throne on behalf of his grandson Philip. It was a more or less legal claim, but a powerful combination of Spanish and French interests was by no means welcome to the British and Dutch and it brought about the thirteen year War of the Spanish Succession; which incidentally led to the Battle of Blenheim and the rise of the Churchill family. So France and Spain became allies and French travelers were at last admitted to the Spanish colonies—though still somewhat unwillingly—with the practical result of introducing many more new plants to Europe, and producing the earliest scientific surveys of the natural history of the Andes. Over the next few years Father Louis Feuillée, Amédée François Frézier, and Joseph de Jussieu were sent out there in turn.

Feuillée was a priest-scientist and his instructions—from the Comte de Pontchartrain, Secretary of State, and the Abbé Bignon,[8] librarian to Louis XIV—were to make geographic and astronomical observations, draw up maps of the exact positions of the ports in Chile and Peru because of the immense treasures brought from there, and to make all possible studies of natural history. His travels appear to have been relatively uneventful, if rather fully occupied, and on his return to France he published his *Journal des Observations* in two volumes and an appendix containing fifty plates, including fuchsia, species of alstroemeria, mimulus, and tropaeolum; the forefather of our now almost too commonplace garden nasturtiums.

Amédée François Frézier arrived in Concepción in 1712 and, so far from being a priest, admitted frankly afterward that he went to South America as a spy, "to pass as a Trader only, the better to insinuate himself with the Spanish governors and to have all opportunities of observing their strength." That he survived suggests he was fairly successful, but what is more important is that among other plants he brought back to France *Fragaria chiloensis*, the large fruited strawberry. Water was short on the six months' voyage home and only a few plants survived the journey; but it was one of these which, crossed with the Virginian Strawberry, became the ancestor of all our fine garden strawberries of today.

[8] Later to be commemorated in *Bignonia capreolata*, the attractive but unfortunately only half hardy red and yellow climber, Trumpet Vine from southeastern America.

Joseph de Jussieu was another of the unfortunates. A volatile character by nature, he was the fourth son of a family of sixteen,[9] and started his career with the study of medicine, gave that up in favor of engineering and mathematics, returned to medicine, and finally made a sudden intensive study of botany—all admirable qualifications for the new scientific survey which was about to be sent out to Ecuador by the French Academy of Science. It was to be a long expedition from the start but longest of all for its young physician-botanist, who left La Rochelle in May 1735 and did not return to France for twenty-six years, when he was insane.

Accounts of his travels are fragmentary. One credits him with collecting young cinchona trees—Peruvian Bark, the source of quinine and at that time the only palliative for the scourge of malaria—and losing them and very nearly his own life in a storm off the mouth of the Amazon. This appears doubtful however since the expedition went by way of Martinique to Panama and thence, after attacks of fever and official delays which enabled de Jussieu to explore the Rio Chagres, over to the Pacific and ultimately to Quito. They worked in Ecuador and Peru for seven years before the party began to break up. Godin, the mathematician, settled in Peru; a physician was murdered; a surveyor killed by accident; a young draughtsman fell in love with a local girl, and the others set out for home, two of them making the first ever journey down the whole length of the Amazon and mapping the river as they went. It seems possible that there might have been some friction since, not for the only time, de Jussieu was left behind; apparently in poverty for he set up as a doctor in Quito. Here he was rather more successful than he had bargained for, since a year or so later with money in hand again he was preparing to leave when smallpox broke out, and the governors not only refused to let him go but threatened severe penalties against anyone who helped him to escape.

There he seems somehow to have received orders from France to go to Lima and collect some surveying instruments from Godin, but on the way he made a wide detour to look for plants instead and after a dangerous journey through desert mountains found his way to a central

---

[9] Of which two elder brothers, Antoine and Bernard, were already famous botanists.

valley of the Cordilleras where he discovered a find, *Heliotropium aborescens (H. peruvianum)*, which, he said, "intoxicated him with delight." [10] When he finally reached Lima, Godin was already preparing to return to France and de Jussieu decided to go with him. They set out for Buenos Aires, an almost impossibly difficult journey across South America from west to east, and in nine months they only reached La Paz in Bolivia where again de Jussieu found the vegetation so enthralling that he lingered to examine it and once more was left behind. Godin went on without him and de Jussieu himself never got to Buenos Aires. On the way there alone he was robbed of his plants and notebooks—it is not clear how the heliotrope got back to Europe—and for the next several years he wandered in poverty through Bolivia before finally reaching Lima in 1755.

Here he learned that his mother and several others of the family in France were now dead, and that collections of plants which he had sent home had been lost at sea. Depression was already closing in on him, and he wrote to his brother Bernard that he was turning to mathematics for solace since "botany had caused him so much vexation." He took up medical practice in Lima again, but his mind was already failing and even though he did at last return to Paris in 1771 he never completely recovered his sanity. It was a heavy price to pay for heliotrope.

It is a relief to come at last to a success story, the fine old Quaker farmer of Philadelphia, a countryman of simple tastes—as he remained all his life—of modest education, who built himself an American and European reputation, and who was described by the all important Linnaeus as being the greatest natural botanist in the world. Moreover, there is a distinct parallel between John Bartram of America, and John Tradescant of Britain a hundred years before: both men of country stock, both of lively curiosity and acute observation, equally of sturdy character, and both to become famous for their contributions to horticulture.

Because of the persistent use of the names John and William, the genealogical details of the family are frankly confusing. The first

[10] From which modern garden heliotropes have been cultivated.

Georg Eberhard Rumpf; blind but still working. From an 18th century engraving. Courtesy of the Controller, Her Majesty's Stationery Office, and the Director, Royal Botanic Gardens, Kew.

RESIDENCE OF JOHN BARTRAM,
BUILT WITH HIS OWN HANDS, A.D. 1730.

John Bartram's house in Philadelphia; frontispiece from *Memorials of John Bartram and Humphrey Marshall* by William Darlington, Philadelphia, 1849.

American John Bartram and his wife emigrated from England [11] and settled in America in 1682 "before there was one house in Philadelphia." John Bartram the botanist, born in 1699, was the grandson of that old pioneer. He married twice, having two children by his first wife and nine more by his second, of which one, born in 1739, was named William. It was this William Bartram who after a somewhat uncertain start became equally famous as an American explorer, naturalist, and man of letters, and who, in fact, ultimately exerted a considerable influence on contemporary literature by his descriptions of Indians and Indian customs and the American landscape. For the sake of clarity and simplicity these are the only two Bartrams who can concern us here, however historically interesting the other connections may be.

John's own mother had died when he was only two, his father had married again and moved to North Carolina, and John seems to have been left in Philadelphia in care of his grandmother from whom he finally inherited the farm which had been left to her by his uncle in 1708. Surprise has often been expressed that in spite of the levels of teaching and access to learning which must then have been available in Philadelphia he remained in the conventional sense comparatively ill educated; it was expressed in his lifetime too, especially after he became famous, when some of his more classically tutored friends were even slightly patronizing about it. The answer appears to be simple enough. He was only nine when the farm came to his grandmother and it seems most likely that his boyhood years were taken up with the hard practical details of seed time and harvest; the life of a working farmer in Pennsylvania of the early eighteenth century left little time for study.

Both John Bartram and William were slightly touchy about it, for many years later William wrote of his father, "He had all or most of the education that could at that time be acquired in country schools; and whenever opportunity offered, he studied such of Latin and Greek grammars and classics, as his circumstances allowed him to purchase; and he always sought the society of the most learned and virtuous

[11] From Derbyshire. The botanist John Bartram is later recorded as having said that he was told by a Scots minister that the Bartram family itself was descended from two brothers Bartram who came to England with William the Conqueror in 1066, one of whom settled in Scotland and the other in Derby.

men." John himself apparently answering some criticism from his friend
and patron, the wealthy Peter Collinson in England, says rather more
sharply, "Good grammar and good spelling may please those that are
more taken with a fine superficial flourish than real truth; but my chief
aims was to inform my readers of the true, real, distinguishing
characters of each genus, and where and how, each species differed
from one another of the same genus." If John Bartram really was
lacking in what is called a formal education he rose above the disability
magnificently.

In 1723 he married a Mary Maris; and in 1723 Benjamin Franklin—
who was later to have a profound influence on Bartram—arrived in
Philadelphia and started work as a printer's compositor. Mary died only
four years later, probably during the "raging sickness" that swept
through Pennsylvania in 1727, and in 1728 we find John buying land of
just over a hundred acres on the Schuylkill River at Kingsessing, then
about three miles from Philadelphia. It was here that he built the house
that is still preserved as a museum and planted the garden generally
considered to have been the first botanic garden in America.[12]

There was already a small cabin on this land, dating from the old
Swedish colony between 1638 and 1655, and on his second marriage—
this time to Ann Medinghall in 1729—John set to work to enlarge and
rebuild it with his own hands, working the materials, splitting rock
slabs, dressing timber in true pioneering style. As appears from the
inscription still to be seen, "John—Ann Bartram 1731," he completed
the building in about two years, although there is a later addition dated
1770, and probably by William Bartram. At the same time he drained
marshland along the Schuylkill to turn it into meadow, and improved
the other land to such an extent that he took heavy crops of hay from
soil which had scarcely produced weeds only a few years before.
Eventually his wheat fields yielded upward of thirty bushels an acre at a

[12] In fact there were others rather earlier. The first, a garden of medicinal herbs, seems
to have been planted by a curious brotherhood of German mystics on the Wissahickon
River. Dr. Christopher Witt—whom Bartram knew and visited—already had a botanic
garden at Germantown, Philadelphia, while there was another nearby at Fair Hill, the
estate of Isaac Norris. John Clayton's garden in Virginia, too, was probably older than
Bartram's. It is safer to say perhaps that John Bartram's garden became the most famous.

time when New York farmers were getting only twenty, and he cropped flax, oats, and Indian corn just as successfully. By 1738 he was purchasing a further 140 acres, and then in the following year adding two more lots of 40 and 10 acres while at the same time profitably selling some of his earlier holdings. In short, a solid man, owner of 261 acres and a fine stone house, and a highly respected member of the community.

The community itself was more than worthy of respect. Philadelphia was fast becoming the intellectual and scientific capital of America, and its leading citizens were in regular correspondence with learned men and societies all over Europe. They included James Logan, a holder of many high offices in Pennsylvania, scholar, botanist and owner of a considerable library from which he gave Bartram a copy of Parkinson's *Paradisus*; Joseph Breintnall, described as "a great lover of poetry, reading all that he could meet with and writing some that was tolerable," and who introduced Bartram to Peter Collinson; Dr. Christopher Witt, whose own library "was furnished with books containing different kinds of learning; as Philosophy, Natural Magic, Divinity, nay even Mystic Divinity . . ."; Benjamin Franklin, post-master, proprietor of the first book shop in Philadelphia, and publisher of *The Pennsylvania Gazette* and *Poor Richard's Almanack*, who was to set up a public fund to finance Bartram's later travels, and who ultimately founded a library, a hospital, and the American Philosophical Society. There were many others; John Bartram was in distinguished company.

Most scientific interest starts more or less unconsciously in early years—Linnaeus, for instance, was known as "the little botanist" at the tender age of eight; but almost everything about Linnaeus was extraordinary—and Bartram himself told Collinson, "I had always, since ten years old, a great inclination to plants," though, he adds, he did not know their proper names, "Having no person nor books to instruct me." William Bartram also said his father knew enough of medicine to treat his neighbors who were too poor to afford professional doctors, which suggests an original interest in medicinal herbs leading on naturally to botany. The traditional story is John's own perhaps slightly idealized account. "One day I was very busy holding my plow (for thee seest that I am but a simple plowman) and being weary I ran under the shade of a tree to repose myself. I cast my eyes on a daisy, I plucked it mechanically and viewed it with more curiosity than country farmers are wont to do; and observing therein many distinct parts, some perpendicular, some horizontal. *What a shame, said my mind, that thee shouldst have employed so many years in tilling the earth and destroying so many flowers and plants, without being acquainted with their structures and uses!* This seeming inspiration suddenly awakened my curiosity for these were not thoughts to which I had been accustomed."

He discussed the idea of botanical studies with his first wife, Mary, but she was against it, no doubt thinking of the farm. "Nevertheless," he says, "Her prudent caution did not discourage me; I thought about it continually, at supper, in bed and wherever I went." Eventually he purchased several botanical works and a Latin grammar, and engaged a neighborhood schoolmaster to give him a three months' course in Latin. He was in his twenties then, botanizing all over his immediate neighborhood, venturing into Maryland, and almost certainly working against a certain amount of wifely disapproval; but his second wife, Ann, does not appear to have objected to his botanical activities so much—it has been suggested indeed that he might have married her for that reason—and he seems to have started his garden about the time of this marriage.

His fruitful friendship with Collinson also started about that time. Peter Collinson was a wholesale wool merchant of London whose main interest was natural philosophy. An enthusiastic gardener, a voluminous correspondent with a wide circle of extremely influential friends, Collinson had trade connections in Carolina, Virginia, Maryland, Pennsylvania, and New England who along with buying his woollen goods were asked to supply him in return with the new American plants which were then exciting so much interest and demand in England. His business contacts were not particularly interested however, their shipments were unreliable, and at length Joseph Breintnall recommended John Bartram. It was a partnership that lasted for thirty-five years.

The trade was tentative at first. Bartram collected what he could on short trips and received payment more or less in kind; seeds for his own garden, books, and tools, lengths of dress material and articles of clothing. Apparently he was not always very well satisfied, as an irritated little comment in one of Collinson's letters suggests. "My cap, it is true, had a small hole or two on the border, but the lining was new. Instead of giving it away, I wish thee had sent it me back again. It would have served me two or three years, to have worn in the country in rainy weather." Then later, when he was travelling farther afield Bartram himself complains, "I assure thee . . . ten pounds will not, at a moderate expense, defray my charges abroad—besides my neglect of business in fallowing, harvest and seed time." He was still the working farmer. But mostly the relationship was more than cordial, as Collinson later wrote, "I can't enough admire thy industry and curiosity in descending to so many minute rarities . . . which are things very acceptable . . ."

Before long the arrangement was placed on a more businesslike footing and Bartram was paid five guineas apiece for boxes containing one hundred varieties of seed, together with maps and drawings, fossils, eggs, minerals, and any other small curiosities he might find. It has been said that Peter Collinson made Bartram as a botanist, but that is not strictly true; Bartram would have been a botanist anyway. What Collinson could and did do was to introduce him to some of the most important patrons of the day. The London wool merchant ultimately published a list of fifty-seven subscribers, headed by Lord Petre, the Dukes of Richmond, Norfolk, Bedford, Argyll, and Marlborough, the Earls of Bute, Leicester, Lincoln and others, Sir Hans Sloane, and his famous protégé Philip Miller of the Chelsea Physic Garden and author of *The Gardener's Dictionary*.[13]

With Collinson distributing his boxes Bartram ultimately introduced upward of two hundred new trees, shrubs, and plants to England, and some of them are still among the best there. *Lilium superbum* and *L. philadelphicum, Phlox maculata,* one of the parents of the fine border

[13] Published in 1724, and another book said to have been the first of its kind in Britain. Frequently revised, enlarged, and translated it remained a standard work for nearly a century.

phlox; *P. divaricata* and *P. subulata, Iris cristata,*[14] the aromatic *Monarda didyma* better known as bee balm, Bergamot, or Oswego tea; rhododendron species, *Magnolia acuminata* and *Gordonia altamaha*— originally *Franklinia altamaha* after Benjamin Franklin, another shrub which has since disappeared completely from the wild and is now only known in cultivation. Again a full list would be tiresome, but there are few parks or gardens in England that do not contain something directly traceable to John Bartram.

Doubtful as the dates and incomplete as the records are, to detail Bartram's travels in full would need several chapters. After his own private botanizing, the earliest collecting for Collinson was still relatively local and it was not until 1735 or '36 that he set out on his first important journey, for which Collinson's friend, Lord Petre, subscribed £10 and promised to find others who would give £10 more each. This journey, after the harvest was safely in, was up the Schuylkill River to its source, and he sent Collinson back seeds and a map of this area, probably the first ever made. The next year found him making several shorter trips to Lancaster County, to New Jersey, and Kent County, but expenses seem to have been worrying him now and a sharp little correspondence with Collinson followed.

That difficulty must have been put right, however, for they were soon discussing the most ambitious project yet: an exploration in Virginia. Collinson himself was particularly interested in this, even to the point of advising Bartram how he should dress. "One thing I must desire of thee, and do insist that thee oblige me therein; that thou make up that drugget clothes to go to Virginia in, and not appear to disgrace thyself or me. . . . [T]hese Virginians are a very gentle, well dressed people—and look, perhaps, more at a man's outside than his inside. For these and other reasons, pray go very clean, neat, and handsomely dressed, to Virginia . . ." If John was unmistakably canny with money

---

[14] *Iris cristata* is among the smallest and most exquisite of all irises. Only a few inches high, its flowers patterned with soft lilac and orange, it is a gem for a lightly shaded spot and cool, peaty soil on the rock garden. *Phlox divaricata* and *P. subulata,* in shades of lavender blue to purple, are also good but rather more obtrusive rock garden plants. These need an open, sunny position.

matters the others also seem to have been slightly worried about him as
a plain countryman.

So, handsomely dressed we hope, John went to Virginia in 1738,
though whether his clothes stood up to the rigors of the journey is
another matter, for on his return he calculated that he had covered
eleven hundred miles in five weeks, resting for only one day. It must
have been a prodigious feat, travelling more than thirty miles a day
alone and through unsettled country, climbing, following forest tracks,
and crossing very considerable rivers. "Up the James River to Gooch-
land. . . . Thence travelling to your Blue Mountains, headed Rappa-
hannock, fell up the branches of the Shenandoah, a great branch of
Potomac, kept the great vale, between the North and South Mountains,
till crossing Susquehanna took the nearest way home." He was nervous
of rattlesnakes, but otherwise it was a profitable journey since that
autumn was an exceptionally good season for seeds.

By now the possibilities of hybridization had been much interesting
botanists for many years, an interest generally considered to be
stemming from a paper presented by the rather splendidly named
Nehemia Grew before the Royal Society in London as far back as 1696.
Hybridization is an uncertain area of horticultural history and one is
unwise to make guesses but, as I have already suggested, it is at least
possible that the European nurserymen knew something about it more
than eighty years before that; working gardeners who keep trade secrets
have never been entirely unknown. As we have seen also Thomas
Fairchild had crossed a Carnation on to a Sweet William, though there
is some doubt whether that was a natural or artificial cross; and Cotton
Mather, the curious New England puritan, witch-hunter, scientist, had
described what were obviously natural crosses between species of
Indian Corn and between squashes and gourds in a letter to James
Petiver.

What is important about John Bartram is that, although the records
are again incomplete, in 1739 he made the first written statement of
deliberate scientific observation and experiment. In a letter to Colonel
William Byrd of Virginia he says, "I have this spring made several
microscopical observations upon ye malle and femall parts in vegetables
to oblige some ingenious botanists in Leyden, who requested that

favour of mee. . . . I have made several successful experiments of
joyning several species of ye same genus whereby I have obtained
curious mixed Colours in flowers never known before. . . . I hope by
these practical observations to open a gate into a very large field of
experimental knowledge which if judiciously improved may be a
considerable addition to ye beauty of ye florists garden." [15] That last
sentence alone shows a man of extraordinary foresight; and how
considerable the addition was may be seen by the fact that today by far
the larger number of plants in our gardens are man-made hybrids, and
that in many genera such hybrids have almost entirely superseded the
species.

In 1739 too the twins, William and Elizabeth, were born; his seventh
and eighth children. Over the next few years he travelled to and fro to
the Jerseys and up the Hudson River to the Catskills, making more new
friends on Collinson's introduction. One of them Dr. Cadwallader
Colden, Surveyor General of the Colonies and a member of the King's
Council of New York observed of him, "It is very extraordinary that a
man of the lowest Education . . . should have such a taste for
knowledge & aquire so great a share of it." Then in 1743 James Logan
sent a peace mission to negotiate with the Iroquois Indians at Onondaga
on Lake Ontario after a skirmish between them and some Virginian
backwoodsmen. These were wild and unknown areas and at Logan's
suggestion Bartram joined the party which consisted of the interpreter
Conrad Weiser, a German who had spent most of his boyhood with the
Maqua Indians, and Lewis Evans, surveyor and map maker, and friend
of Benjamin Franklin.

All three wrote journals: Weiser—who was chiefly responsible for
keeping the Iroquois friendly to the English—a record of the negotiations, Evans details of topography, and John Bartram his observations.
Three copies of this were later sent to England, and such were the
hazards of travel that two were lost to French privateers; the third,
however, reached London safely and Collinson subsequently published
it ". . . at the instance of several gentlemen who were more in number

[15] Bartram Papers, vol. I, the Pennsylvania Historical Society. Quoted in Conway
Zirckle, "The Beginnings of Plant Hybridization" (Philadelphia: University of Pennsylvania Press, 1935).

than could conveniently peruse the manuscript." It was, in fact, an extremely poor publication and Collinson was disgusted by the shoddy job his London printers made of it.[16]

Following streams and Indian trails they reached Shamokin—now Sunbury—where they picked up Chief Shikillamy, who for many years had worked in negotiations between the Iroquois and white settlers; his presence was a great comfort to John Bartram as he had long suspected the Indians of being cannibals. They went on then through "Dismal Vale," "Impenetrable Wilderness" and north ". . . into an Ocean of Woods," finally reaching Onondaga after eighteen days' travel. Here Bartram gives an account of the council, describes a hymn to The Great Spirit "sung in a solemn and harmonious manner" and complains of the Indians' laziness. He also got caught up in a curious little squabble about an Indian belief that rolling stones down the mountainside would bring rain. He tried the trick himself; the rain, in the shape of a violent storm, arrived two days later and when John argued that had there been any truth in the superstition it should have fallen immediately the Indians promptly told him that the white man's almanac often prophesied rain which never came at all. Apart from such minor incidents and snakes, however, it was a profitable journey and he discovered "several curious plants, shrubs, and trees, particularly a great mountain Magnolia, three feet in diameter, and above an hundred feet high." [17]

For the next few years he made only comparatively short journeys and by 1746 even these were becoming hazardous. As yet there had been no serious trouble but the Delaware Indians—cheated out of a huge tract of land by what was known as the "Walking Purchase"—were starting to ally themselves with the French, and in Philadelphia there was sufficient alarm for Benjamin Franklin to organize a militia, while even the peaceful Quaker Assembly voted money for gunpowder. John deemed it wiser to stay at home for a time, though in 1753 he took William, then fourteen years old, for a trip to the Catskills, when they visited Dr. Colden again and met Dr. Alexander Garden,[18] who

[16] Observations, etc., made by Mr. John Bartram in his "Travels from Pensilvania to Onondaga on the Lake Ontario." London, 1751.
[17] *Magnolia acuminata*; the Cucumber Tree.
[18] His name is commemorated in the genus *Gardenia*.

described Bartram and Colden as "men in whom the greatest knowledge and skill are united to the most amiable candour." But with the French and Indian War spreading, further travel was impossible and in 1756 Bartram himself wrote, "I want much to come to Carolina, to observe the curiosities toward the mountains; but the mischievous Indians are so treacherous that it is not safe trusting them, even in their greatest pretence of friendship. They have destroyed all our back inhabitants. No travelling now . . ."

Carolina and the second visit to Virginia had to wait for another four years. He met other botanical notables including John Clayton and a widow lady, Mrs. Martha Logan, who is credited, though probably incorrectly, with having written the first American book on gardening at the age of seventy. She does seem to have been a gardener however. John Bartram was much taken with her—or she with him—and a rather arch correspondence followed with Collinson in which John described her as "my fascinated widow"; he was then sixty-one. The next year, after the English had taken Fort Duquesne, he went down the Ohio River with the officer who had commanded that battle, Colonel Henry Bouquet; Bouquet was a botanist himself and gave Bartram some pecan nuts—the fruit of one species of hickory—which John duly sent on to Collinson. They were the first ever to be seen in the East and they puzzled Collinson considerably; in fact *Carya pecan* has never been satisfactorily grown in England.

William Bartram was now twenty-one and had been causing anxiety for some years. He had enjoyed advantages denied his father—a secure background, a home now with a well-stocked library, a circle of family friends which included some of the most prominent scientific and literary figures in America. He was, moreover, an excellent artist and wished to establish himself as a botanical artist. But John was dubious. In spite of his own success he wanted William to take up some steadier and more profitable work; and it could have been that there was still some trace of his tendency to see himself as "a simple plowman," for at one point he complained to Collinson that he did not want Billy to become what is commonly called a gentleman. The result was that William drifted from one unsuitable job to another, a spell on a plantation with one of his uncles, a trading venture which failed, work as a day laborer, even getting into debt—which horrified and grieved his father.

John Bartram's own career was approaching its climax. Having established an international reputation, he had been corresponding with some of the greatest figures of their time for years: Sir Hans Sloane, Gronovius of Leyden, Buffon in France, Gmelin in Russia, Fothergill in London—one of the greatest physicians of his day and, incidentally, one of the earliest members of the American Philosophical Society—and many others even including the great Linnaeus—Carl von Linné—himself. By now the systems of Linnaeus—in which he proposed that all living organisms should be described by a specific name in Latin consisting of not more than two words, and which attempted to classify plants by the number and arrangement of stamens, ovaries, and associated sexual characteristics—had been generally accepted, though not without a struggle. Even Collinson, who would have been described as advanced, had written to John Bartram shortly after the publication of *Systema Naturae* back in 1735 saying it "is a curious performance for a young man . . ." Linnaeus was then still under thirty. "But his coining of a new set of names for plants tends but to embarrass and perplex the study of Botany. Very few like it."

At first very few did. The uproar was deafening and at times not without its humor. Linné's books were publicly burned in Rome, and his friend Fabricius wrote, "He dared not publish many important observations relating to the general arrangement of Nature because he was afraid of the excessive violence of the Swedish divines." His somewhat over-zestful descriptions of the sexual functions of flowers— "Twenty or thirty females in bed with the same male" for instance, speaking of the stamens and stigma of the poppy—were an offense against decency. "Loathsome harlotry," roared one cleric and another thundered from the pulpit, "Nothing can equal the gross prurience of Linné's mind." The mildest of the attacks called him the "man who has thrown all botany into confusion," though his supporters proclaimed proudly "God created; Linnaeus has set in order." One cannot avoid the suspicion that Linnaeus thought so himself.

Still travelling and dreaming of fresh discoveries John Bartram wrote to Collinson in 1763, "The variety of plants and flowers in our south western continent is beyond expression. . . . If I could but spend six months in Ohio, Mississippi, and Florida, in health, I believe I could find more curiosities than the English, French and Spaniards have done in six score of years . . ." That opportunity was yet to come. In 1765 after a long campaign on his behalf Collinson contrived to get John appointed King's Botanist at a salary of £50 a year, though with some difficulty for George III was not interested and Queen Charlotte was known to favor another botanist named William Young—of whom John Bartram was extremely jealous and said that Young had "got more honour by a few miles travelling to pick up a few common plants than I have by near thirty years' travel with great danger and peril . . ." It was a poor recognition and Collinson was disappointed; but not even his influence could get more; neither could he get John official letters of introduction to the governors of Florida, which had been a British colony since 1763. Nevertheless it was enough to raise one unexpected voice in protest—that of Dr. Garden who wrote to Linnaeus, "He tells me that he is appointed King's Botanist in America. Is it really so? Surely John is a worthy man; but yet to give the title of King's Botanist to a man who can scarcely spell, much less make out the characters of any one genus, appears rather hyperbolical. Pray how is this matter?"

It was enough for John Bartram, too, in spite of Collinson's angry advice, "Thou knows the length of a chain of 50 links, go as far as that goes, and when that's at an end, cease to go any further." In July 1765, he left Philadelphia for Charleston, a journey which took a week by sea, during which he was sick all the time so that he arrived at his "worthy dear friend Dr Gardens very faint." From here he travelled northward up Cape Fear River to Asheville, where William was at work on some kind of trading venture under the watchful eye of an uncle, but growing restless again and more than glad enough to join his father on another botanizing expedition. They went by Jacksonburg to Savannah, up river to Augusta, back to Ebenezer, and then south to Fort Barrington on the Altamaha River. It was here they found *Gordonia altamaha*, already mentioned, and *Nyssa sylvatica*.[19]

[19] The Tupelo. A still relatively uncommon tree, but sometimes seen by the waterside in parks and botanic gardens. It will reach seventy feet and is grown for its magnificent autumn coloring in orange and crimson.

Back in St. Augustine on the coast of Florida John suffered a serious attack of malaria and it was a month or more before he could travel again, but then he and William set out for the main object of their journey: an exploration of the St. John River. This they traced for four hundred miles until they could go no farther, the stream then being choked with water plants. They returned to St. Augustine by February, where Bartram plotted a map of the river for the governor before finally taking the ship for Philadelphia, leaving William behind again. William now wanted to become a planter in Florida and subsequently tried, unsuccessfully, to grow indigo there; "This frolic and our maintenance," Bartram complained, "Hath drove me to great straits."

That was the last of his great journeys. He was then sixty-seven and his old friend Collinson died only two years later in 1768. Long ago, with Benjamin Franklin, Bartram had been one of the nine founder members of the American Philosophical Society, and he was now elected to the Royal Academy of Science of Stockholm in 1769. For some years more he continued to send seeds to Europe, but they were probably from his garden or collected locally; and he was getting to be an old man now, the rifts between England and the Colonies were deepening and widening, and his own opinions against the English were hardening. With growing anxiety about William's restless life he lived on until 1777, dying at the age of seventy-eight, with the War of Independence raging, just as General Howe's troops entered Philadelphia after the Battle of Brandywine Creek. He left the garden to William's next youngest brother, John, who was born in 1743.

In an all too short sketch of a life so full of work and achievement much of equal interest must of necessity be left out; neither, regrettably, is there space here for William Bartram, except to say that through his *Travels*—one of the earliest and certainly the finest record of American experience, landscape, and people in the eighteenth century; a book that achieved world-wide recognition and profoundly influenced Wordsworth, Coleridge, and many later writers—he more than proved himself a worthy son of the old Quaker pioneer.[20] John Bartram need not have been troubled during his later years; he would have been proud of Billy in the end.

[20] First published by James and Johnson. Philadelphia, 1791.

(4)

The Gentlemen Amateurs

The eighteenth century was the age of the gentleman amateur, using that much abused word in its true sense as of a person who follows some interest or study not with a view to personal gain, but merely from a desire for knowledge. At a time when it has become mindlessly fashionable to deride the middle classes—the word "bourgeois" itself only became a term of abuse during the French Revolution when progressively extreme factions set out to inflame the mobs in order to wrest power from the bourgeoisie who had already toppled the aristocracy—we are liable to forget that with a few exceptions all of the foundations of modern science were laid down by well-to-do middle-class amateurs. Such amateurs as founded the Royal Society of London, the American Philosophical Society, the Royal Academy of Science of Stockholm, and many other learned bodies: working and corresponding tirelessly, frequently in Latin, from London to Philadelphia, from Philadelphia to Leyden, Uppsala, Edinburgh, Paris, and St. Petersburg, and steadily advancing the frontiers of learning.

Among the most influential of them was Joseph Banks (1743–1820), in his day one of the greatest patrons of plant hunters and of science, and sometimes a distinctly autocratic patron. A wealthy Lincolnshire landowner, he became interested in botany as a schoolboy; a typical figure of an exciting and expanding age, he was famous by the time he was twenty-eight; a man of tireless energy, and sometimes less amiable characteristics, he made Britain the center of horticultural discovery for the next century. His own travels all-told only occupied a short period of his life; but as a personal friend of George III, honorary director of the new Royal Botanic Gardens at Kew, president of the African Association, and president of the Royal Society—a position which he held for no less than forty-two years—he was very literally a commanding figure in more senses than one.

Like John Bartram, though with greater opportunities, the young

Banks was no scholar; like Bartram too his interest appears to have been in the nature of a sudden conversion. From his own account he was loitering along a country lane one summer evening when, struck by the beauty of the flowers, he said, "It is surely more natural that I should be taught to know all these productions of Nature in preference to Greek or Latin . . ." and then began to teach himself botany, largely with the assistance of country women who gathered herbs for the apothecaries, paying them sixpence for every new specimen they could find him. Finally he discovered an old copy of Gerard's *Herbal* in his mother's dressing room, and thereafter, according to Lord Brougham, "his whole time out of school was given up to hunting after plants and insects, making a *hortus siccus* of the one," (a herbarium of dried plants) "and forming a cabinet of the other." [1]

In those days there was little formal education in botany. It is true that in Sweden Linnaeus was lecturing enthusiastically to a worshipful following of students and disciples—indeed it was difficult to stop that man lecturing—but in England a professorship in one or another of the universities was more often a permanent invitation to the college port than a teaching post. Humphrey Sibthorp, professor of Botany at Oxford, was no exception to this reasonable rule; he is said to have delivered only one lecture in thirty-five years. But that was a situation which young Banks, blessed with money and a habit of getting his own way, disposed of quite characteristically. He "applied to the learned doctor for leave to engage a lecturer, whose remuneration should be wholly defrayed by his pupil," Banks himself, "and it is highly creditable to the professor, and shows his love of the science, in which some of his family afterwards so greatly excelled, that he at once agreed to the proposal." [2]

Sibthorp was more than helpful. There being no person available actually to teach botany at Oxford he furnished Banks with a letter of introduction to Professor John Martyn, who held the same chair at Cambridge, not with the quite impossible thought that Martyn himself should be asked to lecture, but in the hope that he might know of some

[1] Lord Brougham, *Lives of Men of Letters and Science in the Reign of George III* (London, 1846).

[2] *Ibid.* And there is no trace of irony in his lordship's recollections.

suitably lowly tutor to satisfy the demands of this importunate young undergraduate. In due course an Israel Lyons, already distinguished in botany and astronomy, was discovered and brought back to Oxford at Banks's expense: so botany was established there as a teaching subject, and in later years Banks recommended Lyons as astronomer to another friend of his, Captain Constantine Phipps, R.N., who led an Arctic expedition to search, unsuccessfully as it happened, for a route to the North Pole.

When he came down in 1764 Banks was a young man of presence, with a truly admirable income—his father had died in 1761—a town house, and a country estate; his mother and devoted sister, Sarah Sophia, had their own establishment near the Physic Garden in Chelsea. His circle of friends began to expand rapidly, not only the cultured and wealthy gentlemen amateurs of the century, but horticulturalists and gardeners, and in 1766 at the age of twenty-three he was almost automatically proposed for a Fellowship of the Royal Society. The fact that so far he had done nothing whatever to merit the distinction did not in the least matter; he was, after all, supremely eligible in every other way.

When he was duly elected, in April of that year, he was already on the way to Newfoundland in H.M.S. *Niger* with Captain Sir Thomas Adams and the already mentioned Constantine Phipps, then a lieutenant, heir to an Irish peerage, and himself a man of wide scientific interests. We might reasonably ask what a private young gentleman was doing aboard a Royal Navy vessel concerned primarily with looking after British fishing interests in Newfoundland, especially since it is doubtful whether their Lordships of the Admiralty at that time had the slightest interest in botanical exploration. The answer, however, is quite simple. Mr. Joseph Banks had decided that he would go to collect plants and study the Eskimo, and he appears to have arranged the matter with much the same calm certainty as he had reorganized some part of the educational system at Oxford. He had friends in high places.

He kept a journal of the voyage, of which the original is now in possession of the Royal Geographical Society of Australasia; his sister, Sarah Sophia, with whom he corresponded regularly and affectionately, made a copy of it with her own amendments.[3] Some of them are amusing—as where for instance Banks writes of one adventure, ". . . when mere accident preserved my life," and Sarah makes the marginal note "Providence"—and some not so fortunate, as when she says flatly, "mem; there are many references to Latin Names of Plants &c. which I shall leave out." Clearly Sarah did not share her brother's botanical interests, but it is still an entertaining journal of observations: a description of an iceberg ". . . like a body of whitish light," a complaint that after a bout of fever he was so weak that he was "baffled by every Butterfly who chose to fly away," notes on the Newfoundland Indians and the comment that ". . . if half I have wrote about them is true, it is more than I expect," and recipes for chowder and for spruce beer together with the extraordinary and potent variations which could be based upon it.

Some of its style appears in a letter to Sarah.

I hope Mr. Lee[4] has been Very Civil & Given you Nosegays. . . . tell him that if I did not think it might Endanger Cracking some of Your Ladyships teeth I would let him know by you some of the Hard names of the things I have got. . . . I do not know what else to say I am almost Exhausted thank you however for your ague receipt it has one merit however I think for if it would not cure an ague I am sure it would kill a horse. . . . We are here in daily expectation of the Eskimaux Ladies here I wish with all my heart they were Come as I might have sent you a sealskin gown & Petticoat Perfumed with train oil which to them is as Sweet as Lavander water.

Banks's most important journal is his account of the voyage with Captain Cook, a voyage which had as its objects two branches of science in which Banks had no interest whatever, astronomy and geography. It was intended first to observe the transit of Venus—the passage of Venus across the disk of the sun, a phenomenon occurring only at intervals of more than a century—from some suitable location in the Pacific Ocean, and second to find and investigate the great continent which for long theoretical geographers had believed to exist

[3] In the library of the Botanical Department, the British Museum, London.
[4] James Lee. The then well-known nurseryman.

in the southern and western areas of the Pacific; the *terra australis incognita*. The Council of the Royal Society had petitioned King George III for a grant of £4,000 and a suitable ship for these purposes only, and originally nothing was further from their minds than the idea of a botanical expedition. But they had forgotten young Mr. Banks.

He attended his first meeting of the Royal Society in February 1767, when the project was already being discussed, and by June of 1768 the location for the astronomical observations had been fixed at what is now Matavai Bay, Tahiti, and Mr. James Cook selected as commander. It was at this point that the secretary of the Royal Society wrote to the Admiralty. "Joseph Banks Esqr Fellow of this Society, a Gentleman of large fortune, who is well versed in natural history, being Desirous of undertaking the same voyage the Council very earnestly request their Lordships that. . . . He also, together with his Suite, being seven persons more, that is, eight persons in all, together with their baggage, be received on board of the Ship . . ."

In short Banks was proposing to plant himself, his party, and their considerable equipment on to a small and already overcrowded ship for a purpose which the government had not even remotely considered. It is typical of the man that his own arrangements were already far advanced, his "suite" already selected when that letter was submitted to the Admiralty, and that he did not expect to be refused. It is equally typical of the century that he was not. Some of his friends pointed out the hardships and dangers of the voyage, and suggested that he should take the conventional Grand Tour of Europe instead; Banks's reply was again typical. "Every blockhead does that; my Grand Tour shall be one round the whole globe";[5] and duly on July 22 Lieutenant Cook was directed by the Admiralty to receive on board *Endeavour* "Joseph Banks Esq and his Suite consisting of eight Persons and their baggage . . ."[6] That included a library, scientific instruments, and

[5] Edward Smith, *Life of Sir Joseph Banks* (London: Lane, 1911).

[6] This became nine in the end. Besides Banks the full party consisted of Dr. D. C. Solander, a distinguished Swedish botanist and pupil of Linnaeus; H. D. Spöring, a Finnish doctor and naturalist; Sydney Parkinson, a botanical draughtsman; Alexander Buchan, a draughtsman for landscape and figures; Peter Briscoe, James Roberts, Thomas Richmond, and George Dorlton, servants.

apparatus for collecting and preserving specimens, all provided by Banks himself. It was the first privately equipped expedition ever known, although the estimated cost of £10,000 is probably slightly exaggerated.

For a full description of the voyage Banks's own journal[7] cannot be improved upon; they sailed in August 1768 and reached Rio de Janeiro in November. Of Rio he observes: "This town as well as all others in South America belonging either to Spanyards or Portuguese has long been unfamous for the unchastity of its women; the people who we talked with here confirmed the accounts declaring . . . there was (not) one honest woman in the township, which I must own appeared to me a most wonderfull assertion but I must take it for granted as I had not even the least opportunity to go among them . . ." He must have been otherwise occupied for they remained there until December before resuming their journey south.

They were in Tahiti by April 1769, where they remained until August making their astronomical observations, exploring, botanizing and collecting, and where the susceptible Joseph Banks was more than taken by several of the charming young ladies of the island in spite of the fact that he had already got himself devotedly engaged to a certain Miss Harriet Blosset only a few days before leaving England. It was here too that they discovered the breadfruit, *Artocarpus communis*, which eighteen years later was to be the object of Captain William Bligh's voyage in *Bounty*—to collect young plants for introduction to the West Indies as food for the slaves—and lead subsequently to the historic mutiny and Bligh's own epic journey of 3,618 miles to Timor in an open boat.

Early in October they sighted land again and Banks writes, "This morn the land seen from the deck appears to be very large. . . . After dinner dropd calm. . . . In the Evening a pleasant breeze; Land still distant 7 or 8 leagues appears larger than ever . . . all hands seem to agree that this is certainly the Continent we are in search of." That was New Zealand and by the next April, 1770, they had sailed completely

---

[7] J. C. Beaglehole, ed, *The Endeavour Journal of Joseph Banks* (London and Sydney: 1963). Library of New South Wales and Angus and Robertson.

round both North and South Islands; so "to the total demolition of our aerial fabrick called continent."

That was yet to come. Standing westward again they made their next landfall near Point Hicks in southeastern Australia—named after the seaman who sighted it—on April 19. Then north along the east coast, when Banks gives a graphic description of a water spout, landing at and naming Botany Bay and many other points, exploring, collecting, studying the natives—called "Indians" by Banks—and on to the Great Barrier area by August; where at one time they were in danger of being flung on to the reef by immense Pacific breakers and he wrote: "The fear of Death is bitter." Navigating reefs and channels they crept on to Cape York, through Endeavour Straight and its islands to New Guinea, on to Timor and then Batavia (now Jakarta) in Java, where they rested from October to December 26, 1770. The exploration proper had finished when they reached New Guinea and now they were in relatively well-known seas.

The achievement had been extraordinary. Banks had amassed a collection of plants, herbaria, drawings, and natural history specimens such as had never been seen before;[8] Cook had carried out more than his instructions and discovered the Australasian continent without the loss of a single man—that of itself almost a miracle for a voyage of such duration and hazard. But at Batavia and on their first homeward leg disaster in the shape of dysentery and malaria struck the tired, overcrowded ship's company and eight of them died, including Parkinson and Spöring in Banks's party; Banks himself fell sick and Solander was so ill that he barely recovered. However, by the time they rounded the Cape of Good Hope the worst was over. They sighted the British East India fleet in the South Atlantic, sailed with it until they were outpaced, and finally reached England on July 12, 1771, after a voyage of three years less one month; and Joseph Banks was still only twenty-eight.

They stepped ashore at Deal to immediate fame, especially Mr.

---

[8] Collected from everywhere they landed, from Madeira to South America, the Pacific islands to New Zealand, Australia and New Guinea. A complete list, even of those which are now commonplace garden plants such as species of amaranthus, amaryllis, canna, eucalyptus, hibiscus, lobelia, etc., would need a long appendix to itself.

Banks; although, to do him justice, rather from the newspapers than by any deliberate effort of his own. Mr. Banks had brought back "no less than seventeen thousand plants of a kind never before seen"; Mr. Banks was introduced to His Majesty; Mr. Banks was fêted and lionized; he and Solander dined with the celebrated Dr. Johnson and Mr. Boswell; and finally, "Mr. Banks is to have two ships from Government to pursue his discoveries in the South Seas, and will sail upon his second voyage next March." Yet the glory was not without its embarrassments, for Mr. Banks proved sadly fickle to Miss Harriet Blosset who had spent most of his long absence in country retirement engaged chiefly, it seems, in making embroidered waistcoats for him. He spent a whole week without attempting to communicate with the lady and when at last Miss Blosset herself set out for London and wrote to him, very reasonably, asking for an explanation "Mr Bankes answer'd by a letter of 2 or 3 sheets professing love &c. but that he found he was of too volatile a temper to marry." It caused a certain amount of scandal.

Even great men are not immune from self-conceit. The full story of the fitting out of the second expedition in *Resolution* and *Adventure* is complex, acrimonious, and sometimes not without its humor. Briefly, the Admiralty with a very proper appreciation of Captain Cook's abilities placed him in command, but there appears to have been no doubt in Joseph Banks's mind who was really going to give the orders. Public and newspapers alike appeared to confirm him in this, and in the months of preparation the affair at one point very nearly became a political issue. Mr. Banks required extensive alterations made to the command ship; his own accommodation enlarged to a sort of admiral's cabin, extra quarters for his party, decks raised and adjusted, a superstructure built on the main deck itself. Had he been given his way *Resolution* would have capsized in the first moderate wind it encountered.

By May of 1772 he had worked up his party to fourteen persons besides Dr. Solander and himself, including the immensely fashionable society artist Johann Zoffany. There were to be three draughtsmen, two secretaries, six servants and, the final touch of improbability, two horn players. It was to be almost a gala performance, but in the end their Lordships of the Admiralty and Captain Cook had to call a halt. A gentleman of large fortune quartered on a naval vessel and within reason knowing his place was one thing; an extremely self-important public figure who now claimed to have "given pledges to all Europe" was entirely another. When *Resolution* and *Adventure* finally sailed in July they carried neither Mr. Banks nor his suite, but just one astronomer.

Banks took himself and his party—but not Mr. Zoffany—off to Iceland instead, a jaunt which was more in the nature of a fashionable tour than a serious expedition. They botanized, collected specimens, Scandinavian books and manuscripts, visited the geysers and Mount Hecla, and the draughtsmen made drawings of Icelandic landscape and people. In October their ship was ballasted with lava, and they sailed south again, but there was very little to show for it, although the books and manuscripts were later to become the foundation of the British Museum's Icelandic Collection, and the lava found its way to Kew Gardens and to the rockery in the Physic Garden in Chelsea. Solander compiled a *Flora Islandica* which, together with the greater part of the drawings, was never published; and Mr. Banks had a new visiting card made with a map of Iceland engraved upon it.

His short career of active plant hunting was over. The social life in London, the care of his Lincolnshire estates, the affairs of the Royal Society when he was elected to its council, voluminous correspondence and widening scientific interests—with Benjamin Franklin among others—and the honorary directorship of Kew Gardens left him little time for it. He took up that appointment in 1772 on the death of Princess Augusta, widow of Frederick, Prince of Wales, who had laid out the gardens on a grand scale with the help and advice of Lord Bute, a poor politician but a good gardener, who introduced the dahlia to Britain, and was another of John Bartram's correspondents. Banks was to hold this directorship for the remainder of his life; he was to make Kew the greatest botanical garden in the world, and henceforth he was to be one of the greatest—and not always one of the easiest—of patrons to professional plant hunters.

The first collector actually sent out by Banks was Francis Masson, whose name links with that of Carl Pehr Thunberg since for a time they worked together in South Africa. When Banks returned from the great voyage, in spite of the fact that in his journal he does not appear to have been impressed by Cape Town, he suggested that a man should be sent out there. We know very little of Masson's early life save that he was an Aberdonian and had been a gardener at Kew, but according to his own modest account he got the job because he was the only person who applied for it. By contemporary standards it was a good one; he was to receive £100 a year salary, payable on his return to England, and £200 expenses while travelling.

Thunberg was a Swedish physician who was on his way, apparently in a somewhat leisurely fashion, to join the Dutch East India Company in Japan, and when Masson reached Cape Town late in 1772 Thunberg had been here since the previous June. He was also lucky to be alive since on board ship coming out the cook, whether inadvertently or otherwise is not clear, had served up pancakes somewhat curiously compounded with flour and white lead, and Thunberg was a very sick man when he landed. Never a character to allow such minor mishaps to deter him however he set off in August—the African spring—with four other companions on an eight hundred mile round trip.

Thunberg's own version of their adventures included in the four volumes of his *Travels* is apt to be rather more than highly colored but it is always entertaining, especially when on one occasion they were attacked by a maddened buffalo.[9] Two of their horses were killed, but with his never failing presence of mind, courage, and agility Thunberg took instant evasive action by climbing into a tree while his companions fled in terror. One of them "burst into tears deploring the loss of his two spirited steeds" and another was ". . . so strongly affected that he could scarcely speak for several days after." Nevertheless the journey had its rewards, and when they returned to the Cape he brought back a large collection of exotics including *Strelitzia reginae*, the gorgeous bird of paradise flower. The experience of seeing that strange beauty for the first time growing in the wild must have been worth almost any hazard.

Masson had already been here for some weeks and he and Thunberg joined forces, an arrangement to their mutual advantage since Masson

[9] *Travels in Europe, Africa and Asia*, 4 vols. (London: Rivington, 1795).

on his £200 expenses was comparatively affluent but knew nothing of the country, while Thunberg, already with some experience, was very much the reverse. As a result of two of the Cape Dutch governors dying in rapid succession he was receiving no money from Holland, supporting himself by a small medical practice in Cape Town, and probably by selling plants to visiting ship's officers who regularly purchased collections as tourists now buy souvenirs.

Their first journey covered much the same ground as Thunberg had already explored, eastward to Swellendam and then turning north. But Thunberg's impetuosity was soon to get him into trouble, when he was very nearly swept away and drowned while crossing the flooded Duyvenhoek's River. The two accounts of the same exploit make a nice contrast. According to Masson "The Dr imprudently took the ford without the least enquiry, when on a sudden he and his horse plunged head over ears into a pit and [he] was dragged out by his horse." [10] Thunberg's version is rather more dramatic. He announces that being the most courageous of the company and consequently always in the lead he had the ill luck to plunge with his horse into a hippopotamus wallow, an accident which might have proved fatal ". . . if I, who have always had the good fortune to possess myself in the greatest dangers, had not with the greatest calm and composure, guided the animal . . . and kept myself fast in the saddle."

There were further minor adventures—as when Thunberg insisted on sunbathing in blazing sunshine attired only in a handkerchief, as a result of which he was so badly burned as to be helpless for several days—but they pushed on to the boundaries of the colony. Here they explored a magnificent rolling countryside of groves and woods, until their carriers refused to go any farther for fear of the Kaffirs, and they turned back. It had been a successful and profitable exploration and they had made a large collection of new and unknown species, of which the most striking must have been the uniquely colored *Ixia viridiflora*;[11] another startling

[10] *Philosophical Transactions*, vol. LXVI. Royal Society, London.

[11] A color that does not occur in any other known plant; the star-shaped flowers are vivid electric greenish blue with a blackish purple center. *I. viridiflora* is not as vigorous as most of the bulbsmen's hybrid ixias, and it is a rare plant in the wild, but the corms are sometimes offered and they are well worth trying. It is best for pot culture—five or six

and remarkable plant. Then that winter at the Cape, Masson found *Nerine sarniensis* growing on Table Mountain; another important discovery since this had always previously been thought to be a native of Japan. That winter too Thunberg complained that he (Masson) was "not much inclined to make any further excursions this year" (1774) and it rather looks as if he was starting to find the company of the volatile little Swede something of a trial.

However, they set off together again in the spring; this time into unknown country where Thunberg now distinguished himself as a mountaineer, making a hair-raising climb of the precipices of the Riebeck Castell and describing how "My fellow traveller together with his dog stood astonished at my adventurous exploit. . . . My courage was rewarded with a small plant . . ." Masson does not mention the incident at all, contenting himself with saying only that here they collected "many remarkable new plants in particular a hyacinth with flowers of a pale golden colour." Then later, in crossing the desert Karoo under a pitiless sun and sky, they passed through the most tantalizing experience any plant hunter can ever know; they found themselves surrounded by "a great treasure of new succulents" but dared not to stop to examine them as the next water was three days away, they themselves were suffering, and their animals were dying of thirst. Even so they picked up over a hundred new species from the sides of the track as they marched on. They penetrated as far as the Roggeveld Mountains by early December and then, with their horses and oxen exhausted, turned back for the Cape. A few months later they parted, Thunberg sailing on to Java and Japan and Masson leaving for England.

Banks expressed his approval. He announced, "His Majesty's appointment of Mr. Masson is to be accounted among the very few Royal bounties which has not been misapplied." The praise was not always to be so fulsome, but it was a good start, and Masson himself wrote to Linnaeus that he had "been the means of adding upwards of 500 new species to His Majesty's collection of living plants." These included

---

corms to the pot—in good but light sandy soil, planted in autumn, over-wintered in a cool house, and brought out to a sunny position to flower in June.

pelargoniums, mesembryanthemums, heaths and oxalis, stapelias,[12] lobelias, arctotis, and many more. It was the first astonishing revelation of the variety and abundance of the Cape flora.

Thunberg was only in Japan for a little over a year, stationed like Kaempfer on Deshima Island, and having much the same experiences, although he says he was highly thought of and besieged by astrologers and physicians begging his advice about their patients. Botanizing expeditions were always attended by a train of officials, interpreters and guards; and on one occasion his permission was withdrawn because a local governor could find no precedent for a physician, only a physician's mate, to collect plants. Nevertheless he did manage to collect, sometimes secretly, and he noted and later described in *Flora Japonica*—published in 1784—over three hundred species. He spent some time in Batavia too; and of Batavia he tells the grim story how, of the twelve people with whom he dined there before leaving for Japan, only one was still alive when he returned eighteen months later.

He left Batavia in 1777 and, always a leisurely traveller, spent five more months in Ceylon before finally returning to Europe with a large collection of Japanese and Cingalese seeds and plants. Of these, however, most died from gales and cold before reaching Cape Town, and many more were lost in one final storm in the English Channel. Thunberg himself succeeded his old master Linnaeus as professor of botany at Uppsala in 1781, and spent the remainder of his life writing his *Travels*, a *Flora Capensis*, and a number of other somewhat inaccurate botanical works. The genus of greenhouse climbers, *Thunbergia*, is named after him.

Meanwhile after a year or so at home Masson was working in Spain, the Canary Islands, Azores, and West Indies. Little record of these travels exists, but it was 1786 before Banks sent him back to the Cape. Much was changed here too. The American War of Independence was

[12] The stapelias enjoy the dubious distinction of being among the most grotesque of all Nature's plant creations. A genus of seventy-five species of greenhouse succulents, they nearly all have flowers that resemble nothing so much as starfish of one sort or another: blotched, bloated, speckled or hairy. To add to their peculiarity many emit a foul odor of carrion, while another of their oddities is that their seed will often germinate in less than forty-eight hours. Some people, of whom Francis Masson himself was one, find them fascinating, as indeed they are in their bizarre way.

only three years past; Holland, France, and Spain had also been at war against Britain and although peace was now officially restored, suspicion still lingered. A certain mysterious Mr. Patterson, supposed to have been collecting for Lord Strathmore, had been said to be an English spy and the Dutch restricted Masson's own movements to within a radius of forty miles of Cape Town. Apart from that he was treated well enough; within ten days of his arrival he sent Banks sixty packets of seeds, while later he obtained permission to make a long trek to the Hottentot Holland Mountains. Banks—now Sir Joseph; he had been created a baronet in 1781—was not appreciative. He wrote, "These expensive journeys up the country seldom produce an adequate return in really ripe seed," and instructed Masson to work one or two rich areas thoroughly, and added, "I trust you will remain quiet; afterwards you may propose excursions."

Masson dutifully did as he was told. For the next five or six years he remained very quiet, sending a vast amount of material home and meeting other plant hunters at the Cape, including poor unlucky Anton Pantaleon Hove whom we shall meet ourselves shortly. But in 1793 the French revolutionary wars broke out in Europe, and French troops overran Holland. The Prince of Orange took refuge in Britain and authorized a British attack on the Cape to forestall a rumored French landing. The Cape Dutch prepared grimly to fight both French and British if necessary, and Masson, fearing for his collections and perhaps his life, asked to be recalled. He left early in 1795, and Cape Colony capitulated to Britain in September of that year after all.

It was an unlucky move, for Masson was now fifty-six and uncertain of his future. Back in England Banks granted him a year's leave to write his book on the stapelias,[13] a work which he dedicated to the King and added unwisely, "I am anxious to recommend my employment as a collector, and still enjoying, though now in the afternoon of life, a reasonable share of health and vigour, I am now ready to proceed to any part of the globe to which your Majesty's commands shall direct me." His Majesty, or rather Banks, took him at his word. At the best it was unimaginative; at the worst callous. After more than twenty years in sub-tropical climates Masson was sent to Canada.

[13] *Stapeliae Novae*, published in two parts; 1796 and 1797.

He sailed in September 1797, with Britain now fighting France at sea. In the Atlantic his ship was first held up by a French privateer but allowed to sail on, only to be captured soon after by a pirate. Masson and a few others were eventually put aboard a German vessel, on which they were more than unwelcome and suffered appalling hardships from the weather, near starvation, and shortage of water, before being transferred yet again to another ship and at last arriving in New York to a bitter winter in December. In spring of 1798 he set out by way of the Hudson and Mohawk rivers to Oswego, Niagara, and Fort Erie and was in Montreal by October. In December Banks acknowledged receipt of a large consignment of seeds. There the known facts end. Masson's last seven years, where he went and how he lived, remain a mystery. There are records that twenty-four new species, including the beautiful Wood Lily, *Trillium grandiflorum*, were received, and in 1802 Banks wrote to him sharply criticizing the poor quality of his collections; he wrote again in 1805, apparently in answer to one of Masson's own letters, granting him permission to come home. But by then it was too late. Masson died the same year in Montreal, a few days before Christmas.

Masson at least began well; Anton Hove was unfortunate from the start. A Polish-born gardener, also from Kew, he was sent to India in 1787 to study the cultivation of cotton and to obtain seeds and plants in order to introduce it to the West Indies. He seems rather mysteriously to have qualified as a physician at some time, for his name appears in the Indian medical records as Dr. Hove; but in spite of this the officials of the East India Company treated him throughout with a total lack of cooperation.

The country was unsettled and in visiting the northern cotton plantations he was on three separate occasions attacked and robbed of almost everything he possessed. Practically destitute and given no help by the company he was forced at one point to raise loans to support himself and carry on his work as best he could. Then on one journey there was what must have been a peculiarly horrifying experience. This time he was travelling with a young cavalry officer and, after three nights without rest and what seems to have been a more than usually convivial evening with a young local rajah, they were lodged in a hut that was infested with starving rats. Both men slept heavily and when they woke they discovered that every vestige of hair on the captain's head, heavily greased with pomade in the fashion of the period, had been eaten away.

Hove did somehow get a collection together, but after a further series of disasters he succeeded in missing the last transport of the season and only got it off to England after further delay. Predictably when it did at last arrive it provoked an explosion of wrath from Sir Joseph Banks who wrote that he considered Hove's expenses "most unjustifiably enormous" and instructing him to take the first ship home, where it was to be hoped he would be able to explain his conduct. Since it was written in September, Hove did not receive that letter for several months, during which time he had fallen ill and more or less recovered, visited his friend the hospitable rajah in the north again, got together another collection, and hurried south to Bombay with it. Here he had been promised accommodation on an Indiaman—providing this should be at no expense to the company—but when he arrived he discovered that far more important persons than he were travelling, that the price he was asked for a passage was impossible, and that his cases of plants would have to be stowed in darkness in the hold. By now frantic with anxiety he at last sailed on a Danish ship in February 1789, and after continuous bad weather only reached Cape Town two months later.

What follows illustrates the permanent difficulty of getting plants back in good condition. At the Cape he met Francis Masson, on his second visit to Africa; and Masson, now having a large collection ready for shipment, asked Hove to take it with his own aboard the *Norge*. Hove was quite terrified by the suggestion. There was no more stowage space, he explained; the captain was difficult, he himself had already lost many of his own plants through shortage of water, and he dared not take any more aboard, "as the captain was very particular about it." Though Masson might not have known it he was lucky. With fresh rumors of war in the Atlantic, the *Norge* waited weeks at Madeira for a convoy, and then further delayed by bad weather again did not reach southwestern Britain until July, by which time everybody aboard was suffering from scurvy, there was no water at all to be spared for Hove's plants, and they were dying daily. In desperation Hove hired a pilot cutter, at the cost of almost his last thirty guineas, and landed at Plymouth where he made a last attempt to revive his plants; and after all that Sir Joseph Banks's report was "unfavourable."

Unless they had very precise orders, and sometimes even then, sea captains were often unpredictable. William Brass, the Duke of Northumberland's gardener, is another case in point. He was sent out to collect on the Gold Coast by a syndicate including Banks, Northumberland, Dr. John Fothergill, and others, and sailed in 1780 in *Endymion* with an Admiralty order and a letter of introduction to the master, Captain Carteret. But Carteret too had his own ideas. Instead of heading for the Coast he bore away for the West Indies, and it was several weeks before they fell in with two Bristol ships bound for Africa, when Brass, after being presented with a bill for £4 for his keep, was transferred. The Bristol ships were even worse. The Bristolians have always had a name for hard business; they charged Brass an exorbitant price for the passage, his clothes and bedding were ruined by damp and lack of facilities for drying them, and when he finally got ashore at Cape Coast Castle after a five-month voyage he was destitute.

He had been given letters to the governor and a minor post with the East India Company at £30 a year, but neither was much use to him. The governor was as poor as Brass himself, and even tried to borrow from him; while out of his pay, which was mostly paid in trade goods, he was expected to provide himself with a "Euniforme." Somewhere in the background there was supposed to be a further salary to cover his plant collecting, but presumably that was to be paid on his return for he applied to his noble patrons for a grant toward his expenses, writing to Fothergill, "I would willingly Expand my own Sillery (salary) sooner than return without a collection to my credit." He was to wait until August 1781 for a reply, and then it came from his wife, telling him that Fothergill had died the previous December and that his other employers now "seemed very cool about the undertaking." It is not difficult to imagine the poor woman's efforts and inquiries in London, and Brass himself wrote that he was at a loss what to do, "left in a distress'd condition in a distant country with hardly the bread of a common souldier . . ."

Nevertheless he made valiant efforts to discharge his side of the bargain. He sent seeds and reports, made up a herbarium containing more than two hundred and fifty plants, and kept a "Jurnal" in which he noted every possible detail about them and their cultivation. The herbarium was dispatched to Fothergill—presumably before August 1781—but passed to Banks and was eventually examined by the great taxonomist, Robert Brown. He at least recognized the value of Brass's work and named a genus of South American orchids, *Brassia*, after him. But William Brass was long past appreciating the honor; he had died on the way back to England in 1783.

Not all of them were so unlucky. The French Michel Adanson worked the Senegal coast from 1749 to 1753 and returned to France to live out the remainder of his seventy-five years in peaceful if obscure botany. Henry Smeatham, who from 1779 collected in Sierra Leone for the Duchess of Portland, found some four hundred and fifty species but attracted more attention with a paper he wrote on the habits of the white ant, and later turned to aeronautics and invented a dirigible balloon. In Sierra Leone—now founded by William Wilberforce as a colony for Africans who had been released from slavery—again between 1792 and 1796 and recommended by Sir Joseph Banks, the Swedish botanist Adam Afzelius made two separate explorations. He survived a French naval attack on the newly built Freetown, when French sailors destroyed everything they could lay their hands on, brought back many "very extraordinary plants from Africa and truly paradoxical" and thereafter lived to the age of eighty-five. Plant hunting was not necessarily fatal.

In America we have already met William Young in passing; he was the collector under the patronage of Queen Charlotte of England in 1764, of whom John Bartram was decidedly jealous. He had good cause to be. Young was a very minor figure who particularly incensed Bartram when, after little more than three years' experience and a short study of botany in London, he returned to Philadelphia dressed up to the mode of the court, wearing a sword, and talking airily about the £300 a year which the Queen had granted him. It is not difficult to imagine the effect on the independent Quaker society of Philadelphia; yet curiously it was Dr. Garden of Charleston—that friend of Bartram's who had expressed surprise that such an unlettered man as John should have been appointed King's Botanist—who had recommended Young to British botanical circles.

His chief claim to notice was the introduction of the Tippitiwichet, or Venus's Fly Trap, *Dionaea muscipula*, which Bartram had discovered years before. This created a sensation in England, and it is difficult to understand why Bartram's earlier specimens to Collinson were over-looked. Apart from that, Young was not conspicuously successful. "Young has been very diligent," Dr. Fothergill wrote to Bartram, "but has glutted the market with many common things. . . . he put them into the hands of a person who, to make the most of them, bought up . . . all the old American seeds that were in the hands of seedsmen here, and mixed them with a few of W. Youngs to increase the quantity. Being old and effete, they did not come up; and have thereby injured his reputation. I am sorry for him . . . but he is indiscreet." Nevertheless he seems to have found a fairly flourishing trade, for the nurseryman Vilmorin of Paris in 1783 published a *Catalogue d'Arbes, Arbustes et Plants Herbacées d'Amérique, par William Young, Jr, Botaniste de Pensylvanie* listing 173 species of trees and shrubs and 145 herbaceous plants. Young continued to send collections to England until 1785, but then met his death by drowning, apparently in wading for bog plants.

A far more interesting collector in North America in the later part of the century was André Michaux, the son of an estate manager at Versailles. Michaux's young wife had died in giving birth to a son after only one year of marriage and he turned to botany and travel for distraction, studying under the well-known Bernard de Jussieu with the help and encouragement of Louis-Guilliaume de Monnier, King's Physician and director of the Jardin du Roi. His first journeys were in the Middle East, where he found *Michauxia campanuloides*[14] and at one stage was captured by Syrian tribesmen and narrowly escaped

[14] A plant much admired by Victorian gardeners but now uncommon. When seeds can be obtained it is a handsome subject for a sunny and well-drained but not dry border. Best treated as a biennial, sown in spring and transplanted, in good conditions it will grow up to six feet, and carries loose sprays of white tinged purple flowers which are rather more like small reflexed lilies than campanula.

being sold as a slave. Then in 1785 he set out for America as official botanist to the king's nurseries, with an honorarium of 2,000 livres, and instructions to send all his collections to the Royal Gardens at Rambouillet.

He arrived in New York in October with a gardener and the now fifteen-year-old son of his short marriage. Here he was to establish a nursery, but he very quickly decided that the northern winter was much too cold and the next year bought land just outside Charleston, leaving his gardener in charge of the New York depot, and collecting himself in South Carolina. It was here he met John Fraser, a one-time linen draper turned plant hunter who had been financed by subscription and advised to explore Carolina by William Forsyth of the Chelsea Physic Garden. In 1787 the two men set out to explore the Savannah River as far as what Fraser called "the Indian Country." It was to be a short association, for between Savannah and Augusta, Michaux's horses were stolen and Fraser grew tired of waiting for him to recover them and went on alone.

Michaux eventually completed the journey, covering much the same ground as Fraser himself, explored Florida in the following year, and went out to the Bahamas. When he returned to Charleston in 1789 he learned that the French Revolution had broken out, and expecting to be recalled to France he made what he thought would be one last journey through North Carolina and on to Philadelphia and New York. So far from being called back, however, he was so completely forgotten that in the next seven years he never received any further money from France. His son returned to Europe to study medicine while Michaux went on to still more journeys, among them an exploration of Lake St. John and the Mistassen River in the wild lake and forest country north of Quebec. Here he lived only on beaver meat and cranberries for months until driven back by the winter, but he succeeded in doing what had never been done before—plotting the northern limits of many species of trees and plants.

Returning to Philadelphia he now proposed an exploration of the Missouri River to the still undiscovered West, a proposal which was enthusiastically received by the American Philosophical Society and by the then Secretary of State, Thomas Jefferson, but for which only

$128.50 was subscribed. Even on that small sum Michaux was prepared to start, but he was called back by the newly arrived Republican envoy from France, Citizen Genêt, who ordered him off on a curious diplomatic mission instead. He was to approach certain generals in Kentucky carrying letters and instructions concerning a projected French attack on Spanish Louisiana. How enthusiastic Michaux himself might have been is uncertain, but the generals were even less so and nothing came of the plan; Genêt was ordered back to France, and Michaux was left to his travels in peace and poverty.

He set out at last for home in 1796, but almost in sight of France his ship was blown off course in a gale and finally wrecked off the coast of Holland. Passengers and crew were saved, as was Michaux himself—unconscious and tied to a mast—and his last collection. He spent the next six weeks drying it out, and when at last he did arrive in Paris he was received with great honor but nothing else. Revolutionary governments rarely have time for much except revolution, and he found little left of the enormous total of sixty thousand living trees, plants and shrubs, and ninety consignments of seed he had sent back; many of his friends had disappeared; the gardens at Rambouillet had been laid waste; and his former patron, M. de Monnier, was ill and impoverished. Michaux looked after him as well as he could, while working on his two books, the *Histoire des Chênes d'Amérique*, 1801, and *Flora Boreali Americana*, published posthumously in 1803. But he had no part in this new France. He wanted to go back to America but the government refused to finance him and he finally joined an expedition to Australia, left it to explore the Mascarene Islands and died of fever in Madagascar. His journal is again an invaluable account of early travels in America.[15]

There were many more minor plant hunters; among them Michaux's few weeks' companion, John Fraser; Joseph Dombey, Hippolito Ruiz Lopez, and Antonio Pavon y Jiminez who explored South America from 1777 to 1784; the resoundingly named Baron Friedrich August Marschall von Bieberstein and Count Apollon Apollonevitch Mussin-Pushkin, who travelled in Russia toward the end of the century and were

[15] R. G. Thwaites, ed., "A Journal of Travels into Kentucky." in *Early Western Travels*, III, 32 vols. (Cleveland, Ohio: 1904–1907. Reprinted A.M.S. Press. New York).

correspondents of Sir Joseph Banks. Of these von Bieberstein gave us *Chrysanthemum coccineum*, better known as pyrethrum, *Gentiana septemfida*, one of the few gentians that is easy to grow, *Lilium monadelphum*, and the florists' inevitable standby, *Scabiosa caucasica*; while, as their names show, Mussin-Pushkin—who in fact was a mineralogist—introduced *Nepeta mussini*, catmint, and the bulb *Pushkinia scilloides*.

Fraser covered nearly the same ground as many others in America and the West Indies and he must have collected much that was already known for he is reputed to have brought back upward of thirty thousand plants at one time or another. He made collections for Catherine of Russia and her successor Maria, but when Tsar Paul was murdered, his son—and some say murderer—repudiated all previous agreements and Fraser never got his money. In England his subscribers complained that they had received little return for their contributions and he told them that he had "Nothing to save me and my family from ruin but by making an immediate sale of the Collections I had brought along with me in the ship." He founded a nursery for the reception and distribution of American plants near what is now Sloane Square in London, and died in 1811 as a result of injuries received in being thrown from his horse during one final trip to America. Among his introductions were species of rhododendron, hydrangea, oenothera, rudbeckia, and euphorbia.

Dombey, Ruiz, and Pavon were members of a joint Franco-Spanish expedition sent out to South America by their respective governments. Their adventures were so confused, complex, extravagant, and sometimes contradictory, that they demand a volume to themselves and any attempt to give a brief account of them would be doomed to failure before it started. They were unique among plant hunters in that Dombey is reputed to have handed out considerable sums of money with unfailing generosity, though where he got it from remains a mystery, while Hippolito Ruiz Lopez is said to have travelled through the jungles with a wardrobe of five suits (one of silk), three pairs of velvet breeches and seven of plain white, two dressing gowns, sixteen pairs of stockings, fourteen shirts, twelve pairs of shoes, three cloaks, oddments such as hair nets and sleeping caps, and camping equipment that included four table cloths, plate, a chintz bedspread and a silver chamber pot. There seems somewhere to be an echo of Sir Joseph Banks and his two horn players.

To conclude this chapter here is a valedictory little note on one more, David Burton. Burton went out to Australia, arrived there in September 1791, and died of an accidental gun shot in April 1792. He did send some plants back, which reached Kew by way of the nurserymen Lee and Kennedy, and in *Paradisus Londinensis*, published in 1806, R. A. Salisbury observes kindly, "He was a very deserving gardener sent to Port Jackson several years ago by Sir Joseph Banks, who after he had there made an ample collection, with many useful observations relative to their culture, was too soon for us called to botanize in the celestial regions."

(5)
Travellers in the East

Even before Marco Polo had returned from his travels and been captured by the Genoese, so dictating his fabulous tales of the lands of Kublai Khan to a fellow prisoner, Europeans had known rumors of the ancient empires of the East; and for centuries before that exotic trees, shrubs, and fruits had been coming to Europe by way of the old Silk Road through Persia and Venice. In 1583 during the Ming Dynasty the first Jesuit missionary, Matteo Ricci, reached China, and less than fifty years later the Dutch East India Company was spreading out to the Spice Islands. By the eighteenth century the craze for decoration, furniture, and porcelain in the Chinese style was already sweeping Europe, some of it actually hinting at strange and unknown plants, and botanists were asking with increasing curiosity what new discoveries might be made in these mysterious and largely forbidden lands where clearly there was an ancient horticulture.

Ever eager for fresh plants to classify, Linnaeus in particular was keenly interested and as early as 1735 had persuaded the Swedish East India Company to allow periodical free passages for some of his pupils to wherever ships might be trading. In China by now there was a guarded tolerance of Christian teaching, though at best precarious and always unpredictable, and with few exceptions like Robert Fortune priests generally became the collectors here; not surprisingly since most of them were instructed in medicine or the natural sciences during their long and rigorous training. Like so many more popular modern fallacies the conception of the missionary as a narrow and ignorant bigot is merely a literary fantasy.

In spite of the fulminations of the Church against his *Systema Naturae* the first two botanists sent out by Linnaeus were both Swedish clergymen, the Reverend Christopher Ternstroem and the Reverend Peter Osbeck. Neither of them, however, was in China for very long; Ternstroem sailed about 1735 but died on the homeward voyage in

1738, and Osbeck left Sweden in 1750 and was back again by 1752. Nevertheless they did make some discoveries, which Linnaeus included in the first edition of *Species Plantarum*, and Osbeck in particular is recorded as having "made a number of useful and interesting observations, at the expense of his whole salary." Among the many French missionary priests were Fathers Bodinier, d'Argy, Guillamin, and Soulié.

One of the earliest and most important was Pierre Nicholas le Chéron d'Incarville who went to China in 1742 and worked there for fifteen years. A profoundly religious man, he joined the French Compagnie de Jésus in 1726 at the age of twenty, and thereafter spent some years in Quebec, but it was not until he was chosen suddenly for the China Mission in the summer of 1739 that he received any instruction in the natural sciences. Then he started a six months' study of science and medicine, and an intensive course in botany under the man who taught so many French botanists, Bernard de Jussieu again. It was a short training for what was now to be his life's work, but he sailed in January of the next year, and after some months in Macao arrived in Peking (now Peiping) in February 1742, where he was given the apparently rather curious appointment of Master Glass Maker to the Imperial Court. A Jesuit missionary was expected to make himself useful in more ways than one, and the road to Christian teaching had often to be followed by somewhat roundabout means.

One of these, d'Incarville hoped, might be by way of gardening, for he soon discovered that the Emperor was interested in flowers and wrote off urgently to de Jussieu asking him for European bulbs and seeds, although he knew it must be nearly two years before these could reach him. In the meantime there was little he could do. The imperial gardens were forbidden, and between his many duties and the rigid restrictions of Ch'ien Lung's court he found small chance for plant hunting. When the emperor was absent, however, missionaries were allowed slightly more liberty, and he did contrive to make two winter trips to the mountains, while other priests in China also found plants for him. In 1743 and 1745 he sent two collections back; but what happened to them both again illustrates the hazards of eighteenth-century transport. The second was lost in shipwreck, and the first was captured by the British; for Britain was at war with France again, this time in the even more than usually complicated business of the Austrian Succession when, having defeated the French on land in the Battle of Dettingen, the British were now harrying French ships at sea.

In 1746, inflamed by factions which wanted to drive all foreigners out of China, a violent anti-Christian movement began. Even in Peking, to some extent under the protection of the Emperor, d'Incarville went in daily danger of his life and elsewhere in China other priests were relentlessly hunted down; so far from them being free to collect for him d'Incarville wrote, "At present our missionaries have as much as they can do to hide themselves." Neither was de Jussieu particularly helpful for by 1755, having survived the persecution himself, d'Incarville was complaining that he did not know whether the botanist was dead or alive as he had not received a letter from him in the last six years, though by now he himself was corresponding as regularly as conditions would allow with the Royal Society, Peter Collinson, and others in London. The war with France had been over since 1748, but letters by sea were still uncertain and took many months to arrive. Even longer if they went by way of the overland caravan route through Outer Mongolia and Russia to St. Petersburg.

Life in China required a long patience for it was 1753, more than ten years after his arrival, before d'Incarville finally won the imperial favor. Among the seeds sent out to him by de Jussieu at some time were those of *Mimosa sensitiva*, which has the strange habit of drooping and closing up its fine, feathery leaves when touched. This was d'Incarville's chance. The Sensitive Plant was, and still is, a great curiosity; certainly there was nothing like it to be seen in China. With infinite care he raised two plants and ceremoniously presented them to the Emperor; and Ch'ien Lung was "greatly diverted and laughed heartily." So diverted that he demanded to see yet more comic European plants—*M. sensitiva* is in fact a native of Brazil—gave d'Incarville admission at last to the imperial gardens, and promised him all the Chinese plants he wanted. It was a magnificent opportunity at last, but it came too late. D'Incarville wrote at once to the somewhat slow de Jussieu for more bulbs and seeds, but before he could take full advantage of the Emperor's promise he died suddenly, early in 1757, of an illness he had picked up from a sick man he had been tending.

Even the material he did send back was disgracefully neglected. A few of his three hundred herbarium specimens were described and classified, but most were not properly examined until 1897, and many of his seeds were then found to be still unsown. But the graceful *Ailanthus altissima*, the tree of heaven, was raised both in England and France, and he introduced at least one completely new genus in *Incarvillea sinensis*.[1] He is also credited with having introduced the China Aster, *Callistephus chinensis*, but seeds of this had already been sent to Antoine de Jussieu, Bernard's brother, by another Jesuit missionary as long ago as 1731.

After d'Incarville, the first collector in China for any length of time was William Kerr, another Scots gardener from Kew sent out to Canton by Sir Joseph Banks in 1803. Apart from expeditions to Java and the Philippines Kerr remained in China until 1812, and he appears to have led a relatively peaceful life although he also was restricted by the Chinese authorities. According to Dr. John Livingstone,[2] his worst hardship was the meager salary of £100 a year which did not permit him to keep any face with the well-to-do Chinese nurserymen. Having been briefed by Banks to look for oranges, peaches, and other Chinese fruits and to study their cultivation, he was a collector rather than a plant hunter as such, and most of his finds came from the Cantonese nursery or Fa-tee gardens where he discovered a wide range of highly developed material including azaleas, chrysanthemums, tree peonies, gardenias, and bonsai: the miniature trees revered in the East because they are considered to be a microcosm of Nature itself. Though these are generally taken to be Japanese they, or rather the art of dwarfing them, were originally developed in China.

Among the many well-known plants Kerr sent back by way of the East India Company's ships were *Lilium tigrinum*,[3] *L. brownii*,

---

[1] Another handsome perennial which was much better known to Victorian gardeners than it is now under the name *I. grandiflora*. Growing up to one and a half feet it carries rose pink, trumpet-shaped flowers, blotched and marked with white and brownish orange in the throat. It is ideal and showy for a sunny, sheltered border but it must have light, warm, and well-drained soil; cold, stagnant winter wet is fatal.

[2] Chief surgeon to the East India Company at Macao. Livingstone was an authority on China, enthusiastic botanist, and later a corresponding member of the Horticultural Society.

[3] With the exception of *Lilium candidum*, *L. tigrinum* probably has the longest history in cultivation of any other known lily, having for more than a thousand years been grown

Dianthus chinensis, which has given us our strains of modern Chinese
and Indian pinks, *Begonia discolor, Juniperus chinensis,* the yellow
Chinese climbing rose named after Banks, *Rosa banksia,* and many
others including the weedy, invasive and generally rather unpleasant
shrub which bears his name, *Kerria japonica.* Banks expressed himself
kindly as being "well satisfied with his work," and as a reward
appointed him superintendent to the new Colonial Botanic Gardens at
Colombo in Ceylon. But like Père d'Incarville with his admission to the
imperial gardens Kerr did not enjoy the post for long. He took it up in
1812, made a few short botanical journeys, and then died in Ceylon two
years later; as we are told in a brief final note "of some illness incidental
to the climate."

On March 7, 1804, seven men met in a room above Mr. Hatchard's
bookshop in Piccadilly to discuss and then formally propose the
formation of a new, indeed the first, horticultural society in the world.
They included John Wedgwood, the Right Honourable Sir Joseph
Banks—now a Privy Councillor—the Right Honourable Charles Greville, R. A. Salisbury, William Forsyth, W. T. Aiton, and James Dickson.
Of these seven Banks, Greville, and Wedgwood[4] were the gentlemen
amateurs, Salisbury a botanist, Forsyth and Aiton professional gardeners—Aiton at Kew and Forsyth gardener to George III—while Dickson
was a nurseryman and seedsman in Covent Garden.

Neither Forsyth nor Salisbury ever had much to do with plant
hunting, but both are worth a passing note. R. A. Salisbury—the author
of that little epitaph for David Burton in the last chapter—was the only
son of a Richard Markham, a cloth merchant of Leeds, and like Banks
and Linnaeus became interested in botany as a boy. At the age of
twenty he made the acquaintance of a Mrs. Anna Salisbury, a
connection of his maternal grandmother, and this good lady became so

---

as a food crop by the Chinese, Japanese, and Koreans. *L. candidum,* the Madonna lily of
Christian symbolism, goes back for about three thousand years and may be seen depicted,
with the iris, on some of the earliest of Cretan wall paintings.

[4] The eldest of the three sons of Josiah Wedgwood, the great potter, and the associate of
such eminent figures as Erasmus Darwin, Joseph Priestley, James Watt, and Matthew
Boulton. Susanah Wedgwood, John's sister, was to marry one of Erasmus Darwin's sons,
Robert, and thus become the mother of Charles Darwin.

interested in the young man or in science, or both, that she gave him £10,000 to enable him to pursue his studies on the sole condition that he took the surname Salisbury. Not unnaturally he did so immediately.

Subsequently he became an eminent botanist, though a botanist with his own individual little quirks. Whether he thought he was following in the footsteps of Linnaeus or not is uncertain, but whenever he came across a plant name which he personally considered inappropriate, he had no hesitation about inventing another. As a result of this some of the indices of the period are littered with completely useless and confusing synonyms; and it was a habit which called down thunderous rebukes on his head, including one from the Reverend Dr. Goodenough who announced, "Salisbury's nomenclature is, I think, extremely improper, not to say ridiculous. I am sorry that he has persisted in his errors even to printing them. I was present at a very warm dispute between him and Dryander, who in his blunt rough manner finished his argument with, 'If this is to be the case with everybody, what the devil is to become of botany?'"

William Forsyth was a Scotsman with a shrewd eye to the main chance. Having succeeded Philip Miller at the Chelsea Physic Garden —where incidentally he created the first rock garden in England, using old stone from the Tower of London and the lava which Sir Joseph Banks brought back from Iceland—in 1784 he was appointed gardener to George III at Kensington and St. James's palaces. This begins the story of Forsyth's famous "Plaister." The royal gardens had been sadly neglected, particularly at Kensington; most of the fruit trees were in a poor condition and Forsyth found it necessary to remove many branches and generally to head them back severely, which of course left large open wounds. To protect and heal these Forsyth devised a plaster made up of cow dung, lime, wood ashes, sand, soap and urine.

There was no harm in that. Many old gardeners had their favorite recipes for specific purposes, some of them even more improbably compounded. But Forsyth went so far as to claim that his wonderful plaster would actually restore trees which were so old and diseased that little but the outer bark remained, even oak and elm trees, and at this time the provision of sound timber for ship building was a national necessity. In 1789 Forsyth succeeded in gulling a Parliamentary

Commission into recommending that he should be awarded a grant of
no less than £1,500 for his discovery, and not content with that he
published a book about it and advertised the stuff widely. For ten years
or so he and his experiments were famous all over the country, and
Wedgwood must have been sufficiently impressed to invite him to that
inaugural meeting of the Horticultural Society. There were others
however who were more critical, some who said plainly that the plaster
was a hoax, and Forsyth's membership of the young society could well
have been an embarrassment had he not—perhaps tactfully—died in
July 1804, only a few months after it was founded.

The Society had many vicissitudes before it finally became the Royal
Horticultural Society under the "peculiar and personal patronage and
protection" of Queen Victoria, and subsequently the premier and most
respected organization of its kind in the world. But for long before this,
even before the Society had a garden of its own, it was already receiving
many new plants from its growing number of overseas correspondents,
men like Dr. Livingstone, and John Reeves, who was an inspector of tea
with the East India Company in Canton and Macao. As early as 1817
Reeves had offered to forward Chinese plants and drawings of plants by
way of the East India Company's ships. A sum of £25 was sent out and
the first plants which arrived were put into the care of a private
nurseryman and the Physic Garden, while the drawings by Chinese
artists went to form the nucleus of the Society's present unique
collection.

Reeves's most important single introduction was probably *Wisteria
sinensis*, one of the most beautiful climbing shrubs in existence.
Discovered in the garden of a Chinese merchant, one plant was brought
back in 1816 by a Captain Wellbank, and another shortly afterward
came by way of a Captain Rawes. The first plant grew well and was
later propagated by the nursery firm of Loddiges at Hackney, while
Reeves himself sent a third plant which was placed in the Society's
garden, then at Chiswick. This one thrived so abundantly that by 1840
it was described in the *Botanical Register* as "a magnificent specimen
180 feet long, covering about 1800 square feet of wall," and it is said to
have produced no less than 675,000 flowers in the spring of 1839.

There were many such correspondents finding and sending material back, but the losses were enormous. "A voyage from Macao to London was not what it has now become. Doubling the Cape [of Good Hope] was so difficult an operation that the freight of living plants was continually damaged or thrown overboard to clear the decks. And in this way hundreds of plant cases were lost . . ."[5] In 1819 Dr. John Livingstone wrote to Joseph Sabine—then a vice-president of the Society, later to become secretary—"I am of the opinion that one thousand plants have been lost, for one, which survived the voyage to England. Plants purchased at Canton, including their chests and other necessary charges, cost six shillings and eightpence sterling each, on a fair average; consequently every plant now in England, must have been introduced at the enormous expense of upwards of £300 . . ."[6]

The first collector actually sent out by the Society was John Potts who sailed in 1821 by way of Calcutta, meeting Reeves and Livingstone in Macao and Canton, and returned the following year bringing species of camellia and callicarpa, forty varieties of chrysanthemum and a quantity of seed of *Primula sinensis*, the Chinese primrose—a species known to the Society from a painting sent by Reeves in 1819, and from a single plant brought back by Captain Rawes again. The chrysanthemums were lost "in consequence of an accident which befell the ship on her voyage home"[7] and Potts himself, already suffering from consumption, died soon after arriving in London; but the first plants of *P. sinensis* ever to be raised in Britain came from his seeds, and these became the source of all of our fine modern strains of this plant. He was followed in 1823 by J. D. Parks, who was more fortunate in every way and returned with a collection of new chrysanthemums, more camellias, a number of greenhouse plants and orchids from Java, and the singularly unattractive Victorian house plant—now said to be becoming fashionable again—*Aspidistra lurida*.

After these two men, mainly owing to its political instability and increasing suspicion of foreigners, no further attempts were made to collect in China for twenty years. During that time the Wardian case

[5] *The Gardener's Chronicle*, no. 13. 1856. An obituary to John Reeves, who had recently died at the age of eighty-two.

[6] *Transactions*, vol. 3. Horticultural Society. 1820.

[7] *Ibid.*

was invented—a neat and easily portable little glass box which was to reduce plant losses to a minimum, to extend areas of commerce by making possible the introduction of tea plants to India, and later to have a profound effect on world health by permitting the distribution of cinchona seedlings to malarial areas. The Wardian case was the answer to most of the problems which had beset plant hunters for generations; and once it was in operation it seemed so obvious that the only surprise is that it was not discovered until 1838.

Nathaniel Ward was by profession a doctor in one of the poorest parts of London and by inclination a naturalist. His greatest pleasure was to tramp out into the countryside and bring back specimens to study at home. On one occasion, wishing to watch the development of a chrysalis, he buried it in soil at the bottom of a covered glass jar. Within a few days he noticed that seeds were starting to germinate in the soil, and that they very quickly grew into strong, vigorous plants. Ward began to experiment—mainly, it seems, on the respiration of plants—and by 1838 had produced the first Wardian case: simply a closed glass box with a metal frame. The principle is exactly the same as the fashionable "bottle gardens" of today. Once the plants are set in the soil and the case shut up they are protected against most outside conditions, they need little or no water since the system is a continuous cycle—moisture given off by the leaves in the form of vapor condenses on the glass and runs back into the soil—and given that they are not placed in direct sunlight they can be left to look after themselves with a minimum of attention for months on end. It was beautifully simple; and it worked.

After the war of 1839–1842, when Britain and China fought for control of the opium trade, Hong Kong was ceded to the British, Chusan occupied, and four more treaty ports opened to Europeans. Although it was an uneasy peace and the government suggested delay, John Reeves now retired to England, immediately advised the Horticultural Society to send out another collector, and the man chosen for this exacting and possibly dangerous mission was Robert Fortune, once again a Scotsman, and working in the Society's garden. He arrived in Hong Kong in July 1843 with £100 a year salary, a supply of the new

Wardian cases, a list of precise instructions running to twenty-four paragraphs, and a fowling piece and two pistols. These last were a concession he had extracted with some difficulty before he started, for the Society had considered that a good stout stick was all he needed for defensive purposes, and he himself had written firmly to Lindley, the secretary, ". . . we must not forget that China has been the seat of war for some time past, and that many of the inhabitants will bear the English no good will . . . a stick will scarcely frighten an armed Chinaman."

Fortune describes his travels in the first of his several books *Three Years Wanderings in the Northern Provinces of China* (1847).[8] To start with Hong Kong proved unproductive, as did the area of Amoy—which he describes as one of the filthiest towns he has ever seen and complains that "At every corner the cooks and bakers were pursuing their avocations, and disposing of their delicacies; and the odors which met me at every point were of the most disagreeable and suffocating nature." Then:

> Having travelled all over the country adjacent to Amoy, and completed my researches . . . I sailed again towards the Formosa Channel, on my way to our most northern stations of Chusan, Ningpo and Shanghae. The Monsoon, however, had now changed from south-west to north-east and . . . we met one of those dreadful gales so well known to navigators of these seas. Our newest and strongest sails were split to pieces, the bulwarks washed away, and in spite of the best seamanship, and every exertion, we were driven back far below the bay from which we started about a week before. I shall long remember one of those fearful nights . . .

Perils at sea were followed by misadventures on land. Driven into what he calls "Chimoo Bay" for shelter and repairs he went ashore to look for plants near "Chinchew" (Chuanchow, now Tsinkiang) and was here set upon by "the Chinchew men." He tells it all with a curious, quiet understatement. "From their manner I suspected that their

[8] A more recent edition is 1935. *Three Years' Wanderings in China* (Shanghai: The University Press).

intentions were not good . . ." They certainly were not; attempting to rob Fortune they surrounded his servant, "presenting their knives and threatening to stab him if he offered the slightest resistance. . . . my poor plants collected with so much care were flying about in all directions. . . . I felt there was no denying we were in dangerous company. . . . Accordingly I made straight for the village where we had left the boat, and my servant took good care to follow close on my heels. As we approached the landing place the boatman came to meet us in high spirits, saying he had expected us long ago, and was fearful that the Chinchew men had either robbed or murdered us." Nevertheless even that adventure had its compensations, for among the plants he did carry back were "several fine roots of *Campanula grandiflora*,[9] which grows wild amongst these hills, and a new species of Abelia (*Abelia rupestris*)."

He reached Chusan in late autumn—the first of many visits in following years when he was to write enthusiastically of the hills clothed and glowing with azaleas—and spent a cold and miserable time in Shanghai. Even here some of the nurserymen were shy of the *fankwei* or foreign devil, for "as I approached, a boy, who was on the watch, scampered away to the gardener's house and gave notice of my appearance; and long before I reached the gate it was closed and barricaded, and not persuasion nor entreaty could remove their fears . . ." He got in eventually with the aid of a Chinese attached to the British Consulate and found several very valuable plants. By January 1844 he was back in Hong Kong dispatching his first consignment, and the Wardian cases had more than proved their worth in saving plants. Then there was an unwise visit to Canton where he was chased by a hostile crowd, stoned, and narrowly escaped with his life.

Back in Shanghai in the spring he discovered another trick of the Chinese gardeners. He had heard of several valuable varieties of the much prized Moutan, or tree peony, and a Chinese artist had made him

---

[9] Chinese bell flower, or balloon flower, now *Platycodon grandiflorum*, which Lindley considered to be the finest herbaceous plant sent back from China. Easy to raise from seed, asking little but reasonably good, well-drained soil in a sunny position, it carries large, shallow bell flowers which finally open out into a starlike form. The typical color is soft blue, but there is a white variety.

drawings of them.[10] Fortune took these to a nurseryman who, "prom- ised at once to procure living plants for me, but said they would be very expensive, as he would have to send to Soochow [now Wuhsien] a distance of nearly one hundred miles, for they were not to be procured in the vicinity of Shanghae, and a man would be absent at least eight days. At the specified time the Moutans arrived, and proved most valuable kinds.. . . . Great was my surprise when I afterwards found that these plants were brought a distance of not more than six miles from the walls of Shanghae, and that the celebrated town of Soo-chow was, in fact, supplied with Moutans from the very same place."

Journeys followed to Ning-Po, where he studied the cultivation of tea—*Camellia sinensis*—and then to Soochow, which had the reputa- tion of producing everything that was most beautiful in China, from women to flowers. Foreigners were still only allowed to travel thirty miles inland from any treaty port, and the famous town was well beyond this limit, but Fortune disguised himself as a Chinese and inveigled his boatmen into taking him there by a mixture of bribery and cunning. He was robbed on the way, while Soochow itself did not live up to its reputation and he returned to Shanghai and Chusan. After a bout of fever he was in Hong Kong again by November sending off his second season's collection and then, having experienced one winter in Shanghai, left in January 1845 for Manila where he collected specimens of the beautiful white moth orchid, *Phalaenopsis amabilis*, a plant that was already known in England but still extremely rare. That summer found him revisiting all his old haunts for one final bout of collecting, and then going to Foo-chow, the last of the treaty ports. Here he found the crowds insulting and dangerous again and he took a passage on a Chinese timber junk bound for Shanghai, observing that "the natives continued to the last troublesome and annoying."

Sickening for fever once more Fortune took to his bed on board and prompt on time, Chinese style—two weeks later—they sailed. The

---

[10] The true Moutan or tree peony is *Paeonia suffruticosa*, but there are several other species such as *P. lutea* (yellow) and *P. delavayi* (crimson), growing up to five or six feet high. *P. suffruticosa* naturally bears rose pink flowers, but Fortune speaks of lilac, purple, and other colors, which could at least seem to suggest that Chinese nurserymen were hybridizing as early, if not earlier, than American and European gardeners.

South China seas at this period were infested with pirates, and what follows is in the best tradition of travel stories.

About four o'clock in the afternoon the captain and pilot came hurriedly down to my cabin and informed me that they saw a number of *Jan-dous* [pirates] right ahead, lying in wait for us. . . . I therefore considered it prudent to be prepared for the worst. I got out of bed, ill and feverish as I was, and carefully examined my fire-arms. . . . I also rammed down a ball upon the top of each charge of shot in my gun, put a pistol in each side pocket, and patiently waited the result . . .

Chinese passengers, captain, and crew were all feverishly hiding their money and valuables wherever they could.

All was now dismay and consternation on board our junk, and every man ran below except two who were at the helm. I expected every moment that these also would leave their post; and then we should have been an easy prey to the pirates. "My gun is nearer you than those of the *Jan-dous*," said I to the two men; "and if you move from the helm depend upon it I will shoot you". The poor fellows looked very uncomfortable . . .

The pirates now seemed quite sure of their prize, and came down upon us hooting and yelling like demons, at the same time loading their guns, and evidently determined not to spare their shot. This was a moment of intense interest. . . . The nearest junk was now within thirty yards of ours; their guns were now loaded, and I knew that the next discharge would completely rake our decks. "Now," said I to our helmsmen, "keep your eyes fixed on me, and the moment you see me fall flat on the deck you must do the same". . . . We had scarcely done so, when bang! bang! went their guns, and the shot came whizzing close over us, splintering the wood about us in all directions. . . . "Now, mandarin, now! they are quite close enough", cried out my companions, who did not wish to have another broadside like the last. I, being of the same opinion, raised myself above the high stern of our junk; and while the pirates were not more than twenty yards away from us, hooting and yelling, I raked their decks fore and aft, with shot and ball from my double barrelled gun.

Had a thunderbolt fallen amongst them, they could not have been more surprised. Doubtless many were wounded, and probably some killed. . . .

They were so completely taken by surprise that their junk was left without a helmsman . . . and, as we were still carrying all sail and keeping on our right course, they were soon left a considerable way astern. . . . Another was now bearing down upon us as boldly as his companion had done. . . . I determined to follow the same plan with this one, and to pay no attention to his firing until he should come to close quarters. The plot now began to thicken; for the first junk had gathered way again, and was following in our wake . . . and three others, although still further distant, were making for the scene of action as fast as they could. In the mean time, the second was almost alongside, and continued giving us a broadside now and then with their guns. . . .

My poor fellows who were steering kept begging and praying that I would fire into our pursuers as soon as possible, or we should all be killed. As soon as they came within twenty or thirty yards of us, I gave them the contents of both barrels, raking their decks as before. This time the helmsman fell and doubtless several others were wounded. . . . their junk went up into the wind . . . and was soon left some distance behind us. . . . Two other piratical junks which had been following in our wake for some time, when they saw what had happened, would not venture any nearer; and at last, much to my satisfaction, the whole set of them bore away.

At Shanghai he packed up all of his plants and sailed for Hong Kong, where he sent off eight cases of duplicates and kept eighteen more to take back home under his own care. These contained two hundred and fifty living plants; and once again the Wardian cases proved their value, for only thirty-five died on the voyage. He reached England in May 1846 with one of the finest collections, and certainly the healthiest, ever to be brought back. Azaleas, camellias, chrysanthemums, peonies, and roses, the "Japanese" anemone *Anemone hupehensis*, Dutchman's breeches, *Dicentra spectabilis*, and the platycodon. And among a wealth of popular shrubs *Jasminum nudiflorum*—winter jasmine, which gardeners then rather curiously treated as a valuable greenhouse subject before they realized that it is one of the hardiest winter flowering shrubs in existence—Forsythia, the first Weigelia, the winter flowering honeysuckles *Lonicera fragrantissima* and *L. standishii*, together with many others.

Back in England he was offered and accepted the post of curator at the Chelsea Physic Garden, and settled down to the production of his first book, the *Three Years Wanderings*. Besides the tale of his adventures—sampled in the foregoing extracts—this contains two chapters on the cultivation and manufacture of tea, and this so interested the officials of the British East India Company that in 1848 they asked him to go to China again and find seeds and plants of the best tea varieties and ship them to India. In many ways this was a more hazardous journey than the first. The best tea districts were a considerable distance from the coast and restrictions on the movement of foreigners were still in force. Fortune once more travelled disguised as a Chinese—a trick of which he was really rather proud. Again there were mishaps and adventures—including one bizarre occasion in a cargo boat on the Tsien-tang River when he observed two fully occupied coffins removed for off loading from beneath his bunk—but the second mission was as successful as his first. Having dispatched two consignments to Calcutta he finally followed them up himself early in 1851 with, it is said, no less than 2,000 plants and 17,000 seedlings.

That number is probably somewhat exaggerated; but the directors of the East India Company were more than satisfied. They asked him to return to China and after only a little over twelve months in England—during which he published his second book, *A Journey to the Tea Countries of China*—he left again in 1852. He was away for four years, but this third trip was neither as interesting nor as productive as the two previous, for by now the Tai-ping Rebellion had broken out and it was impossible to risk any long explorations. But except for the incidentals of robbery and hostile crowds he does not appear ever to have been in any serious danger and he made a number of short trips, mostly to places he already knew, and on one of these collected seed of *Rhododendron fortunei*. Back in England once more, having travelled by way of India where he spent eight months, he now published his third book, *A Residence Among the Chinese* in 1857.

He was in China again during 1858–59, this time at the request of the American government which was interested in tea growing in the Southern states, an experiment which came to nothing, as by the time Fortune's plants arrived in America pressures were already building up

to the outbreak of the Civil War. In 1860 Fortune himself went to
Japan, where he met J. G. Veitch[11]—who was collecting on behalf of his
family firm of nurserymen—and P. F. von Siebold. Siebold we shall
meet ourselves later, but Veitch and Fortune had surprisingly little to
say about each other, possibly because in a sense they were business
rivals since Fortune was now sending his own collections to nursery
gardeners. In spite of danger now from the Daimyos, or hereditary
feudal princes who regarded it as their patriotic duty to kill any
foreigner whenever they could, his account of this journey in *Yedo and
Peking* (1863) seems surprisingly tame compared with his exploits in
China; and most of the plants he collected were chrysanthemums
purchased from nurserymen.

After a break of three months in Shanghai he spent one more season
in Japan—during which there was a brush with the British vice-consul
when he visited Tokyo without permission and somewhat tactlessly
stayed at the American legation—and then returned home by way of
one last visit to China. After nineteen years of wandering he arrived in
England in January 1862 to spend the remainder of his life in
comfortable retirement. Perhaps all the more comfortable because
being a hard-headed Scotsman and a typical Victorian he had made,
besides the popular success of his books, considerable sums of money
from the sale of oriental antiques and works of art which he had also
picked up on his travels.

After Fortune came two great French plant hunters; Jean Marie
Delavay, and Jean Pierre Armand David. Both were priests and both
were more or less contemporaries in China although they do not seem
to have met until 1881 in Paris. While Delavay was primarily a
missionary who was deeply interested in botany David was also an
all-around natural scientist with a preference for zoology. Nevertheless,
he too had intended to make the foreign missions his life work, and it
was almost by chance that he became a naturalist instead. He was born

[11] Veitch made many valuable introductions including *Lilium auratum*, *Magnolia
stellata*, and several species of primula. He made a second journey to Australia and the
South Seas in 1864–66 collecting stove house plants, but shortly afterward developed
tuberculosis and died in 1870 at the age of thirty-one.

just on the French side of the Franco-Spanish border in 1826, and his family encouraged his early enthusiasm for natural history. When David joined the Order of St. Vincent de Paul in 1848 he was ultimately sent to teach science in a college at Savona, in Italy. It was from here that he wrote to the superiors of his Order that ". . . all the time I dream of Chinese missions. . . . I think of giving my life while working at the salvation of infidels. . . . I am getting on in years and am almost twenty-seven, and long to go to the Celestial Empire, Mongolia and similar places . . . in order to learn new languages, customs, and scenes . . ."

It was ten years before his wish was granted; but then he was called to Paris, ordained as a missionary, and met a Monseigneur Mouly, who was preparing to leave for Peking where he was to open a school for boys. Armand David was to go with him to teach science, one other priest mathematics and physics, and one more, music and clock making. It seems to have been a curious mixture. But David was also introduced to the great French sinologue Stanislas Juline, who in turn introduced him to scientists of the Musée d'Histoire Naturelle, who asked him to send back anything of interest he could find in China.

He arrived in Peking in 1862, and with his customary energy began to investigate the surrounding countryside soon after. In September he travelled to another station of his Order—the Congrégation des Lazaristes—up beyond the Great Wall, followed it the year after with a five-month trip to Jehol (now Chengteh), and sent back material so remarkable that the scientists of the Museum now went to the Minister of Public Instruction and asked him to obtain permission from the superior general of the Order for David to make an expedition to Inner Mongolia, then almost entirely unknown. The permission was granted, and funds were allocated by the government through the Museum; so Père David, far from his early ambition of giving his life to the salvation of the infidels was to devote the remainder of it to botany and zoology.

David himself seems to have been uneasy about it at first, for he wrote in the introduction to his Journal ". . . it was not to engage in natural history research, and much less to undertake voyages of scientific exploration, that I came to China over four years ago. It was my ambition to share in accordance with my abilities the hard and meritorious day to day work of the missionaries who for the past three centuries have endeavoured to convert the great population of the East to Christian civilization. . . . But all sciences concerned with the works of creation increase the glory of their Creator, for to know truth is to know God . . ."[12]

Quietly ignoring five serious illnesses in eight years, the dangerous hostility of the remote Chinese, and periodical outbreaks of local rebellion—when he observed that if one took any notice of such things he would never get anywhere—he made three great expeditions, usually only in company with one or two Christian Chinese assistants. The first, to the deserts of Mongolia; the second, which lasted for more than two years, to the borders of Tibet; the third in the central provinces. Of the first he says himself, "The results of my eight months' journey were not remarkable," and of the three the second was most successful when he penetrated to the unknown marshes of the east, exploring en route the wild gorges of the Yangtze Kiang, and climbing Hong-shantin, a mountain which rises to fifteen thousand feet, on the slopes of which he found the strange tree which is most closely associated with his name, *Davidia involucrata*.[13]

By this time China had been more or less open to Europeans for twenty years or so, and in Peking and the treaty ports they were relatively safe but in the outer districts, threatened by wandering armies of bandits, the corruption of local officials, and unpredictable outbursts of fanatical hatred against Christians, life and freedom was often more than uncertain. In his diary of the second journey David writes, "A European cannot realise to what lengths the spirit of vandalism and senseless destruction will carry these hordes of brigands and pitiless assassins. . . . A few years ago when they came to Kuikiang they killed

[12] *Journal d'un Voyage en Mongolie fait en 1866* . . . par M. L'Abbé Armand David, *Missionaire de la Congrégation des Lazaristes* . . . Bulletin des Nouvelles Archives du Musée, vols. III and IV. Paris, 1867 and 1868. *Journal d'un Voyage dans le centre de la Chine*, etc. Bulletin, vols. XIII, X and XI. 1872, 1873, 1874.

[13] The pocket handkerchief tree, so called because although the flowers themselves are small and insignificant they are carried between two long, white, papery bracts. A *Davidia* in full bloom looks as if it is festooned with hundreds of waving, flapping linen handkerchiefs. George Forrest was to go out again many years later to find and bring back seeds.

The tree discovered, lost, and found again. *Davidia involucrata*, the Pocket Handkerchief Tree. Courtesy of the Controller, Her Majesty's Stationery Office, and the Director, Royal Botanic Gardens, Kew.

so many people that the corpses of their victims, it is said, filled the
whole of the principal lake, which measures three to six miles in
circumference . . ." And again in a later entry, "The ill will of the
Chinese follows us everywhere. Today we are alarmed at the news, false
or true, that an important mandarin of the Chengtu government is
trying to persuade the princes of Man-tzu to exterminate all Christians
established in their states . . ."

Nor were the Chinese the only danger. In approaching Hong-shantin

My Wang Thome and I . . . go up into a wild valley . . . following the
rocky banks of the half frozen stream, we reach the foot of a series of
foaming cataracts. . . . we try to climb the steep mountains on either side
of this narrow valley, hoping to find a passage over the difficult cascades,
but in vain. For four hours we pull ourselves up from rock to rock as high
as we can go by clinging to trees and roots. All which is not vertical is
covered with frozen snow. Fortunately the trees and shrubs prevent us
from seeing too clearly the abyss over which we are suspended, sometimes
holding only by our hands. We . . . repent twenty times having tried to
ascend these awful precipices, where we can see no sign of the foot of
man. . . . The danger is extreme. Sometimes we are plunged into half
melted snow, or the trees which we clutch break and we roll to another
tree or rock. Fortunately my robust young man is seeing it through better
than I might hope from a Chinese; twice, however, I hold him back when
he is slipping to the edge of the gulf. He says if we do not die that day we
never shall . . .

Being utterly exhausted we are forced to descend so as not to be
overtaken by night in these awful solitudes. . . . No sound breaks the
silence, except for the distant roar of the cascades and the croaking of the
brown carrion crow. I also distinguish the lowing of a wild ox, but am
careful not to say anything to my Chinese assistant so as not to add to his
discouragement and fear. On such occasions it is easy to pray; we do this
with fervour and then give ourselves up to Providence. We descend the
immense wall of over three thousand feet as we have climbed it, from tree
to tree and rock to rock. . . . At last, after an hour of this inhuman
descent, we reach the base of the mountain and the banks of the foaming
torrent. Our clothes and hands are torn and the guns are in a sorry state.
We are soaked with sweat and water and, in spite of the snow we have
swallowed, have a burning thirst. But we are safe, and we thank God for
having let us escape from danger.

Although he collected many new plants, Père David was primarily studying birds and animals, and one of his notes in this context is of particular interest. "My Christian hunters . . . bring me a young white bear, which they took alive but unfortunately killed in order to carry it more easily. The young white bear, which they sell to me very dearly, is all white except for the legs, ears, and around the eyes, which are black. . . . This must be a new species of *Ursus*, very remarkable . . ." It was indeed. It was that animal most beloved of children all over the world, the panda; the first ever to have been seen by a European. Then later, on the mountain Hong-shantin, he describes the northern slope. "There is an inclined plain . . . now covered with fine herbaceous plants . . . a white *Veratrum* of a new species, a fine blue aconite, several gentians with large blue flowers, two very pretty *Papaveraceae* [I believe *Meconopsis*] with flowers of delicate lavender. The rocks are covered with several species of yellow flowered saxifrages . . ."

Toward the end of this journey he fell ill of a mysterious sickness and several times records with distress that he cannot get up to say Mass. It affected his legs with extreme pain, but after a rather curious treatment with poultices made of ginger and onions moistened with brandy he recovered sufficiently to make one last trip to the mountains before returning to Chengtu in November of 1869, and then crossing China to reach Che-Foo on the coast in the following July. It was here he received news of the recent massacres at Tientsin, when the missions there had been burned and the missionaries slaughtered, and temporarily broken by ill health and the deaths of so many of his personal friends and associates he sailed for France.

In France he received many honors, among them being elected to the Académie des Sciences in 1872. That year too he set out again for what was to be his final expedition in China, this time to the central provinces. But the greater part of his life's work was already accomplished, for by August 1873 he was sick again, and worsened steadily until November when his condition was so critical that he received the Last Sacraments. He did recover, but remained too ill for any further exploration and eventually returned to Shanghai and set out for France again in 1874. Back in Paris he lived quietly in the house of his Order for the remaining twenty-six years of his life, leaving it only occasionally

The Min-shan gorges, Central China, explored by Dr. J. F. Rock. Photo J. F. Rock by courtesy of the Royal Geographical Society, London.

Opposite: The Tsang-po, Tibet, from Kingdon-Ward's 1924 camp. Photo Frank Kingdon-Ward by courtesy of the Royal Geographical Society, London.

for shorter journeys; one to Tunisia and another to Constantinople. One plant collector at least who came home to die, where he would have wished, at the age of seventy-four in 1900. Estimates of his collections vary as to the authority, but according to the historian of Chinese plant hunting E. H. M. Cox these must have amounted to at least 2,000 species, while the French botanist A. R. Franchet calculated that a thousand others must have been lost when on one occasion his boat was sunk on the Han River. Among those we still have are *Clematis davidiana*,[14] *Cotoneaster salicifolia, Stranvaesia davidiana*, a handsome and vigorous evergreen shrub with masses of crimson berries in the autumn, several species of rhododendron and primula, *Lilium davidii*, and *L. duchartrei*.[15]

Jean Marie Delavay had been in China since about 1867. He was stationed near Canton, and unlike David was never released from his missionary duties; but he was nevertheless an enthusiastic botanist who had been first encouraged to collect by Dr. H. F. Hance of the British Consular Service in Canton and Hong Kong. For some years Hance purchased almost everything Delavay collected until, on leave in Paris in 1881, the priest met Armand David who introduced him to Adrien René Franchet—director of the Musée d'Histoire Naturelle—and persuaded him to forward his collections to France in future. On his return to China he did so to such effect that Franchet later estimated he sent more than 200,000 herbarium specimens, of 4,000 species in which not less than 1,500 were unknown. His material indeed was so vast that Franchet started a *Plantae Delavayi* in 1889 which remained unfinished at the time of his (Franchet's) death in 1900 while many of Delavay's specimens were still not fully sorted and classified until long after.

[14] Now more correctly *Clematis heracleifolia* var. *davidiana*. An interesting clematis which instead of being a climber grows more like a herbaceous perennial and is suitable for the border. It will make a bushy plant up to four feet high carrying small, soft blue tubular flowers not unlike a hyacinth. It is still somewhat straggly in growth, however, and is best with a little support.

[15] *Lilium duchartrei* is one of the best of the less known species. It has few fads, will tolerate lime and, given only gritty soil well enriched with leaf mold, quickly spreads by stolons underground to form a colony. Each stem growing to two feet, or sometimes higher, carries up to ten white flowers marked and spotted with purple. Reginald Farrer called it the Marbled Martagon Lily.

For ten years he explored the hill country of northwest Yunnan, where he discovered such plants as *Primula malacoides, P. nutans,* and others; *Aster delavayi, Incarvillea delavayi, Iris delavayi,* several rhododendrons, and not least the blue poppy, later named *Meconopsis betonicifolia,* which became almost a legend before Kingdon-Ward finally rediscovered and established it in our gardens many years later. Delavay concentrated mainly on the mountain Tsemai Shan, described as the garden of Yunnan, which he climbed sixty times, and maintained that even then he had scarcely started to explore its alpine flora. Many of his discoveries sent as herbarium specimens were left for other collectors to bring home as plants, for in 1886 he suffered an attack of bubonic plague which paralyzed his left arm. In permanent ill health he left for France in 1891, but only two years later insisted on going back to China, where he died at Yunnan-fu in 1895.

Throughout that century there were other less well known collectors in China and Japan. One of the earliest was the Bavarian Dr. Phillip Franz von Siebold, who was employed by the Dutch East India Company as a physician in Batavia. Having by the early eighteen twenties temporarily lost most of her possessions and influence in the East, Holland in 1825 proposed a special embassy to Tokyo to treat for better trading conditions, and Siebold was invited to go with it, chiefly because his known skill as an ophthalmic surgeon was expected to give him prestige with the Japanese, among whom eye troubles of one sort or another were then prevalent. Accounts of his activities vary—one for instance credits him with marrying a Japanese girl, and others do not so much as mention it—but there is little doubt that he was an odd choice for a country where the old restrictions were still very much in force. He was arrogant and unscrupulous, and medicine was only a means to the end of his main interests of ethnography, politics, and plant hunting. It was a dangerous combination for Japan in that period.

He arrived at Deshima in August 1826 and soon built up a following of pupils and grateful patients who were happy to present him with plants. On the excuse of visiting the sick, he was gradually able to travel farther, to collect more, and also to pick up a great deal of information about Japanese politics. As was customary, the embassy—like that with which Kaempfer travelled—left Deshima and Nagasaki in the spring, travelled overland to Tokyo, and then remained there for several weeks for the rigidly prescribed ceremonies and negotiations before returning to the Dutch trading station. Siebold himself, however, appears to have stayed on, and over that summer and autumn to have built up another following including the court astronomer and other dignitaries. Again it was a dangerous game, for he persuaded them to find him maps of Japan and the adjacent islands, and that was treasonable. In Japan at this time all maps were strictly prohibited to foreigners.

The climax came in autumn, 1828. Siebold's more innocent collections were already aboard the ship that was to take them back to Deshima, but a sudden storm blew up which drove her ashore and before she could be refloated the forbidden maps were discovered. Siebold is said to have worked feverishly all one night making copies and concealing them among his plants; but many of his unfortunate friends were tortured and others committed hari-kari. It was an acute embarrassment to the Dutch government which promptly repudiated Siebold. The Japanese held him from December of that year until December of 1829 when, lucky to escape with his life, he was released under sentence of permanent banishment from Japan.[16] Yet somehow he still managed to send one collection of plants away—shipped just after he was imprisoned—and took another with him when he left, probably from the garden at Deshima which Thunberg had started years before.

He arrived back in Antwerp during the summer of 1830 and part of his collection went to one of his patrons, the Duke of Ursal at Brussels, while Siebold himself, apparently as a result of some fresh quarrel, took his share to Ghent. At this time Belgium was a province of Holland—or rather of the Low Countries—and that year the Belgians rebelled against Dutch control, and a war of independence broke out which the local horticulturalists seized upon as an excellent excuse to confiscate the remainder of Siebold's plants. He moved on again somewhat hurriedly to Leyden, but as wars go this one was short and relatively good-humored, and on the conclusion of a peace treaty which made

---

[16] From an account in *Allgemeine Deutsche Biographie*.

Belgium an independent state, Siebold claimed back at least some of his property. He got about 80 of 260-odd species, set up a garden with them at Leyden, produced a stream of works on the natural history, politics, geography and language of Japan, and a *Flora Japonica* beautifully illustrated with plates by Japanese artists.

He succeeded in making himself a considerable popular hero and authority, particularly with William II of Holland who granted him a number of honors and favors including a title of nobility and a decree empowering him to form a "Royal Society for the Encouragement of Horticulture"—which in effect was little less than a monopoly on the importation and distribution of all material from the Far East. The government was to send out and pay collectors, Dutch East India Company ships were to carry the plants at reduced prices, the botanic gardens in Java were not to distribute any which interested Dr. Siebold, and all these were to come to Siebold and Company at Leyden from whom alone they could be obtained. The arrangement collapsed eventually when subscribers to the Society became dissatisfied, but the Leyden nursery continued to flourish and through it many new species were introduced to Europe: bamboos, lilies, azaleas, hydrangeas, and hostas, the numerous plants which bear Siebold's name like the magnificent white *Magnolia sieboldii, Prunus sieboldii, Forsythia sieboldii,* and others.

By 1853, however reluctantly and still with the opposition of the feudal princes, Japan was beginning to abandon her traditional policy of isolation. Partly as a result of diplomatic pressure, more decisively from the appearance of American warships under the command of Commodore Matthew Perry in Tokyo Bay, negotiations were started to open ports to Western trade. Siebold at once began to make plans to return to Japan himself. His sentence of banishment was automatically revoked by the new treaties, but still mindful of his past exploits the Dutch government was understandably dubious of allowing him out there in any official position. Nevertheless he got himself a post with the new Netherlands Trading Company and in 1859 at the age of sixty-three arrived back in Nagasaki. Here he met Fortune, Veitch, and probably Richard Oldham—another collector sent out from Kew Gardens—although he is said to have been extremely unpopular with the rest of the

European community. Then in 1860, mainly through his Japanese friends, he was invited to Tokyo to introduce Western sciences, advise on internal affairs, and smooth foreign relations.

What exactly happened then is still not quite clear—again there are conflicting stories of intrigue—but he appears to have smoothed relations to such good effect that the Dutch authorities ordered his recall and, when he refused to comply, requested the Japanese government to dismiss him. Eventually he was persuaded to go to Batavia, ostensibly to discuss some diplomatic post which in fact never existed; and here in the time-honored governmental fashion of dealing with awkward personages he was passed from one department to another until at last in disgust he returned to Europe in 1862, cut all of his connections with Holland, and retired to Bavaria. He was still obstinately planning another journey to Japan when he died there in 1866.

There are, of course, other names. Augustine Henry; Richard Oldham; Charles Maries; J. H. Veitch; Professor C. S. Sargent of the Arnold Arboretum; Thomas Hogg; and Dr. G. R. Hall. By the end of the century there was a steady export of oriental plants to America as well as Europe and the last three men were mainly concerned with this trade in Japan, Professor Sargent in particular specializing in the Japanese flowering cherries. J. H. Veitch—the eldest son of that James Gould Veitch who died in 1870—was making a world tour purchasing plants on the way, and Henry was a doctor, stationed at Ichang on the Yang-tse River in 1881, who discovered *Lilium henryi* and a number of new species of Chinese shrubs; he was a regular correspondent with botanists and nurserymen in England and America, and later became an adviser and mine of information to other collectors in China. Maries was sent out by the firm of Veitch in 1877, travelled widely in China and Japan with few particularly outstanding results apart from the discovery of *Primula obconica*,[17] and finally retired to take up the post of Superintendent of Gardens to the Maharajah of Gwalior in India.

[17] A plant which for some reason Reginald Farrer detested. *"P. obconica"* he declares in *The English Rock Garden*, "is an evil thing." Its modern strains are among the most popular of cool greenhouse plants.

Richard Oldham was another of the unlucky travellers. Formerly a gardener at Kew he arrived in Japan in 1861 full of ambition and with hopes of a brilliant career, but somehow he seems to have incurred the dislike of Sir William Hooker—then director of the gardens—from the start, and thereafter nothing went well for him. Although in three years he sent back upward of thirteen thousand herbarium specimens, most of his finds had been anticipated by earlier workers in the field, his few good discoveries were neglected, and some were later credited to other collectors. Inexperienced, constitutionally unfit, and underpaid—his entire expedition cost less than £750—he carried out his contract faithfully in Japan, China, and Formosa, and died at Amoy in 1864 at the age of twenty-six.

(6)

The Treasure Lands
of America

While the missionaries were exploring China, on the other side of the world the West was also starting to be systematically opened up. Between 1801 and 1875, when most of the great discoveries had finally been made, there were no less than twenty-seven collectors working here, even without counting those travellers to whom plant hunting as such was merely incidental. Wallace and Bates on the Amazon were naturalists; Captains Meriwether Lewis and William Clark, who made the first epic crossing of America from east to west in 1804–1806, were primarily concerned with finding a route to the Pacific;[1] and Colonel J. C. Frémont of the United States Corps of Topographical Engineers generally had political or military objectives for his journeys—though his journals are fine tales of adventure, describing buffalo hunts and night raids, snow-bound passes and the thirst of blazing deserts.[2] With so many names some of necessity can have little beyond a passing mention though all deserve more.

The lush tropical forests, the mysterious rivers, and the mountains of South America were an irresistible lure and here, for instance, we must do all too little justice to the adventures of the German geologist and physicist Alexander von Humboldt, and Aimé Bonpland, the French botanist. Humboldt's fame as a geographer has far outstripped his relatively modest contributions to horticulture, and Bonpland in the end seems to have been rather less enthusiastic about writing up his

[1] Lewis and Clark nevertheless brought back a number of plants. Among others those which now bear their names, Lewisia and the popular annual Clarkia, *Gaillardia aristata*, *Mimulus luteus*, *Calochortus elegans*, *Erythronium grandiflorum*, and the now all too familiar Snowberry *Symphoricarpus alba*.

[2] J. C. Frémont, *Narratives of Exploration and Adventure*, A. Nevins, ed. (New York: Longmans, Green, 1956).

Frémont was also a perceptive botanist. Along with several species of desert plants from the Mojave he discovered the two beautiful genera of shrubs, *Freemontia* and *Carpenteria*, although it was left to later collectors actually to introduce them.

botanical discoveries than he was as a travelling companion. They were both optimistic and both young, Bonpland twenty-seven and Humboldt thirty-one, and perhaps that explains why their first venture was to set out to find the unknown waterway which was rumored to connect the Orinoco of Venezuela with the Rio Negro and the Amazon in Brazil. With no previous experience of jungle travel they started from Caracas in February 1800, at a later stage taking only four Indians and a pilot for their canoe, to make a journey which less than fifty years before had cost the lives of 312 men out of a 325-strong Spanish expedition sent out with the same objective. They did not find the river of course—it does not exist—but they did accomplish a valuable scientific exploration before working back to the coast.

Although hampered by shipping difficulties due to yet another naval war—this time between Spain and Britain, Spain having been forced into an uneasy alliance with Napoleon—they then made their way to Cuba, where Humboldt befriended John Fraser (see Chapter 4) who with his son had recently been shipwrecked and was destitute. Their next move in 1801 was to Colombia and on to Lima, where they hoped to pick up the ships of a French expedition to Australia thought to be sailing by way of Cape Horn and the Pacific (already having taken the eastern route round the Cape of Good Hope these ships never appeared) and after waiting for them until 1803 the two wandering inseparables left for Mexico. Here they climbed volcanoes, made observations and botanized for nearly another year before finally turning for home—though in a somewhat roundabout way, for they called at Havana, went on to Philadelphia to meet members of the American Philosophical Society, and visited President Thomas Jefferson, who was himself a man of great intellectual versatility as a writer, amateur scientist, philsospher, and architect.

They eventually arrived at Bordeaux in August 1804 with thirty-two cases of specimens of all kinds and notes sufficient for eleven books in twenty-nine volumes, most of these Humboldt's work. Bonpland was subsequently made superintendent of the Empress Josephine's gardens at Malmaison, but after her death in 1814 returned to the Argentine where he married a native woman, settled, and died in 1858. Humboldt went on to carve out a career as the greatest scientific explorer and geographer of his time and lived to be ninety. He is said to have introduced more than forty new species of plants, but the few that have proved to have any horticultural value were all collected in Mexico; they included *Lobelia fulgens*, *L. splendens*, and several varieties of dahlia, which were later grown by the Empress Josephine though not by any means for the first time in Europe.

After Humboldt and Bonpland, Allan Cunningham and James Bowie were next to arrive in Brazil, sent out by Sir Joseph Banks in 1814. Their journeys however were comparatively short, and Banks himself did not think the results were worth the hardships involved although in fact these two collectors brought back the gloxinia, *Sinningia speciosa*, and the handsome flowering tree *Jacaranda acutifolia* (syn. *J. ovalifolia*). They were followed in the Argentine in 1825 by John (or James) Tweedie, a man who seems to have developed a thirst for travel fairly late in life for he was fifty when he arrived in South America after having for some years previously been head gardener at Edinburgh Botanic Garden. From the scanty records remaining it is not quite clear whether he was sent out by the garden, by a syndicate, or whether he went as an independent collector scenting a profitable and adventurous business in providing the new tropical plants which were then becoming so fashionable in English hothouses and conservatories.

Either way he must have been contented and successful enough, since he remained there for the rest of his life, only writing sadly on one occasion that even the discovery of new plants "could not prevent him falling into a sort of melancholy as it was his sixtieth birthday 9,000 miles from home and among people worse than savages." He must also have been a remarkably tough old gentleman for on one other occasion, at some time unspecified, he refers to being shipwrecked in a storm four hundred miles up the Uruguay River "when the skies at noon were as black as midnight"; and when he was well over seventy he started with one companion for Patagonia, a jaunt which might have given Humboldt himself pause for thought. This time he was held up by floods, provisions ran out, and he and his unknown friend or guide were very close to starvation until they stumbled on a group of dwarf pines, sheltered among them and lived entirely on pine kernels until the waters went down. Most of Tweedie's discoveries were stove house subjects, now rarely seen except in public gardens, but he also introduced the Pampas Grass so much admired by the Victorians and today becoming fashionable again, *Cortaderia selloana, Tritelia uniflora*,[3] *Petunia violacea*, the origin of our modern bedding petunias, and the so-called tree tomato, *Cyphomandra betacea*.[4]

After Tweedie there was a succession of plant collectors in various parts of South America; Poepigg, Bridges, Mathews, Gardner, Hartweg, Lobb, Spruce, Pearce, and Roezl. The information about most of them is at its best uncertain, and at its worst contradictory, but Eduard Frederich Poepigg was a young German doctor, again with an itch for travel, who sailed first to Cuba and spent five years in the West Indies and North America before finally arriving in Chile in 1827. He found orchids in the valleys of the Andes and alpines on their heights; and with such excitement that he was "often compelled to relieve his full heart by uttering loud shouts of joy, to which his faithful dog, the sole companion and witness of his delight, responds by many a yelp of exaltation." In 1829 he went to Lima, worked northeast into the Amazon area, in 1830 embarked on the Huallaga River and vanished for two years into the forests, finally settling for eight months in a remote Mayan village where he was the only European in a vast province "without shoes and without clothes, often without a monkey to dine on." He was back in Leipzig by 1832 with a large collection of plant and animal specimens and material for a number of later botanical works, but his most spectacular introduction (by seed to Germany) was the giant water lily *Victoria amazonica* which had already been seen by earlier travellers but never before collected. Poepigg also claimed that the first specimens in Europe of the Monkey Puzzler tree, *Araucaria*

[3] Now *Ipheion uniflora*. An attractive little bulbous plant, indestructibly hardy, with white or pale mauve star-shaped flowers. It is best for naturalizing in an open situation on banks. In the rock garden it should be planted with caution since given a situation which it likes a dozen bulbs will quickly develop into hundreds and it then becomes almost impossible to eradicate.

[4] Now being re-introduced, and occasionally offered by nurserymen as something new, rare, and exotic. It is not hardy, however, and is best in a greenhouse where a winter temperature of 50° F. can be maintained. In warm areas it may be grown in tubs outdoors. Given these conditions it makes a handsome shrub up to six feet high, and carries purple and orange flowers followed by edible fruit which is rather sweeter in flavor than the ordinary tomato.

araucana, were raised from seeds he sent back, though there is some doubt about this.

Thomas Bridges was described as a "very enterprising young man" who having "spent some years among the plants already in England . . . solicited some gentlemen to whom he was known . . ." for funds to assist him to travel.[5] The funds apparently were forthcoming and enterprising he certainly was, for when he arrived in Valparaiso in 1828 he set up as a brewer of small beer to support himself until plant collecting began to show satisfactory returns—the only plant hunter ever to turn to brewing although many of them might have been forgiven for taking to drink. It was 1832 before he went out on his first long journey, to the little known area of Valdivia, returning to Valparaiso the following year with three hundred species of plants. He next put in a spell as superintendent on an estate before making one more trip north along the coast and then returning to England in 1842. He was back again, however, two years later, moving on from Bolivia to explore the rivers of Venezuela where he too found and collected seeds of the giant water lily. These he brought back to England and sold at the not unreasonable price of 2s. each, though he complained afterward that he never received credit for their introduction, probably because only two of them germinated and even those plants died before flowering.[6] He married in England and took his wife back to Valparaiso, where he started a nursery (not only for plants) but moved on to California in 1855 and from there made a further two-year exploring trip to British Columbia; then, still restless, he visited Nicaragua in 1865 and died at sea of malaria on the way back to San Francisco.

About Andrew Mathews little is known except that he too was an independent collector who had at one time been a gardener with the Horticultural Society, that he arrived in Lima in 1830, made a number of journeys in Peru over the next ten years and finally died in rather mysteriously unexplained circumstances in 1841. Meanwhile another collector who had taken a medical degree before turning to botany, and another who was financed by private subscribers, was exploring in

---

[5] *The Gardener's Magazine*, vol. VI, 1831.

[6] There is no record of what happened to the seeds Poepigg took back to Germany, but *Victoria amazonica* was not successfully raised in England until 1850–51.

Brazil. George Gardner's interest also was mainly in stove house plants, and he is chiefly notable for the vast number he collected in one long and industrious journey that lasted for three years. Arriving in Rio de Janeiro in 1836 he stayed there for twelve months getting to know the country and then went north by sea to Aracaty, inland by the rivers to Crato, southeast to the wild diamond mining areas, and finally south on the long march back to Rio—a total distance by canoe, horse, mule, and on foot of some two thousand miles. Back at his base it took three months to sort his collection, which consisted of upwards of sixty thousand specimens. Once these were safely on the way he set off on one last trip to the luxuriant area of the Parahyber River before leaving for home himself in 1841, taking another six cases of living plants. Many of these did not survive the journey, but he successfully introduced a number of orchids, including *Oncidium forbesii* and *Sophronitis coccinea.* That was his first and last expedition, for shortly after his return to England he was appointed superintendent of the Peradeniya Botanic Garden in Ceylon and in 1849, at the age of thirty-seven, died there in what really seems to be a rather curious way: "of an apoplexy while taking off his boots."

Theodor Hartweg travelled mainly in Mexico, but by 1841 he was exploring in Ecuador and sending back stove house plants and orchids, including the superb pale rose *Cattleya maxima.* At about the same time William Lobb[7] was working farther south for the nursery firm of Veitch; as none of Veitch's collectors were ever asked to keep journals, the record is vague. We know that Lobb crossed the continent from east to west—a formidable journey from Rio to Chile—and that there he went south to the araucaria forests and procured a large quantity of seed, the results of which may still be seen in many old suburban front gardens today. Returning to England in 1845 he sailed again for Rio the same year, crossed again to Valparaiso and went south to Valdivia, northern

---

[7] William's brother, Thomas Lobb, was also working for Veitch at this time in India and Sikkim, and later in Java and the Malay Peninsula. From Veitch's lists it appears that he introduced many new orchids in the genera *Vanda, Pleione, Dendrobium* and *Cypripedium,* but he was another who did not keep records and most of the references to him—many of these contradictory—come from fellow collectors and resident officials. He must have made some extremely arduous journeys, and finally retired having lost a leg as a result of exposure on his last long jungle trek.

Patagonia, and the island of Chiloe. Here he made a large collection of the trees and shrubs that were Veitch's main interest, *Saxe-Gothaea conspicua*—named after Prince Albert—a number of other fine new conifers, and the handsome greenhouse climber the Chilean bellflower, *Lapageria rosea*. He was back in England again by 1848 and in the following year went out for the first of his two trips to California.

With Richard Spruce however we are on firmer ground, for he left an account of his travels which was later published after his death, and which compares with H. W. Bates's *Naturalist on the Amazon* as one of the great journals of Amazonian exploration.[8] The son of a Yorkshire schoolmaster, he was primarily interested in mosses and lichens, gave up teaching himself because of persistent ill health, and after travels in Spain was encouraged to go to South America by Sir William Hooker and the botanist, George Bentham. It seems a curious choice for a sick man, but he arrived in 1849 and remained there for fifteen years, working up to the borders of British Guiana—now Guyana—and Venezuela, exploring the Orinoco and the Rio Negro, following the sources of the Amazon to Ecuador and the Andes in Peru, and from first to last sent back no less than seven thousand species of plants to Kew and private subscribers.

Some idea of that sort of travel may be gained from Spruce's own description of it. "Let the reader try to picture to himself the vast extent of the forest clad Amazon valley . . . and how the vegetation is so dense that it is rarely possible to see more than a few paces ahead. . . . I have heard an Indian relate that, having gone out one morning to cut firewood, he had wandered about the whole day before he could find his hut again. . . . When there are several persons in company . . . the turning of a large tree may completely hide the leader from view, although only a few paces ahead. . . . the bush is almost constantly wet, however clear the sky may be overhead." Small wonder that Spruce suffered from rheumatism in the forests. But not all of it was hardship, for at Manaos he writes, "Among the dancers were two very pretty Mamaluco girls. . . . During the course of the night I danced with every one." Neither were all occasions so pleasant, however, for at San

[8] *Notes of a Botanist on the Amazon and Andes*, A. R. Wallace, ed. (London: Macmillan, 1908).

Fernando de Atabapo he fell sick with fever, was dangerously ill for five weeks, and describes his "nurse" with some feeling. "This woman . . . I shall not easily forget. She was a Zamba—that race by which nine-tenths of the most heinous crimes are said to be committed in Venezuela," and apparently her favorite amusement while he was lying helpless was to "fill the house with her friends and spend the time in discussing or abusing him; calling him all the vile names in which the Spanish language is so rich. Among other things she would call out: "Die, you English dog, that we may have a merry watch night with your dollars . . ."

Spruce's greatest work, and one for which he has been almost forgotten, was with the Cinchona Tree. "Towards the end of the year 1859, I was entrusted by Her Majesty's Secretary of State for India with a commission to procure seeds and plants of the Red Bark tree [*Cinchona succirubra*] . . ." The medicinal value of Peruvian bark— quinine—had been known for centuries. As early as 1639 the Countess of Chinchon, wife of the Spanish Viceroy in Peru, had taken it back to Spain to treat the fever-stricken workers on her estates; Jesuit missionaries had carried it to Rome where malaria was endemic; in England the apothecary Robert Taylor had cured King Charles II of ague with it; and incidentally made his own fortune. But it was far beyond the reach of most people, and the forests were said to be dying out. Earlier plant hunters had tried to get living plants and failed; some never found the trees, others died in the attempt and one was murdered. Spruce set about the commission in his imperturbable Victorian way; "I proceeded to take the necessary steps for entering on its performance." He located the surviving forests, waited for a Mr. Cross who had been sent out from England with fifteen Wardian Cases and then between June and the end of December 1860 collected a hundred thousand seeds, raised six hundred seedlings, and shipped them down the river on rafts to Guayaquil in Ecuador. Plantations were subsequently established in India and later, more successfully, in Malaya and the first steps to combat the world wide scourge of malaria—before its connection with the Anopheles mosquito was discovered—were taken.

Spruce remained on the Pacific Coast until 1864 and then returned to his quiet Yorkshire village, where he spent the last twenty-nine years of his life as a permanent invalid, working quietly on his own specialized botanical studies, greatly admired by his learned colleagues, but otherwise in obscurity and comparative poverty.

The two other collectors in South America were Richard Pearce, about 1860 to 1868, and Benedict Roezl in 1870. Pearce was another of Veitch's men and once again his movements and even dates are uncertain but he had a wide brief to look for everything from timber trees to orchids. He is known to have made three trips, and along with other plants to have sent back the three begonias from which all our tuberous rooted hybrids today are descended, *Begonia boliviensis, B. pearcei,* and *B. veitchii; Hippeastrum pardinum,* the parent of our modern strains of this handsome bulbous subject—and generally but erroneously called amaryllis—and *Nierembergia repens.*[9] On his third trip, this time for the firm of William Bull, Pearce died of yellow fever in Panama after only four days' illness and when probably still little more than thirty.

Roezl may be more correctly described as a predator than a plant collector, chiefly remarkable for the astonishing speed at which he travelled even allowing for much improved communications in the later half of the century, and for the vast shipments he sent back—indeed it seems surprising that he did not totally denude some areas of plants altogether. After his first lightning trip to South America, when he covered more than two thousand miles through Colombia and Peru in six months, it is difficult to pin Roezl down to anywhere; but since he based most of his forays on Mexico we shall meet him again, with Theodore Hartweg, among the other collectors in the southern and Spanish states of North America.

Though disturbed by wars, piracy, and continual changes of nationality the islands of the Caribbean had been worked over since the seventeenth century; first by Thomas Willisel, gardener to the Earl of Carberry who was governor of Jamaica, and then by Dr. (later Sir) Hans

---

[9] A beautiful plant for the rock garden. The hardiest of the *nierembergia* species, with glossy leaves and handsome white flowers tinged with rose pink, it requires little but good moist soil and a shaded position.

Sloane, and by James Harlow. Harlow had already been out to Virginia in 1687 and in 1690, Sir Arthur Rawdon—an enthusiastic Irish gardener and botanist and lifelong friend of Sloane's—sent him to Jamaica. For a long time nothing was heard of him, and Sir Arthur wrote to Sloane in 1692, "I much wonder what is become of James . . . I fear he has a design to cheat me, for I cannot hear the least thing from him . . ." But later that year James returned and Rawdon continued glowingly that he ". . . not only brought over a ship almost laden with Trees and Herbs . . . but also a great number of samples of them, very well preserved in Paper . . ." Father Charles Plumier and James Read were there about the same time, followed by William Houstoun, a ship's surgeon; and then Robert Millar, sent out by a syndicate including Sloane, Lord Derby, and Lord Petre, and the Austrian physician and botanist Joseph von Jacquin between 1730 and 1754. Then there was Francis Masson of the South Africa explorations in 1778—who, "When the French attacked Grenada . . . was call'd upon to bear arms in its defence, which he did, & was taken prisoner fighting in the trenches"—and Humboldt and Bonpland in Cuba in 1798.

All this time the flora of Mexico was practically untouched, mainly owing to the Spanish government's curious habit of occasionally encouraging investigation and then firmly suppressing the results, a policy not unknown to some governments today. Francisco Hernandez in 1570—who brought *Tigridia pavonia* back—the Jesuit Father Barnardez Cobo,[10] who spent forty-five years in Mexico and compiled a natural history of the New World in ten volumes which never saw the light of day; Dr. Martin Sesse y Lacasta and Jose Mariano Moceno in 1788 all suffered particularly in this way, although these last two almost certainly sent the seeds of dahlia, *Cosmos bipinnatus*, and *Zinnia elegans* to Europe.[11] The curtain did not really start to lift until the arrival there of Humboldt and Bonpland for their quick ten months' exploration in 1803.

[10] Cobo's name is commemorated in the attractive and easily grown Cup and Saucer Vine, *Cobaea scandens*, with green and purple flowers.

[11] As said before, Lord Bute grew the first dahlias in England in 1798–99. He was British Ambassador to Madrid from 1795 to 1797, and the seeds were there given to his wife, the Marchioness of Bute.

Mexico became independent of Spain in 1821, although Augustin d'Iturbide proclaimed himself "emperor" immediately afterward and it was not until 1823 that an unsettled republic was finally set up. Whatever its faults, this at least partially opened up the country, and one of the earliest to take advantage of it was the engaging young Irish doctor, Thomas Coulter, who arrived in 1825 and remained for ten adventurous years. Coulter had taken a medical degree in Dublin, moved on to Geneva where he studied botany for seventeen months, planned a supremely ambitious trip through South America and up to Mexico and California—which did not materialize—and finally settled more modestly for a three-year contract as physician with a mining company newly set up in England to reopen mines left derelict since Mexican independence.

It was a lawless country—at the Veta Grande mine near Zacatecas, Coulter reported twenty-one murders in a single month—but it suited the energetic young Irishman. He seems to have turned his hand to everything, giving free treatment at the company's expense to the impoverished Mexicans, finding time to study mining techniques and assaying, making adventurous journeys from one mine to another, and botanizing on the way: in fact sometimes lingering to botanize too long. In the end he was removed from one mine and sent on to Zimapan in the Hidalgo region. But there was no harm in that, the Hidalgo was a better botanical area, and it was from here that at his own cost Coulter sent his first two collections of cacti back to old friends in Europe; one of seventy species to the garden of Trinity College, Dublin, and another of fifty-seven to the botanist who had trained him in Geneva, A. de Candolle.

He remained at Zimapan until his contract expired, and then for the next three years his movements are obscure. He seems to have tried out several financial enterprises, with some success at first, but of which he remarks in the end that "four robberies and a shipwreck helped to balance my accounts without the help of a bookmaker . . ." In August 1831 he turned up at Guaymas in the Sonora province of Mexico, having decided to return to botany and his earlier ambition of exploring California, since 1822 a part of Mexico itself, and still primitive, with settlements of only a few hundred people around the military posts, no more than twenty or so mission stations, and a single road along the coast.

Coulter landed at Monterey, but there were few flowers about at this time of the year and he went south to San Gabriel—now part of Los Angeles—to study the prospects for the spring. Back in Monterey by November he met the Scots plant hunter, David Douglas, just returned from his Sacramento trip, and the two men took a liking to each other and worked together until March 1832, when Coulter left again for the south, this time beyond San Gabriel to the San Luis Rey River and upstream to Pala. It was almost certainly about here that he found the magnificent shrub which bears his name, the California tree poppy, *Romneya coulteri*. From Pala he turned south along to the sand plain of Carizel, crossed a hundred miles of waterless desert to the Colorado River, and forded this just below its junction with the Gila; and thus was probably the first botanist to enter Arizona. Then he returned to Monterey by the same route, having been out for only seventeen weeks, a remarkably short time considering the distances he covered.

He planned to return to Mexico that year and again the record is uncertain, but in April 1833 he was in Mexico City, trying to set up a fresh mining project with two partners in Guanajuato, and still hoping to take a fortune back with him when he returned to Ireland. Nothing was less likely. The two partners absconded, while Coulter himself was needed as a doctor for an outbreak of cholera. The cholera moreover was further complicated by a revolution, during which Guanajuato was besieged and Coulter's house, being directly between a fort and the revolutionary lines, took the fire from both sides. Not surprisingly he returned to Britain in 1834, taking with him fifty thousand herbarium specimens, and samples of nearly a thousand species of woods. These he got safely to Ireland, but the case containing his diaries and botanical notes was lost in transit between London and Dublin and never recovered. He handed over the entire collection to Trinity College and was appointed its curator, but died nine years later in 1843 at the age of fifty.

The last important collectors in this area were Theodor Hartweg and the bustling Roezl. We have already met both of them in South America although in fact—such is the difficulty of keeping chronological and geographical sequences in order—they went on there from Mexico. Hartweg arrived in Mexico in 1836, reached Guatemala in 1840, extended his travels to the Andes in 1841, and returned to Mexico for a further short visit of only six months in 1845 before moving on to California by the following year. Descended from a German gardening family, he had worked at the Jardin des Plantes in Paris, and then as a clerk at the Horticultural Society's London garden before being sent out by the society to collect hardy plants and orchids, which were now becoming a fashion with wealthy horticulturists in Europe. Orchids also were Hartweg's own main interest, and on arriving at Vera Cruz he sent off his first collection within two weeks; he found one of the finest in a hat worn by an Indian and tracked the man to find the plant itself. But by this time war now began to threaten between Mexico and France, French ships blockaded the Mexican ports and the only vessels allowed to leave were British; they, however, were so overloaded that Hartweg's consignments had to take their chance. Two sent in February and April of 1838 did not reach England until February of the next year, when most of the plants were dead, and another sent in September never arrived at all.

Mexico also was becoming increasingly dangerous, with roving bands of robbers, Indians who would stone any foreigner on sight, and some fresh local revolution a daily possibility. Alarmed both by plant losses and for Hartweg's safety the society decided to send him south to Guatemala, but the instructions did not reach him until January 1839, when the war with France had already started and there was a revolution in Guatemala too. After a journey with every possible obstacle in his way Hartweg finally reached Guatemala City in January 1840, and it was from here that he extended his travels to South America that year. In spite of all his difficulties he still sent back 140 species of orchids, a number of cacti and conifers, seed in such quantity that the Horticultural Society distributed 7,000 packets to members, including *Fuchsia fulgens, F. splendens, Lupinus hartwegii* and the scarlet *Penstemon hartwegii*.

Benedict Roezl was more than interested in orchids and collected them on a vast scale, together with anything else he could get his hands on. Having been apprenticed as a boy in the gardens of the Count of

Thun in Bohemia, he had then worked in a number of important continental gardens, and finally emigrated to Mexico in 1854 to establish a nursery near Mexico City. He next took a plantation to grow sugar, coffee, and tobacco, introduced a textile plant, *Boehmeria tenacissima*, and then invented a machine for the extraction of its fibers; in fact the thing extracted Roezl's left arm, for while demonstrating it in Havana in 1868 he got his hand caught in the machinery spinning at sixty revolutions a second. So it was half crippled and at the age of forty-four that he embarked on his career of wholesale plant removal.

In 1869 he went via Havana and New York to the Sierra Nevada where he collected some of the most important of his hardy plants; *Lilium roezlii*, and *L. humboldtii*, so called by him because he found it on the hundredth anniversary of Humboldt's birth. Then he dashed south to Panama and Colombia. From here in 1870 he sent to Europe 10,000 mixed orchids and 500 other species, and followed these up soon after with a further 3,000 odontoglossums. August that year found him back in San Francisco embarking by steamer for the Columbia River and Portland, now the railhead from the east but still surrounded by unexplored forest. Here he collected *Lilium columbianum* and conifer seeds before making another unpredictable dash 1,100 miles back to the Sierra Nevada to look for more of such seeds there. By November he was sailing once more from San Francisco for another journey in Colombia, where he found more orchids.

In 1872 he spent four months in Europe and realized all his assets, intending to invest his whole capital in further journeys. Returning to New York he crossed America by rail, stopped off at Denver, and with quite extraordinary naïveté gave most of his money to a Danish innkeeper to look after for him while he went on an excursion to the mountains. When he returned the innkeeper had decided to take an excursion too, and was never seen again. How Roezl recovered from this calamity is not clear—though he must have been getting used to it, for in the course of his travels he was robbed no less than seventeen times—but he went on undeterred to New Mexico, where he found the magnificent silver fir, *Abies concolor*; revisited the Sierra Nevada, which he combed for more conifers and lilies; went back to Southern Mexico for orchids and sent a further 3,500 to London. He then crossed Panama to Caracas, where he garnered a further eight tons of orchids, and turned again by way of Cuba to Mexico and picked up the double poinsettia and a further ten tons of other plants. After a detour to New York he made one more trip to Panama and Peru—where he is said to have collected 10,000 bulbs—and then turned for Europe. But in three months he was back, heading for the Sierra Nevada once more, and then on to a new part of Mexico, near the Colina volcano, where he paid the local Indians from ten to fifteen francs a hundred for orchids and collected a further 100,000. What seems surprising is that they grew so abundantly there; after Roezl it is very doubtful whether they do so now.

Roezl returned home finally in 1874. His huge collections—not only orchids, but other stove plants, together with fuchsias, calceolarias, begonias, tropaeolums and conifers in wholesale quantities—found a ready market all over Europe, but he did not make the fortune he had hoped for; no plant collector ever can. He spent the last eleven years of his life in quiet retirement at Smirchow, near Prague, probably exhausted.

As we have already seen, the eastern states of North America had been explored since the time of the first Virginia settlers and later by the Philadelphia and Charleston pioneers and botanists. It would be too much to say these were worked out by the beginning of the nineteenth century, but interest was turning to the still only partly opened West beyond the great plains and rivers, deserts and mountains. From 1802 to the last quarter of the century—when plant hunting seems to tail off all through the Americas—of the ten men working north of Mexico only one between 1802 and 1814 was still collecting in the East, though it is uncertain whether even he could truly be described as a plant hunter.

This was John Lyon, originally gardener to William Hamilton of Philadelphia, whose garden, The Woodlands, then contained one of the finest collections of native and foreign plants in America. Hamilton was a difficult and demanding employer, and in 1802 Lyon left him to set up as an independent collector, with an eye to the British market. He seems to have concentrated on quantity rather than variety; we hear of him shipping 3,600 plants of *Magnolia macrophylla* in one consignment, and it looks as if he was another of the type which does more to kill off species than preserve them. In 1806 and again in 1812 he took collections to Britain, but the profits can scarcely have been encouraging considered as the outcome of years of work; the first made £923. 9s., and the second only £613. 6s. 9d. Since Lyon worked over much the same ground as Fraser and Michaux it is extremely difficult to disentangle his introductions from theirs, but it seems reasonably certain that among the comparatively few new species he introduced were *Chelone lyonii, Dicentra eximia* and *Iris fulva*.[12]

Before David Douglas arrived in America the two most interesting collectors were Thomas Nuttall and John Bradbury, the first a poor journeyman printer of Liverpool and the other a cotton mill worker from Stalybridge near Manchester, close contemporaries who for some part of their time travelled together. In his early twenties Nuttall emigrated to Philadelphia in 1808, attracted by the city's fame as the center of scholarship and publishing in America, and hoping to practice his trade there. He was already interested in botany, but knew little about it. The story goes that on his first walk he found a flower which neither he nor anyone in his boarding house could name and he was advised to take it to a Professor Barton, who lived nearby; a meeting that made Nuttall a botanist and Barton his friend and patron for life. Nuttall was an enthusiastic pupil and as early as 1809 Barton sent him on two collecting trips, though Nuttall seems to have financed both of these out of his own earnings as a printer.

A more ambitious journey was planned for 1810 and this was paid for by Barton, who gave Nuttall equipment and weapons, eight dollars a month and his expenses. The objective was Winnipeg, but for a young man who had no experience of wood craft or frontier conditions, who could neither swim nor shoot—he used the double barrelled gun with which Barton had provided him mostly for digging up plants—it proved to be impossible. He left Philadelphia in April, travelled by stage coach to Pittsburgh, went on by boat, finished by walking with his possessions on his back, reached Detroit exhausted in late June, and after resting

[12] Sometimes offered under its synonym *I. cuprea*. An interesting iris for moist soil or the waterside, having flowers of an unusual coppery red; there is also a violet form, var. *violacea*.

continued by birch bark canoe up Lake Huron to Mackinac. Here the
Canadian shores of Lake Superior were prohibited by the British North
West Company, and the British military posts were far from encouraging to strangers travelling on American passports; but Michili-Mackinac
was a trading post and the headquarters of John Jacob Astor's fur
company, which at this time was about to send an expedition of
thirty-four men along Lewis and Clark's route to the Pacific Coast.
Nuttall decided to travel with the Astorian party and it was at the end
of the first stage, at St. Louis on the Missouri River, that he met John
Bradbury.

Bradbury was eighteen years older than Nuttall, and had been
studying botany in his spare time since a youth. He had attracted the
attention, as a worthy and diligent person, of Sir Joseph Banks and
William Roscoe of the Liverpool Philosophical Society. Under their
patronage he was sent out on what appears to have been the standard
arrangement—£100 a year for three years—by the Philosophical
Society and Liverpool Botanic Garden not only to collect plants but also
to look in the South for new cotton growing areas essential for the ever
expanding Lancashire industry. He left a wife and eight children behind
him in England, and there is no doubt that he regarded his assignment
as the most exciting opportunity of a lifetime. Arriving in the late
summer of 1809, with letters of introduction from Roscoe, he stayed at
Monticello for two weeks with President Jefferson, who always
welcomed botanists and scientists. Jefferson was interested in encouraging the development of the West; he suggested that Bradbury should go
to St. Louis instead of New Orleans, and the cotton interests were
shelved in favor of botany.

St. Louis was to be the winter base for the main body of the Astorian
expedition and, having reached the city on the last day of 1809 himself,
Bradbury had been there for nine months—botanizing and dispatching
his collections to Liverpool from St. Genevieve farther down the
Mississippi—when the Astorians arrived. He too was invited to join it
and, as inexperienced in pioneer travel as Nuttall, when he was offered
an undreamed of opportunity to explore far into the unknown West, the
offer was too good to refuse. The cotton interests were now completely
forgotten. Hampered by incessant rain and flooded rivers, the party left

in March 1811, during the next few weeks joined up with two more separate groups waiting to meet it, and then numbering nearly sixty went on in four boats, with Nuttall in one and Bradbury probably in another, for little is heard of Nuttall at this stage although Bradbury kept a record of the journey.[13] Early in June they were joined and their numbers increased to ninety by a somewhat dubious Spanish fur trader, Manuel Lisa, and his own party, which included Henry Brackenridge. Brackenridge, who also left an account, had joined partly for the adventure and partly because he had already met Bradbury in St. Louis and was looking forward to making botanical excursions in his company.[14]

Numbers, however, did not make for harmony, for Lisa represented the rival Missouri Fur Company. He had left St. Louis a month after the Astorian expedition and had driven his men almost to mutiny in his efforts to catch up before they entered territory where the Sioux Indians were thought to be hostile. Yet even when they did combine neither party trusted the other an inch, and only three days after meeting, Lisa and the leader of the Astorians got into a violent quarrel which, but for the intervention of Brackenridge and Bradbury, might have led to shooting on both sides. Thereafter both parties kept their distance except when they seemed actually to be threatened by the Sioux; and when Bradbury went off on side excursions Brackenridge stood guard over him with his gun.

By mid-June they had reached the point from which the Astorian expedition must now continue its journey overland, with eighty horses collected from the trading post of Fort Mandan. Realizing that it would be impossible to carry his collection of several thousand plants across the Rockies, and moreover finding the botanizing in this area so good that he could not tear himself away, Bradbury here attached himself to Lisa's party and finally elected to embark himself and seventeen cases on two boats loaded with furs which Lisa was sending back down river to St. Louis in charge of Brackenridge. Nuttall too found the district a good hunting ground and stayed on at the fort after Bradbury had gone, later penetrating farther up the Missouri, where he found *Yucca glauca*,

[13] *Travels into the Interior of America* (London: Sherwood, Neely, and Jones, 1817).
[14] *A Journal of a Voyage up the Missouri*, 2nd ed., 1816.

and where he seems to have imagined that he was already in the Rockies, though in fact the mountains were still many hundreds of miles away.

Bradbury and Brackenridge left on July 17, and three days later were overtaken by a storm. In torrential rain and wind they narrowly escaped being wrecked on the rocky banks, and fought to build up the gunwales of the boats with extra boards and blankets which they had to hold in position with their hands. Even so they were nearly swamped and Bradbury was much concerned for Brackenridge. He wrote later, "Poor young man, his youth and the delicacy of his frame ill suited him for such hardships, which nevertheless he supported cheerfully." Brackenridge was equally worried about the other. In his turn he said, "Poor old man, the exposure was much greater than one of his years could well support. His amiable ardour in the pursuit of knowledge did not permit him for a moment to think of his advanced age . . ." Bradbury was then forty-three.

Back in St. Louis by the end of July there was a letter waiting for Bradbury informing him that his patrons had "determined to withhold any further supply," presumably because of his lack of interest in cotton. Already ill, he laboriously planted his collection in ground offered by some generous resident and then collapsed with fever—a few weeks before Nuttall returned to St. Louis. It was November before Bradbury started to recover, perhaps encouraged by a further letter saying that his remittances were after all to be continued, and that of his previous consignment to Liverpool from St. Genevieve more than one thousand plants were growing and seeds were germinating in great numbers. More hopefully he set out down the Mississippi for New Orleans, and was then involved in the earthquake which destroyed the town of New Madrid on 14–15 December 1811, and again barely escaped with his life.

He reached New Orleans in January 1812 and embarked for New York, but was prevented from sailing for England by the outbreak of the War of 1812, which arose out of conflict over British naval policy in the Atlantic. In New York Bradbury entered into some sort of business venture only to be cheated by his partner, and then when peace was concluded in 1814 made one last journey into Illinois. In the meantime back in England William Roscoe had loaned the herbarium specimens Bradbury had sent home to the botanist Frederick Pursh, who published descriptions of Bradbury's forty-one new plants in an appendix to his own *Flora Americae Septentrionalis* thus, as Bradbury said bitterly, "depriving me both of the credit and profit of what was justly due to me." He returned to England to publish his own book of travels in 1817 and then returned with all his family to America, where he became director of the Botanic Garden at St. Louis. He died in 1823 in Kentucky at the age of fifty-five.

Nuttall was altogether more fortunate. Arriving in St. Louis in October he remained only until Bradbury began to recover from the fever and then left, so avoiding the earthquake and arriving in New Orleans in time to sail direct for England before the outbreak of war. Before leaving he sent a generous half of his collections to Professor Barton in Philadelphia and took the rest to England, donated some to the Liverpool Botanic Garden and sold the remainder through the Frasers, who were now well known for American introductions. Nuttall himself compiled their 1813 catalogue, which listed also some of Bradbury's plants, and these in turn were later described in the botanical magazine; thus Nuttall too was given credit for other species found by Bradbury, including the handsome trailing Evening Primrose *Oenothera missouriensis*. Among Nuttall's own discoveries were *Camassia fraseri*, *Rudbeckia columnaris*, *Mentzelia nuda* and several more species of *oenothera* and *penstemon*.

He returned to Philadelphia in 1815 and in 1818 published his *Genera of North American Plants*, having the distinction unique among botanists of setting a large part of the type with his own hands. This was the third and best American flora—the first by Michaux and the second by Pursh—and with that and a comfortable reputation behind him, together with subscriptions from a growing circle of friends, Nuttall set out on a further adventurous journey to the West. Leaving Philadelphia in September 1818 he reached Lancaster by stage coach—at that time as far as it went—and then walked on to Pittsburgh, where he purchased a skiff for six dollars and hired a boatman to take him down the Ohio. At Louisville he spent nearly all of his remaining capital in buying a flat-boat and cargo, apparently comprised chiefly of whisky, salt, and flour, for he speaks of selling them all at a good profit farther along the river, and by mid-December had turned down the Mississippi. It was a miserable journey as most of the scattered settlements had been abandoned owing to floods and earthquakes and the prospect was "such as to inspire the mind with horror," but in January he reached the Arkansas River, and arrived at the real object of his journey, Arkansas Post, by the beginning of February just as the first spring flowers were starting to appear.

From there he worked up the river first by getting a passage in a skiff—with some difficulty, for his appearance "in the meanest appearance of a working boatman and unattended by a single slave" was suspicious—then with a trader named Drope calling at the scattered settlements, sometimes seventy miles or more apart, and finally continuing upstream with two French boatmen to Fort Smith, which was to be his base for the next six months. The fort commander was helpful and in May Nuttall left with a contingent of troops moving overland toward the Red River to clear settlers from an area which had been assigned as an Indian reserve. The hint of trouble behind that is overlaid by Nuttall's observation that by now the prairies were "enamelled with innumerable flowers," *Coreopsis tinctoria, Rudbeckia maxima*, oenotheras and penstemons.[15] Whatever duties the troops had, Nuttall's single-minded enthusiasm was still for botany; on the return journey at one point he stayed behind for only two hours to dig up plants, and lost his way trying to find the next encampment. He was rescued by a kindly farmer, but then had to wait for nearly two weeks before he could join up with a hunting party heading for the Arkansas. Nothing more clearly illustrates the loneliness of these wide spaces, little more than one hundred and fifty years ago, than the fact that even this party took the wrong track and found it difficult to get back to Fort Smith.

By July he was off once more, now with a trader's agent making his way upstream to the Verdigris River. After excursions from here, and an attack of fever, he set out again in August with a trapper on a cross-country journey to the Cimarron. This was very nearly fatal, for

15 "A Journal of Travels . . . in the Year 1819," in *Early Western Travels*, XIII, 32 vols. (Cleveland, Ohio: 1904–1907; reprinted A.M.S. Press, New York).

the weather was intolerably hot and their provisions went bad, the trapper's horse was lame, they were afraid of attack by Indians, and Nuttall's fever came back so severely that he was delirious. Moving on at less than six miles a day they reached the Cimarron early in September, made a canoe and started downstream, the trapper on the river and Nuttall, only slightly recovered, but still looking for plants, riding along the bank. They got back to a trading post more dead than alive, and after a pause to recuperate, Nuttall returned to Fort Smith. Thereafter the homeward journey was relatively uneventful; back to Arkansas Post, down the Mississippi to New Orleans by February 1820, and on to Philadelphia by sea.

In 1822 Nuttall was appointed curator of Harvard University's Botanic Garden at Cambridge, Massachusetts, and remained there for twelve years, only making short excursions and visiting England three times. Then in 1833 came an opportunity of realizing his most cherished dream, to reach the Rocky Mountains. One of his friends, Captain Nathaniel Wyeth, was to lead an expedition for the Columbia River Fishing and Trading Company to establish stations beyond the Rockies, and Nuttall promptly threw up his post at Harvard to join the party. Fully equipped, with two hundred and fifty horses and seventy men—surveyors, hunters, and naturalists, including the ornithologist J. K. Townsend who kept a record of the journey[16]—the expedition took on something of the nature of a holiday tour by contrast with Nuttall's earlier travels. They started in April 1834 from Independence on the Missouri, crossed the mountains as planned, and reached Fort Vancouver by September. Nuttall was away for two years, exploring in David Douglas's area of the Columbia River and spending two winters in the Sandwich Islands (Hawaiian Islands), before returning by sea from California and rounding Cape Horn in the same ship as the Harvard student, Henry Dana, who later was to become famous as the author of the book, *Two Years Before the Mast*. He reached Boston in September 1836, having by this journey alone added a further 1,000 new species to the American flora.

That was the end of his active career. In 1841 he inherited the estate

[16] "Narrative of a Journey Across the Rocky Mountains," in *ibid.*

of his Uncle Jonas, with whom he had been printer's apprentice as a boy, on condition that he should live for at least nine months of every year in England. He did not want to leave America, but since he had resigned his post at Harvard the Wyeth expedition had left him a poor man, and after one final six months' visit to Philadelphia—three months to the end of one year and three months into the next, so complying with the terms of the will—there was nothing for it but to fall in with Uncle Jonas's wishes.

The best known of all collectors in America was David Douglas, born in 1798, and the son of a village stone mason in Scotland who was apprenticed as a gardener's boy at the age of ten. Douglas contrived to pick up a remarkably good education by his own efforts, obtained a post at Glasgow Botanic Garden by the time he was twenty-one, and there attended the botanical lectures of Dr. W. J. Hooker—later Sir William Hooker, the director of Kew Gardens who advised Spruce to go out to South America. In 1823, when Joseph Sabine, then secretary of the Horticultural Society, was looking for a collector Douglas was strongly recommended and after a period in the society's garden was sent out on his first trip to America. This was mainly occupied in touring gardens and nurseries in the vicinity of New York and Philadelphia, with one longer excursion to Lake Erie and over to Amherstburg on the Canadian side before returning to Buffalo and then New York. After a second visit to Philadelphia where he met Nuttall—whom he describes as being "very communicative"—he visited John Bartram's garden and was back in England by January 1824.

Satisfied with his work the Horticultural Society then planned a more ambitious project for him. China was first considered but thought to be too dangerous and finally, with the co-operation of the Hudson's Bay Company, it was decided to explore the Columbia River area in British Columbia. Staying little more than six months at home Douglas set sail again on the *Mary and Anne*, which was to put him ashore at Fort Vancouver before cruising on farther north. After an eight months' voyage, rounding Cape Horn and calling at Juan Fernandez and the Galapagos Islands, by mid-February 1825 they were off the Oregon coast but then adverse winds made it impossible to cross the Columbia River bar for nearly another two months. That was always a dangerous operation; on a later voyage, in 1829, the same ship was wrecked there with the loss of all hands.

At this time the company post at Fort Vancouver was being transferred to a point ninety miles up river, and here Douglas made his base for the next two years. He spent the first summer exploring the lower Columbia, made trips to the Grand Rapids in the Cascade Mountains and covered two thousand miles in his first season before returning to Fort Vancouver in September, where the *Mary and Anne* had returned from her northern cruise and was preparing to sail for England. Douglas sent back nearly five hundred plants, seeds, letters, journals, and skins of birds and animals, but by then he had injured his knee on a rusty nail and the wound had developed into an abscess which troubled him for some months to come. This injury was the first of many such mishaps and it is hard to avoid the perhaps slightly unkind suspicion that Douglas rather enjoyed a good calamity.

Nevertheless with his first consignment dispatched he started off again for a district he had not been able to visit during the summer, as the Indians had been fighting among themselves. Now the villages were deserted, there was no food to be had, and he was forced to live on berries and roots. In his second season, during which he covered four thousand miles in all, he began to have trouble with his eyes; first inflamation caused by blown sand and then snow blindness later in the mountains. On one trip game was scarce, the rivers too rough for salmon fishing, and he was reduced to living on ground rats and a little boiled horseflesh. On another, having heard from the Indians of some magnificent pines growing in the forest he went off to find them, but this time blistered his hands so badly trying to make a raft that he sent his Indian guide back for help and, left alone, fell down a ravine while hunting a buck and lay unconscious for five hours before some other wandering Indians rescued him.

Still undaunted he made a fresh attempt some days afterward and finally reached the area in which "this most beautiful and immensely large tree" grew. It was *Pinus lambertiana*, second only to the giant redwoods in size and magnificence, one of the many trees introduced by Douglas that were to change the appearance of the European landscape. But the only cones to be seen grew right at the top, two hundred feet above his head, and determined to have them he shot them down with his gun. He secured three, but he also attracted the attention of a party of eight extremely hostile Indians, and he seems to have had an uncomfortable half hour or so before he could finally shake them off.

He left Fort Vancouver finally in March 1827 travelling east with the highly organized Hudson's Bay Express, a party of some forty men which came overland across Canada from Hudson Bay each year, bringing mails and supplies, and returning by the same route. They went by canoe, but Douglas walked for the first twenty-five days, only taking to the water when his feet got sore, and at Fort Colville he found *Fritillaria pudica*, *Erythronium grandiflorum*, and *Claytonia lanceolata*. By the end of April they started across the Rockies on foot, on the first day fording one icy river fourteen times in ten and a half miles, and seven more on the next; on the third nearly losing the track in six feet of snow. In May they were met by a Canadian guide with horses for the next part of the journey; and after that stage they took to canoes again, going on by way of Fort Edmonton and east across half Alberta and the whole of Saskatchewan to the northern tip of Lake Winnipeg.

It was on this cross-continental trek that Douglas met another collector and an old acquaintance in the person of Thomas Drummond, who had been in Canada for two years as botanist with Sir John Franklin's second Arctic expedition. At a rest post called Carlton House it must have been a curious meeting, as the summer before Douglas had sent off a box of herbarium specimens and seeds by the Hudson's Bay Express, and this had somehow been passed on to Drummond for safe keeping. Douglas's dissatisfaction when he heard of the arrangement is apparent for he wrote suspiciously, "hope my box is safe . . . do not relish botanist coming in contact with another's gleanings." It was safer than he might have hoped for, since Drummond had already saved many of the specimens from ruin by changing damp papers, and then went on still further to win Douglas's somewhat grudging approval by generously sharing all of his own information. Some weeks later they were to meet again at York Factory, on Hudson Bay, and sail home in the same ship. But in the meantime there is one other really magnificent picture of those last stages in Canada. Douglas had always travelled with a minimum of clothes and personal possessions, and by now had lost many of those, but one treasured outfit he still contrived to keep intact: a complete suit in the Royal Stuart tartan—not by any means one of the more restrained weaves. This he now wore, being in more populated regions, and was agreeably surprised and satisfied by the sensation it created; "scarcely a house I passed," he remarks complacently, "without an invitation to enter, particularly from the Scottish settlers."

His return to England was a triumph. Botanical circles were "literally startled by the number and importance of his discoveries," while the Horticultural Society had so many seeds that it found some difficulty in distributing them all. Certainly many of our most familiar plants today which had previously been known only to botanists were now brought into general cultivation, *Cornus alba* and *Mahonia aquifolium*; the Monkey Musk, *Mimulus moschatus*, that in later years was to adorn almost every cottage window in England, *Lupinus polyphyllus*, *Eschscholtzia californica*; the Douglas fir, *Pseudotsuga taxifolia*, and many other species of handsome landscape conifers. One of his introductions alone, the Flowering Currant, *Ribes sanguineum*, was then considered to be well worth the entire cost of the expedition, which was less than £400.

Even so the Horticultural Society was at first dubious about sending him out again, considering that the days of active plant hunting were already over and that seeds from any accessible country could now be more easily obtained by correspondence. But Douglas had set his heart on an exploration of California and in the end left again in October 1829 with one fresh commission from the society and another from the Colonial Office to make a survey of the Columbia Valley.[17] It was to be an erratic journey; and his last. The ship in which he sailed reached the Hawaiian Islands in April 1830, anchored there for a month—just time enough for Douglas to become fascinated by the islands and their flora—and finally reached the mouth of the Columbia River in June. Thereafter Douglas raced unpredictably from Fort James in the north to Santa Barbara in the south with side trips to the islands in between.

---

[17] In preparation for this Douglas that year had studied surveying with Captain Edward Sabine, brother of John Sabine, then secretary of the Horticultural Society.

That summer he was unable to leave the coast for several weeks owing to tribal fighting among the Indians, while the lower part of the country had been almost depopulated by an outbreak of fever which had wiped out entire villages; but at last he managed to get as far as one of his old hunting grounds on Lewis and Clark's river and by October when his ship sailed on her return journey sent back three cases of seeds. Then he left for the milder winter of the south and by December was in Monterey. California then still belonged to Mexico and Douglas had to apply for a permit to travel, which took so long to obtain that it was April 1831 before he was permitted to make any but the most restricted local excursions. He spent the season collecting in the Sacramento area before hurrying back to Monterey by November, where he hoped to meet a Hudson's Bay Company ship to take him to the Columbia again. No ship arrived but he met Thomas Coulter, who seems to have been the best of company until the following March, when he moved off again on his own travels.

By August Douglas was tired of waiting and took a passage to the Hawaiian Islands. From here he sent home his Californian collection, some 670 species, many of them new including *Garrya elliptica*, and a number of showy annuals still popular today; godetia, *Limnanthes douglasii*, mentzelia, nemophila, phacelia, platystemon, etc. After a sharp attack of rheumatic fever—and a curious and quixotic resignation from the Horticultural Society in support of his friend and patron Joseph Sabine, who had also resigned—by October he was back on the Columbia River, where he spent the winter and early spring in geographical work and surveying, and in planning a still more ambitious journey. Before he left London it had been suggested that he should return from America through Russia by way of Alaska and Siberia; he had brought with him letters of introduction to Baron Wrangel, the governor of Alaska, and when these were sent on to the baron they produced an enthusiastic response and the offer of a Russian ship to take Douglas to Siberia. Excited by the prospect of new geographical and botanic discoveries he set about his preparations completely undeterred by a warning—again of changeless Russia—that Siberia was like a rat trap "which there is no difficulty in entering but from which it is not so easy to find egress," and by the fact that he had now completely lost the sight of one eye. The damage started by sand and snow blindness in 1826 had been finished by the harsh sun of California.

He left in March 1834 intending to head for the mouth of the Skeena River, from which he could reach Sitka in Alaska by sea. Travelling by canoe, then with an overland cattle party, and finally by canoe again, he got barely past the halfway point and suddenly turned back; exactly why is uncertain. Early in June he was descending the Fraser River once more, and on June 13 his canoe was dashed to pieces, he himself was battered and nearly drowned in a whirlpool, and although his surveying instruments were saved, his botanical collections, journals, and all personal possessions were lost. He reached Walla Walla discouraged and far from recovered, but spent the remainder of the summer trying to make good his losses before returning to Fort Vancouver and embarking in September for the Hawaiian Islands, where he hoped to recuperate. But misfortune still dogged him. The crossing was unusually stormy; the brig was forced to run back for San Francisco, where she remained until the end of November, and it was late December before Douglas finally arrived in Hawaii.

His death, a little more than six months later, was peculiarly and horribly violent. What really happened will now never be known, but it was then a custom of the Hawaiian natives to dig pit traps for the dangerous wild bullocks which roamed the island; descendents of the cattle originally landed there by the navigator, Captain George Vancouver. Douglas came upon one of these pits, in which a terror-maddened animal was already trapped, apparently approached too near to the edge, slipped down himself, and was gored and trampled to death. None of the explanations is quite satisfactory. It has been said that he was pushed, which seems unlikely; in a recent and exhaustive study of his life and character it is suggested that he was in great mental distress at the time.[18] But Douglas was certainly calamity prone. And the final picture is of his small Scots terrier, still sitting patiently and guarding his master's travelling bundle close by, when the body was discovered.

While Douglas was exploring in British Columbia and California,

[18] William Morwood, *Traveller in a Vanished Landscape* (London: Gentry Books, 1973).

Thomas Drummond was working in Texas. Of Drummond's early life very little is known except that about 1814 he was a nurseryman in Forfarshire. After his return from Sir John Franklin's Arctic expedition in 1827, when he sailed home with Douglas, he was made curator of Belfast Botanic Garden, but then left that in 1831 to become an independent plant collector sponsored by Glasgow and Edinburgh Botanic Gardens and private subscribers, who were to receive plant specimens at the modest rate of £2 a hundred. He had been attracted to Texas by some plants collected by the Swiss botanist, Jean Berlandier, but he started in America by way of New York and Philadelphia, and spent his first two seasons collecting mainly in the Ohio valley and southeastern states before finally reaching there in 1833.

He could not have chosen a worse year. It was a time of floods, which afterward became known as the Great Overflow, of political disturbances, and of a cholera epidemic. Drummond's £2 a hundred was hard earned, for he caught cholera himself and barely recovered, suffered two periods of near starvation, and was later afflicted by an outbreak of boils and an ulcerated leg. His one piece of good fortune was when he just missed joining a surveying party to the interior which was massacred by the Indians. In spite of all that he seems to have remained unquenchably optimistic, and to have been so taken with the country that he applied for a grant of land in Texas, intending to return to Scotland and bring back his family to settle in America. But he planned to visit Florida first and in January 1835 went by sea to Apalachicola, and then in February moved on to Cuba. By June of that year Dr. Hooker in Edinburgh received three boxes. They contained not plants, but the remains of Drummond's scanty possessions, and were followed by a letter from Havana dated 11 March 1835 enclosing Drummond's death certificate and referring to particulars given in an earlier letter which in fact was never received. Nothing more is known of Drummond's death, and many of the beautiful Texan plants he discovered have proved difficult in cultivation, but one at least is still with us today in the shape of our colorful and brilliant annual phloxes; *Phlox drummondii.*

. The remaining three collectors, Hartweg, Jeffrey, and Lobb, all revisited the areas explored by Douglas for the express purpose of following up his finds. Hartweg was sent out by the Horticultural Society; John Jeffrey by a number of Scottish gentlemen calling themselves the Oregon Association, who were interested in new conifers with which to plant their estates; and William Lobb again by the nursery firm of Veitch that wanted to introduce the conifers discovered by Douglas to commerce, since all his specimens previously had gone to gardens and private subscribers.

Hartweg seems always to have run into wars and revolutions and this final trip in 1846 was no exception, for America was now at war with Mexico for possession of Texas, New Mexico, Arizona, and California. In his first season he could not venture far afield first from Monterey and later from San Francisco, and in the second he worked the Sacramento valley. Nevertheless he amassed a fairly considerable collection which included the first *Cupressus macrocarpa,* two species of ceanothus, the Californian Fuchsia, *Zauschneria californica*[19] and a number of annuals; he is also, though dubiously, credited with the introduction of the redwood, *Sequoia sempervirens.* He returned to England by way of Guatemala in 1848 and shortly afterward retired to his native Germany, where after his twelve years of travel he spent the peaceful remainder of his life as Inspector of Gardens to the Duke of Baden at Schwetzingen.

John Jeffrey was another who does not seem to have given full satisfaction to his employers. The Scottish gentlemen arranged a passage for him in a Hudson's Bay Company ship and he arrived at York Factory on Hudson's Bay in August 1850 and then followed the usual route across Canada—including 1,200 miles on snow shoes with a four dog sledge team—to reach Douglas's hunting grounds after a twelve-month journey. He seems to have been fairly successful in his first season and sent five packages from Fort Vancouver, but though he dispatched them all by different routes no less than three failed to arrive. Starting the next spring hopefully he worked his way south

[19] An interesting and attractive plant, bearing small, bright orange scarlet tubular flowers, for the sunny rock garden. It is supposed to be rather less than half hardy, but is easy to raise from seed and given a sheltered pocket and a fair supply of broken fragments of rock among which it can retire for the winter it will often survive for several seasons.

Sequoiadendron giganteum in the Calaveras Grove. Courtesy California Department of Parks and Recreation, photo by Gene Russell.

through Oregon and down the Sierra Nevada, but though Douglas had found this a rich area the collections Jeffrey sent home were again disappointing. Reaching San Francisco in October 1853, he was ill for some part of the autumn, and sent off his final consignment in January 1854. That is the last that was ever heard of him. When one of the gentlemen of the Oregon Association, William Murray, arrived personally in San Francisco early that year Jeffrey was nowhere to be found.

Several explanations were offered for his disappearance: that he had died of thirst in the Colorado Desert, that he had been murdered for the sake of his mules and equipment, or that he had been killed by the Indians. But in any one of those cases he would not have arrived in San Francisco at all, and what seems much more likely is that he was caught up in the Californian gold rush and abandoned plant hunting for what promised to be more profitable pursuits. Nevertheless he did send back more than a hundred extremely interesting varieties of seeds and bulbs including *Delphinium nudicaule, Dodecatheon jeffreyi, Fritillaria recurva,* and the Quamash, *Camassia leichtlinii.*

After his two successful trips to South America most of what little we can glean of William Lobb's movements in the western states comes from brief references in books by members of the Veitch firm—*Manual of the Coniferae,* 1881, and *Hortus Veitchii,* 1906—and if any more detailed records ever existed they have almost certainly been lost. He arrived in San Francisco in the summer of 1849, the year of the first gold rush when eighty thousand prospectors came to town, five hundred ships lay in the harbor deserted by their crews, and the lawlessness was uncontrollable. But he seems to have been one of the few men there who was not interested in the fever, for he turned his back on all of it and went south to San Diego. From here he visited the Santa Lucia mountains in the summer of 1850, and San Juan in 1851. The next year he went to Oregon and up the Columbia River, where he found one of the few trees Douglas had missed, *Thuja plicata,* the Western Red Cedar.

He was back in California by 1853 when he heard of a new "big tree" somewhere in the mountains and set off to find the comparatively small area of California where these magnificent giants grow, and are now protected—the Calaveros Grove. Finding seeds and young plants he got them back to England successfully, and although Lobb made many other introductions it is by this tree that he is usually remembered. In fact some seeds had already been received but it was from Lobb's specimens that Dr. Lindley of the Horticultural Society first described and named it *Wellingtonia gigantea*, after "the greatest of modern heroes," the Duke of Wellington.[20] That was Lobb's final achievement. In 1854 he returned from England to settle in California, and although his contract with Veitch ended in 1857 he continued to send back occasional consignments of seeds and plants until his death in 1863.

By this time it seems to have been thought that most of the great discoveries in America had already been made, as they possibly had. After Lobb in the western states and Roezl in Mexico and South America there was little more important activity here; but in the Far East there was still a rich field to be explored.

[20] Now *Sequoiadendron giganteum.*

(7)
The Other Quarters

The French "poivre" for pepper comes from the name of Pierre Poivre (1719–1786), one of the most adventurous of the spice seekers, and it has been said that much of the early exploration of the East was first inspired by the demand for spices: cloves, cinnamon, nutmeg, and ginger. Spices and trade were followed by the explorers and naturalists, and at the end of the eighteenth century they were starting to penetrate deeper into the jungles of the East Indies, the uplands and forests of Africa, and the still unknown interior of Australia and New Zealand. While America was providing, in general, most of the hardy trees, shrubs, and plants then being introduced, these other quarters of the world were to yield their own contribution of beautiful and sometimes bizarre genera and species. A yellow forget-me-not and an encrusted plant which from a distance looks like a sheep out of New Zealand, insectivorous nepenthes from the Indies, succulents which look like stones and other curiosities from Africa.

Christopher Smith initially went out from Kew to the Moluccas in 1795 to collect and distribute plants of nutmegs, cloves, and other spices, and did so to such purpose that he sent 127,000 plants to England, Calcutta, Madras, and Penang besides collecting more than 28,000 other unusual species, though few of them are now of much garden interest.[1] Smith was followed in 1803 by Leschenault de la Tour, a botanist who had sailed with the French expedition to Australia under Captain Baudin,[2] but who fell ill on the homeward voyage, was left behind at Timor and subsequently went on to Batavia to make an exhaustive botanical exploration of Java over the next three years.

---

[1] Smith and James Wiles, originally gardeners at Kew, went first with Captain Bligh on his second breadfruit expedition in 1791–93. There was no mutiny this time and *H.M.S. Providence* safely carried a shipload of young breadfruit trees from Tahiti to Jamaica.

[2] This was the expedition Humboldt and Bonpland had hoped to join in 1801 when they waited so long for its ships to appear at Lima in Peru.

William Kerr was working at about this time in the Philippines after his first season in China. Then it was nearly twenty years before the orchid hunters started to arrive, with Thomas Lobb and Hugh (later Sir Hugh) Low the first among them.

Low was a man of singular ability, who went out to Borneo as a plant hunter and remained to become one of its greatest administrators. His father had started life simply as a gardener, later to become foreman and eventually managing director of Mackie's Nursery, near London, and Hugh Low himself sailed for the East solely to collect plants for the firm. He arrived in Kuching in January 1845, and there met the soldier James Brooke who had brought the piratical coastal Dyaks at least nominally under control, and who in 1841 had been granted the province of Sarawak by the Sultan as his own private kingdom. That meeting was later to change Low's entire career, but for the following two years he explored the Borneo jungle—said to be so dense that an orang-utan could swing the whole length of the country from one tree to another without once touching ground—penetrating deeper than any other European before him, and making friends with the natives in spite of their fearsome reputation. "The Malays," he wrote, "natives of the western coast of Borneo, do not practise many of the vices for which their nation in general has become so famous. In their character they are a mild and quiet people, devoid of the cunning and treachery of the natives of Sumatra, whom the dissolute inhabitants of the capital more closely resemble." [3]

Still only twenty-four, Low returned to London in October 1847 and when his book was published early in the following year it was rightly considered to be a remarkable achievement. Rajah Brooke was in London at this time, much fêted by the young Queen Victoria, and on being urged to become his secretary Low returned with him to Sarawak that February. He remained on the island of Labuan for the next twenty-eight years, making some excursions to the mainland, becoming the first European to climb Mount Kinabalu—again with the help of his native friends—and sending a few plants back to England. What had started as a profession now became a hobby, and plant hunting had to

[3] *Sarawak; Its Inhabitants and Productions* (London: Bentley, 1848).

give way to his increasing official duties. His introductions were mainly orchids, together with some clerodendrum and rhododendron species and the giant pitcher plant *Nepenthes hookeriana.*

Low's near-contemporary Thomas Lobb, of the two brothers sent out to collect by the nursery firm of Veitch, has been mentioned elsewhere (Chapter 6) though it is nearly impossible to trace any coherent record of his movements. We know that he set out in 1843 and thereafter until 1860 he seems to have hopped from the Malay Peninsula to Java and possibly Bali, back to England at some time between 1847 and '48, and then off again for three years in India, during which time he somehow managed to turn up also in Burma and Malaya once more. Then he is reported in North Borneo, Sarawak, and the Philippines with fresh visits to Singapore, Borneo and Sumatra. In 1856 he was in Borneo again, attempting to repeat Low's ascent of Kinabalu but forced to give up as the natives refused to help him, and then some time before 1860 he lost one leg, apparently as a result of exposure on a more than usually arduous jungle journey—though exactly where and how remains unknown—and retired to his native village in Cornwall, where he lived to a great age and died in 1894. Nevertheless he was a remarkably successful collector and James Veitch said of him that he had enriched British greenhouses with more beautiful plants of Indo-Malayan origin than any other collector before or since; orchids, rhododendrons, nepenthes, and scores of other exotics.

At that time fuel supply problems did not exist, and hothouse exotics were becoming almost a gardening craze. Collectors' lots of plants, roots, tubers and pseudo-bulbs, sorted and roughly classified, were now to be had regularly at the plant auctions, and you could bid for bundles with the not altogether unlikely chance that you might find yourself with something that had never before been seen outside its native jungles. Veitch's in particular were quick to see the possibilities here, commercial as well as horticultural, and they sent out several more collectors in rapid succession. In 1877 Frederick William Burbidge and Peter Veitch—a cousin of J. G. Veitch, who was making a leisurely tour of the world—followed by Charles Curtis and David Burke in 1880. They too brought or sent back supplies of orchids, nepenthes, and crotons, but with the exception of Burke remained in the East Indies for only a short time, and Burbidge alone published a record of his single season in Borneo, *Gardens of the Sun*, in 1880. Burke, however, was another of the dedicated plant hunters of whom little is known—all the more tantalizing as he is said to have become a solitary eccentric and "one of those natures who live . . . with the natives as a native and apparently prefer this mode of life." [4] He continued to collect and send plants back for seventeen years, up to the time of his death in a little known area of Amboina at the early age of forty-three.

The unfortunate Francis Masson (Chapter 4) had left Africa early in 1795, three years before the next collector, James Niven, arrived at the Cape. Niven was a Scots gardener employed by the Duke of Northumberland until he was engaged to collect by George Hibbert, a wealthy amateur in the then pleasant country village of Clapham near London, who was a great expert on the magnificent South African genus of greenhouse shrubs, *Protea*. With one short break Niven worked in Africa for fourteen years, the first five for Hibbert and then for a syndicate that included the nurserymen Lee and Kennedy and, rather curiously since the Napoleonic Wars had broken out again after the short Peace of Amiens, Napoleon's Empress Josephine. He was described as a "most affable and friendly hearted man" and he seems to have served his employers well for he discovered thirty new ericas— Josephine was particularly interested in heathers and had a large collection in her garden at Malmaison—five new proteas and species of gazania—the popular so-called Jewel Flower now treated as a half hardy annual—lobelia and moraea. In 1812 he returned to England and gave up botany and gardening completely in order to go into business with his brother in his native Scotland, where he died in 1827. His obituary notice says sadly that "on the instant her husband's corpse left the door of the house . . ." his wife died too, "leaving five orphans." One of the orphans, however, was then twenty-eight.

Two years before Niven himself left, one of the Cape's most versatile explorers and plant hunters arrived in the person of William John Burchell, the son of a London nurseryman who had lived for the

[4] J. H. Veitch, *Hortus Veitchii* (London: 1906).

previous five years on St. Helena—the island which was to become Napoleon's prison in 1815—first as a merchant, then schoolmaster, and finally as official botanist. Later the author of a much admired two volume book of travels, Burchell was a man of wide interests and enthusiasms: trader, geographer, ethnographer, artist, zoologist, and not least botanist.[5] He travelled at his own cost, working from an ox wagon proudly flying the British flag, carried with him a library of fifty books, and his great pleasure after the day's trek was done was to entertain a circle of admiring Hottentots with airs on the flute; there are shades of Sir Joseph Banks and his two hornplayers there.

He made short preliminary excursions in his first season and then in January 1811 set off with a party of missionaries on a journey that was to last for four years. It was during the early part of this exploration that he made one of his most interesting discoveries—on one occasion picking up what he thought was a pebble and then realizing that it was in fact a living plant, *Mesembryanthemum turbiniforme*, one of the most extraordinary examples of natural mimicry in existence.[6] Joined by other wagons on the way and travelling through what was for the most part trackless wilderness the party reached the mission station of Klaarwater in September and after a long stay here—while he explored areas previously unknown to any European—Burchell set off again in February of the next year against the advice of the missionaries, who regarded the project as suicidal madness, to make a long trip southeast. Steering by compass through unknown country and reputedly danger-ous tribes—which he found in fact to be only miserably poor and timid, and again much affected by his flute playing—he reached the settle-ment of Graaf Reinet in March and was safely back in Klaarwater by May. This time the missionaries were far from welcoming; Burchell suspected that they were unduly disappointed in their prophecies of disaster, and he left again in June exploring northward once more through unknown territory to the native town of Litakun.

[5] *Travels in the Interior of Southern Africa* (London: 1822–24; reprinted, Batchworth Press, 1953).

[6] Now included in *Lithops*, a group of which all species more or less resemble stones or even fragments of rock, some so closely that it is difficult to distinguish them from the soil in which they are growing. Seed is sometimes offered, and they are not difficult to grow in a warm and sunny window given careful attention to watering and a porous compost. None reach more than an inch or so high and all bear attractive white or yellow flowers.

Here his own account of his travels finishes, but it is known that he made his way as far north as what later became British Bechuanaland before returning once more to Klaarwater, heading south to the Great Fish River, and working back some six hundred miles along the coast to Cape Town. He sailed for England in August 1815 with a collection of more than 40,000 herbarium specimens, 500 drawings, 2,000 species of seeds and 276 of bulbs. With typical generosity he gave all of these but the most ornamental away and grew on the remainder himself in his father's nursery in London, although few of them except the mesembryanthemum seem to have remained in cultivation.

Burchell's successor, James Bowie, was a man of very different character. Another gardener from Kew, he had originally been sent by Sir Joseph Banks to Rio de Janeiro with Allan Cunningham, whom we shall meet later. In 1816 Cunningham was directed on to Australia and Bowie to South Africa, and arrived in November of that year to remain until 1823. With one exception, when he travelled up country to Burchell's area of Graaf Reinet and beyond, he worked mainly the eastern coastal districts to the new British settlement of Grahamstown and on to the Great Fish River, and his chief claim to interest is the friendship he struck up about 1818 with a Mr. George Rex at Knysna, eastward along the coast from Cape Town. Mr. Rex was not the best of companions for a modest young botanist, being an illegitimate son of King George III who had been persuaded to remove himself to South Africa for his own and everybody else's good, famous alike for his riotous life and the considerable number of his part-colored descendants. Bowie must have enjoyed his company for he stayed at Knysna several times, six months on one occasion and four on another. It was on Rex's land that he found *Streptocarpus Rexii*,[7] which together with *Clivia nobilis*, the handsome Kaffir Lily,[8] discovered near the Great Fish River, ranks among his most important introductions.

[7] One of the progenitors of our fine hybrid strains for the greenhouse. Note also that it is *rexii*, not merely *rex* which would indicate fancifully that it is the king or greatest of streptocarpus. *Rexii* links it specifically with George Rex, and by the strict rules of nomenclature would indicate that he discovered it, which is doubtful. Probably the only example of a very beautiful plant being named after a royal error.

[8] A common name which it shares with the entirely different plant *Schizostylis coccinea*.

In spite of Mr. Rex he sent many collections back, including numbers
of new succulents, but on the death of Sir Joseph Banks in 1820 Kew
Gardens lost the impetus of his inspired directorship, the money
available for plant collecting was drastically reduced, and Bowie was
recalled. He arrived in London in August 1823 and there sadly took to
bad company again, as it was reported long afterward in the *Journal of
Botany*, passing his time "among the free and easy companions of the
bar parlours, recounting apocryphal stories of his Brazilian and Cape
travels . . ." Eventually he decided to go back to the Cape, advertised
to that effect in the *Gardener's Magazine*, and returned in 1827. But by
now he had little perseverance, less tact, and no business head, and
from that time on he sinks into obscurity.

During Bowie's first period in South Africa the Horticultural Society
sent out another collector to Sierra Leone, George Don, who sailed on
H.M.S. Iphigenia commanded by Captain Edward Sabine—brother of
John Sabine, secretary to the Society—and arrived in Freetown in
February 1822. It was an unfortunate assignment altogether, for though
Don made a number of collections he was continually hampered by
recurrent bouts of fever, and his last and best collection was completely
lost during the long voyage home when Sabine was ordered to return by
way of South America, the West Indies, and New York, finally reaching
England in February 1823. Then in the following year, when Don
published a paper in the *Edinburgh Philosophical Journal* describing
some new species of plants he had discovered, the Horticultural Society
promptly sued him for breach of contract but made no further use itself
of any of his records.

There were many other collectors in Africa but few remained for long
and some were amateurs; Bowie complained bitterly of "an officer of
the army who has sometimes 40 soldiers at a time told off to collect for
him." The only two remaining names of importance in the later half of
the century are Friedrich M. J. Welwitsch and Thomas Cooper. Little is
known about either of them. Welwitsch was a middle-aged Austrian
botanist who had been director of various botanic gardens in Portugal,
arrived in Angola in 1854, and started an enthusiastic exploration of the
neighboring territories which lasted for the next seven and a half years.
He received a magnificent allowance of £46 a year from the Portuguese

government which he supplemented by selling collections of plants, seeds, insects, and specimens in London. A brilliant botanist, he has however been almost forgotten apart from his strangest discovery, the unique and really rather unpleasant *Welwitschia mirabilis*, a plant described as resembling a giant mushroom bearing leaves fringed with ribbon-like filaments, almost impossibly difficult to grow and now very rarely seen.

There is even less information concerning Thomas Cooper, except that he was engaged by the wealthy amateur, W. Wilson Saunders, and worked in South Africa from 1859 to 1862. In that short time he somehow covered more ground than any previous collector with the exception of William Burchell, and some of the plants he discovered are still with us today—to name only two the asparagus fern, *Asparagus plumosa*, and the fine hardy bulbous plant with a spire of pendulous white bells, *Galtonia candicans*, which is a handsome addition to any perennial bed. Cooper died in 1913 at the great age of ninety-seven and by that time he had probably forgotten most of his adventures himself.

Australia too was now attracting its own botanists and explorers, some who worked there for only a few weeks or months and one, Allan Cunningham, who stayed for fifteen years. George Austin and James Smith, the two gardeners sent out by Sir Joseph Banks in 1789—of whose history nothing at all is known—that David Burton who in Chapter 4 was called "to botanise in the celestial regions," Leschenault de la Tour with the French expedition in 1801–1802, Brown, Bauer, and Good with Captain Flinders in 1802–1805. After these the first of any importance was George Caley, a curious, difficult character more often in trouble than out of it and with a distinctly roving eye. Banks, who appears to have treated Caley with extraordinary tolerance, once said of him, "Had he been born a gentleman, he would long ago have been shot in a duel."

His father was a horse dealer and Caley himself went to work as a stable boy at the age of twelve, and so developed an interest in botany through searching for herbs with which to physic the horses. Then in 1795 he sent Banks some plant specimens he had mounted, and asked if Sir Joseph could help him find botanical work in London. Banks found

him a place as gardener's laborer at Chelsea Physic Garden, explaining
that this was a humble beginning but it was the way many a famous
botanist had started, and then later offered to have him transferred to
Kew, at 9s. a week. That Caley refused on the grounds that the money
was less than he was getting at Chelsea. He was already interested in
the New Holland (Western Australia) plants now being discovered and
next asked Banks to have him sent out there as an official collector, to
which Banks answered reasonably enough that he could not conscientiously recommend a man who had had no scientific training. On this
Caley took himself off home in a temper, accusing Sir Joseph of "not
acting in a proper manner," with the surprising sequel that in
November of 1798 Banks wrote that he had arranged a free passage for
Caley to Port Jackson (now Sydney), and that he himself would pay him
a salary and provide him with a letter of introduction to the governor. It
can only suggest that Banks saw some qualities in Caley that were
hidden to less perceptive eyes.

Caley was due to sail in a few weeks, but in the end his ship did not
leave until the following September, and even then was forced to put
back owing to storm damage in the Bay of Biscay. Passengers were
transferred to the more appropriately named *Speedy* and they eventually arrived at Sydney in April, 1800, Caley by now having distinguished
himself by falling violently in love with a widow whose husband had
died on the voyage, an infatuation which seems to have been regarded
as scandalously precipitate. Once landed, with his salary conscientiously
paid by Banks throughout all the delays, Caley was given every possible
assistance and during that year made a number of excursions in the
surrounding territories. He was energetic enough but his uncertain
temper must have been an intolerable nuisance to his companions, for
between March and May 1801 he sailed on a survey cruise of the
southern coast and appears to have spent the better part of his time
quarrelling with two other naturalists aboard this ship. Then in August
of the same year the local governor "advised" him to investigate the
flora of the Hunter River which was a very considerable distance away.

In 1803 Banks received seeds of 170 species of plants, including the
attractive evergreen greenhouse shrub, *Epacris purpurascens,* and in the
following two years Caley made a number of pioneering journeys into

central Australia, bestowing his own highly descriptive names on some of the areas: Dark Valley, Devil's Wilderness, and Skeleton Rocks.[9] By 1805 he was anxious to return to England but when in the following year Banks wrote that owing to his own increasing age he no longer required the services of a collector and offered Caley a pension of £50 a year for life, whether he came back or remained in Australia, Caley elected to stay. By now he was involved in a further passionate affair, this time a determined but unsuccessful courtship of a spirited young woman convict named Margaret Catchpole, who had originally been transported to Botany Bay for stealing a horse.

But he was equally capable of unpredictable loyalties. In 1805 Captain Bligh, of the mutiny and breadfruit expeditions, was appointed governor-general of New South Wales. Bligh was in fact a very able man with advanced ideas on colonial administration, but after his easy-going predecessor he imposed them so harshly that in 1808 part of the New South Wales Corps under Major George Johnstone mutinied and deposed and imprisoned him. Caley, who had hitherto been one of his bitterest critics, now became his staunchest advocate, did his best to get public support for Bligh—an almost impossible task—visited him in prison, and eventually returned to England in 1810 mainly in order to give evidence at Johnstone's court-martial.[10] He was later appointed director of the St. Vincent Botanic Garden in the West Indies, and here too his curious affairs and increasing troublesomeness became notorious. Nevertheless he was a very able botanist—Sir Joseph Banks would not have tolerated so much had he been otherwise—and among the plants named after him is a small genus of botanically interesting orchids, *Caleana*, mainly remarkable for their irritability. Probably the best known of his introductions today is the popular house plant, *Platycerium bifurcatum*, the Stag's Horn Fern.

There can be no greater contrast than the next collector to arrive in Australia, Allan Cunningham. Of Scots descent, the elder of two brothers—with a tragic tale to come concerning the younger—he had originally studied law but turned to botany, and had been working at

[9] Ida Lee, *Early Explorers in Australia* (London: Methuen, 1925).

[10] Bligh was subsequently promoted to rear and then vice admiral, but never served afloat again, presumably to avoid any further mutinies.

Kew with the younger William Aiton on the preparation of the second edition of *Hortus Kewensis*. With the end of the Napoleonic Wars Sir Joseph Banks was ready to send out more collectors and Cunningham and Bowie were posted to Rio de Janeiro where they worked for two years before, as we have already seen, Bowie was posted to Africa and Cunningham to New South Wales. He arrived in December 1816 and paradoxically there is little to say about him almost because there is too much. He made prodigious journeys with exploring parties—generally on foot since horses were still at a premium in the colony and far more useful for carrying supplies and equipment than as riding animals—and his series of expeditions into unknown territories of the new continent did much to open up Australia in the early days. But most of his discoveries were of botanical rather than horticultural interest and apart from the inevitable hardships of such journeys—marching through swamps or shoulder high scrub, occasional shortages of food, and pressing on over desert in search of water—there was relatively little incident, perhaps largely as Cunningham himself was such an efficient, orderly and blameless character, who in appearance and manner is said to have more resembled a rather diffident clerk than a determined explorer.

To come round to the tragedy of Cunningham's younger brother, Richard, we must go back to Allan's first journey in Australia and then move on some years later to New Zealand. Only a few months after his arrival Allan Cunningham was instructed by the governor to work with a party which was about to set out for the west under Surveyor General John Oxley, and when they reached the last outpost of human habitation on the Lachlan River they were joined by a private soldier named Charles Fraser who had been stationed here. Where or how Fraser acquired his botanical knowledge is uncertain, especially since the privates of that period are popularly supposed all to have been drunken and ill-educated ruffians, but Cunningham described him as being very much attached to his "pursuits of the Flora," and he must have had some sort of connections since he was to work with the party as collector for the third Lord Bathurst, then secretary for the Colonies. Cunningham ranked as King's Botanist and in 1818 Governor Macquarie—who was never particularly helpful to him and seems to have been somewhat jealous for his own new colony—appointed Fraser Colonial Botanist and placed him in charge of a new botanic garden at Parramatta.

The two men themselves were personally friendly and remained in touch with each other throughout the following years although now their separate journeys were to lie in different directions, Fraser to explore on behalf of the colony while Cunningham sailed on five successive coastal surveying expeditions and then, in 1826, went on to New Zealand. He arrived in August with letters of introduction to the missionaries at the Bay of Islands from the Reverend Samuel Marsden in Sydney, another kindly and helpful man with whom Caley had quarrelled. Cunningham's own personality did the rest. In less than six months he established a reputation among the local Maoris which was to pass from tribe to tribe, and enabled him to wander safely through the virgin forests and explore as he pleased. When he sailed for Sydney again in January 1827 he wrote that he was "greatly gratified by the kindness of the missionaries as well as by the general esteem in which he was held by the natives." It was an esteem which was to last as a legend and to prove more than valuable to Richard when he arrived in New Zealand himself nearly seven years later.

By 1828 Allan was asking permission to return home, and when this was finally granted in 1830 he sailed from Sydney in the following year and reached England in July to find that much was changed. His father and his patron, Sir Joseph Banks, were both dead, the Royal Botanic Garden was under a new director, and Richard—who had gone to Kew when he was only fifteen and remained there ever since as a clerk—was, understandably, restless and frustrated. Then scarcely had Allan settled in a cottage near the garden before he had news from Australia that Charles Fraser had fallen ill on the way back from a collecting expedition and died suddenly at Parramatta. The vacant post of Colonial Botanist was offered to him by the new governor, Sir Thomas Brisbane, successor to Macquarie. It was tempting, but Richard, now thirty-seven, had never yet been given his chance and Allan refused the position in his favor.

As might be expected after twenty-two years at Kew Richard was a first class botanist, but again a very different personality from his brother. Reckless, curiously unobservant, and almost totally lacking in the first essential of any plant hunter or explorer if he is to survive, a strong sense of direction. Nevertheless he was recommended for the post by Allan and William Aiton at Kew, sailed for Sydney with a consignment of plants for the colony, and arrived in January 1833. He appears to have spent his first few months at Parramatta quietly enough and later that year was appointed to *H.M.S. Buffalo*, which was leaving for New Zealand with an expedition to look for and fell a cargo of the Kauri pine, *Agathis australis*, a fine, straight tree growing from eighty to one hundred feet high and at that time much in demand for making ships' masts and spars. It was reported to grow abundantly about the Bay of Islands, and a botanist was sent with the party as it was thought, surely rather improbably, that no one else would be able to recognize the tree.

At the Bay, however, it was discovered that all the available pines had already been felled and *Buffalo* cruised on along the coast to Wangaroa. Here a very curious incident occurred; "Circumstances obliged Mr Cunningham to quit the store ship altogether",[11] and the captain finding it impossible to fell suitable trees here either, sailed off and left him behind. Hooker describes this as botanical zeal on Cunningham's part, but it would have been an extraordinary excess of zeal which led him to go ashore alone at a spot where the entire crew of the ship *Boyd* had been massacred only a few years before. What looks more likely is that Richard's ideas of discipline did not match up with the master of the *Buffalo*, who decided that the ship could get on just as well without him. Quite oblivious of his danger, as he always was to be, Richard set up camp and hired a canoe and a crew of natives to take him back along the coast. Here at least the gods smiled on him, for protected by the still lingering legend of his brother—"Canni-mama" as the Maoris called him—he arrived at the Mission Station on the Bay of Islands quite safely, finding the beautiful greenhouse *Fuchsia procumbens* growing in its only known natural locality, on the way. From the Bay he made several more excursions, collecting plants for the Sydney Botanic Garden generally from areas already explored by his brother

[11] J. D. Hooker, "Companion to the Botanical Magazine," vol. II (London: 1836).

years before, and finally returned to Australia and his own terrible death in May 1834.

This came barely a year afterward when he joined an expedition under the now surveyor general, Major Mitchell, to explore the Darling River. In totally unknown territory, where it was essential for men to keep together, he was a worrying member of the party even in the first few days—always falling behind or straying, losing sight of the main body and then having difficulty in finding the camp at nightfall. Several times Mitchell warned him that unless he was more careful he would never live to return to Sydney, and at the later inquiry into his death it was said that "he was not so often with his companions as away from them."

Little more than a week after starting the party camped one night without water and Richard, as usual, had fallen behind. They waited for him, and he caught up next morning. By that time Mitchell had gone on ahead to prospect, and Richard called out cheerfully that he too would push on to overtake him. He never did. Mitchell had reached the dried out bed of the River Bogan and there left quite clear signs that he had moved along it to the north, but Richard did not see or did not understand them and worked away himself to the west. Mitchell found water easily enough and the party camped by it for twelve days while searching for Cunningham. They found no sign of him and nothing certain was known of his fate until months later when a special rescue party was sent out from Bathurst. Then it was discovered that after following the dried out River Bogan for twenty miles or more he must have wandered about aimlessly until his horse died of thirst, and had at last fallen in with a family of aborigines who had taken him in and given him food and water. But by then he was already delirious, and during that night he became so violent that the frightened natives killed him, as they thought to protect themselves.

It took two years for his death to be confirmed and the news to reach England, and then the post of Colonial Botanist was again offered to Allan Cunningham. Now he accepted it and returned to Sydney early in 1837 only to find that his work included landscape gardening and the production of vegetables for the governor and his staff, leaving little or no time for the botanical exploration which he felt should be his main

interest. A new governor who was sympathetic to these views arrived
the following February, but the discussion of what his duties ought to
be seems to have dragged on, and in April Cunningham went to New
Zealand. But by now the underlying cause of his frail physique was
starting to show itself in symptoms of tuberculosis, and that year the
winter rains were cold, incessant, and heavy. He did manage some
collecting, for he found the orchid, *Dendrobium cunninghamii*, and he
planned to visit all the neighboring mission stations. Whether he was
able to do so or not is unknown, but he must have struggled as far as the
Keri-Keri River as it was here that he found the curious and striking
climbing shrub, *Clianthus puniceus*, known variously as Parrot's Bill,
Lobster Claws, or Red Kowhai from the appearance of its clusters of
red flowers.[12] He returned to Sydney in October a very sick man and
though he still hoped to join a further expedition in March of 1839 he
wrote finally, "I am past further exertion. . . . can neither undertake
any more expeditions nor walk about in search of any more plants . . ."
and died in the following May at Sydney.

One of Charles Fraser's expeditions was to survey the Swan River
area, and he followed this river to its source through a beautiful green
landscape, with water everywhere and many new plants. It was mainly
due to his favorable report that the British government sent out the
party of colonists, under Admiral Sir John Stirling, which arrived in
August 1829 to found Perth and Freemantle. One of them was James
Drummond, who was to be Superintendent of Gardens and had
instructions to lay out a botanic garden with seeds supplied by the
Horticultural Society, mostly vegetables and fruit, but also with some
flowers, including chrysanthemums and dahlias, the first ever grown in
Australia. Drummond—the brother of Thomas Drummond who had
explored in America and was to die mysteriously in Cuba (Chapter
6)—was forty-five when he embarked with his family on this project and
had already been curator of the botanic garden at Cork in Ireland for
twenty years. J. C. Loudon, the editor of the *Gardener's Magazine*, who
greatly admired Drummond, prophesied that within a few years he
would become a Justice of the Peace and thereafter rise to high office in

---

[12] One of the few plants known to have been grown by the Maoris, Sir Joseph Banks
had seen it in cultivation, but it had never been discovered growing wild before.

a new United States of Australia, clearly thinking over-optimistically of other colonists who had emigrated to America a century or more earlier. The reality, however, was something very different, and little more than a year afterward the post of Superintendent of Gardens was abolished and he was made Government Naturalist at a salary of £100 a year; then in 1832, with the new colony struggling for its existence, this appointment also went the same way and Drummond found himself penniless with a large family to support. He is reported as having been desperate, but he must somehow have recovered, for in 1835 he was farming a three thousand acre grant of land and by 1837 he had set up as an independent collector in one of the most botanically interesting areas of Australia. Plants from the Swan River were much in demand by gardeners, and enthusiastic amateurs among the colonists were already sending packets of seeds home; notable among these was Mrs. Georgiana Molloy—probably one of the earliest women gardeners in Australia—who was put into touch by the governor's wife, Lady Stirling, with her cousin Captain James Mangles, himself a horticulturist and botanist. In one consignment alone Mrs. Molloy sent Mangles sufficient seeds to divide into fifteen lots for distribution among friends and nurserymen in England; these included *Anigozanthus manglesii*, the curious greenhouse Kangaroo Paw with downy red stems and green flowers resembling a kangaroo's paws, the well-known "everlasting" useful for dried flower arrangements, *Helipterum manglesii*, and among many others almost certainly the attractive little bedding and border plant in deep purple blue like a miniature cineraria, Swan River daisy, *Brachycome iberidifolia*. Mangles carried one cargo back to England from Drummond consisting of a large bale of unclassified seedlings and forty-four pounds of seeds in 220 species which he was asking Mangles to sell for him. The transaction appears to have annoyed Lady Stirling, who considered that Drummond was exceeding his friendship, and he was later accused of sending seeds under names which turned out to be "mere fiction." Subsequently Captain Mangles found Mrs. Molloy to be a rather more reliable source of supply.

Whatever the truth of that might be Drummond certainly became, with Allan Cunningham, one of Australia's greatest explorers, though there is no record of his travels until William Jackson Hooker—who became director of Kew Gardens in 1841—started to publish extracts from his letters. Again a recital of his expeditions would be little better than a list of more or less unknown place names, but he covered immense distances, usually with his eldest son, John, and mostly in areas where the natives were friendly enough, though on one trip through northern territory they took an armed escort against tribes which were both murderous and cannibalistic. He was reputed to be an avaricious character and often complained that the sale of plants barely covered his expenses, but still went on collecting, even after his greatest personal tragedy at the age of sixty-eight when John Drummond, who had now been travelling with him for more than twenty years, was speared and killed by a native. Undeterred, the old man made plans for yet another journey, and was still sending seeds to England in 1861. He died in Perth two years later at the age of seventy-nine.

Australia's greatest botanist was Ferdinand (later Baron) von Mueller. Mueller had been advised to emigrate with his sisters from their native North Germany to the warmer climate of Australia, and did so very reluctantly, for he already had a considerable reputation in his own country. Once there, however, he was captivated by the flora and remained for the rest of his life. He was another of the eccentrics: pedantic, an almost impossible travelling companion, entirely lacking in a sense of humor, and totally dedicated. When he arrived in Adelaide about 1845 he first found work as a chemist, but with single-minded persistence spent all his leisure and income on botanical exploration to such effect that by the time he was appointed botanist to the State of Victoria he had already covered twenty-five thousand miles in seven years. He claimed also to have acquired a wide experience of every Australian plant which could be eaten safely in times of necessity, and enjoyed the distinction of being one of the few men ever to have dined on the pseudo-bulbs of the orchid *Cymbidium caniculatum*.

Mueller collected honors and degrees no less systematically than he collected and classified plants, and these were heaped on him in plenty over the following years. He became internationally famous, but he had little idea of gardening and less interest, and when he was appointed director of Melbourne Botanic Garden in 1857 he attempted to turn it into an exhibition of pure botany without the slightest concession to the interests of lesser mortals, a proceeding which caused so much trouble that eventually he was "relieved of the post in response to popular clamour." Nevertheless he was by now far too important to offend lightly and he was duly installed in a specially built library and herbarium just outside the gates, where he became something of a local curiosity and worked for the next twenty-three years writing innumerable books, but never setting foot inside the garden itself again. He is thought to have added more than two thousand species to the Australian flora, but as most of them have now been reclassified, and his own botanical names reduced to synonyms, it is difficult to determine what most of them were.

The only remaining collectors of any note were two members of the Veitch family, James Gould Veitch in 1864 and his son James Harry in 1893. Neither of them stayed in Australia for long. James Gould landed at Sydney and spent a month inspecting local gardens before sailing north to the new settlement of Somerset on Cape York, which had been founded only the year before and consisted of "five gentlemen, two ladies, and eighteen marines," two others having recently been killed by the natives. Veitch stayed here for some weeks and filled four Wardian cases with palms, orchids, and other tropical plants but on the whole was not impressed by the northern flora. Returning to Sydney by 1865 he next sailed for a four-month cruise among the Polynesian Islands from which he made a valuable collection, some of which are still popular as house plants today—codiaeums, cordylines and dracaenas. He married shortly after his return to England, with the symptoms of his ultimately fatal tuberculosis already starting to appear, and James Harry Veitch was born in 1868.

James Harry does not appear to have been a particularly enthusiastic collector. He was in Australia for six months and made only two excursions, one by rail to Mount Barker and the other on a short camping trip when he wrote that "stooping to collect . . . in the blazing sun is not a pastime to be chosen," a difficulty which a number of other plant hunters must have noticed. He seems to have decided that most of the worthwhile discoveries in Australia had already been made and to have spent the remainder of his time visiting nurseries and gardens in Melbourne, Sydney, Adelaide, and Perth before moving on in June 1893 to New Zealand—where he found the winter snows just as inconvenient as the Australian summer heat.

With coastlines unusually long for their total area and fierce and warlike natives who were suspected of cannibalism, most of the early exploration of the two islands of New Zealand had been from the sea. Banks's and Captain Cook's expedition was; so was that of the French naval surgeon Edouard Raoul—who gives his name to Raoulia, a genus that embraces encrusted plants from minute carpeters to the large white hummocks called vegetable sheep—with Captain Lavaud. The first real attempts on the interior were made by the Cunningham brothers from 1826 onward but their visits too were short ones, based on Australia, and it was not until 1839–40 that the distinctively New Zealand botanists began to work: John Carne Bidwill, Dr. Ernest Dieffenbach, and the young missionary, William Colenso.

Colenso was from Cornwall, originally a printer by trade before turning to mission work, and he was sent out to New Zealand, supplied with a printing press and type, by the British and Foreign Bible Society about 1833. He was to learn the Maori language, translate the New Testament, then set up and print, and finally distribute it through the missions. It was a fairly ambitious program but he seems to have completed it by 1837, shortly before Allan Cunningham's second and last visit to the Bay of Islands. Whether Colenso was particularly concerned with botany before he met Cunningham is not clear, but he certainly began to show a growing interest soon after. Before he started either his active mission or his active botanical career Bidwill and Dieffenbach both arrived in 1839.

The son of a Devon merchant, Bidwill had emigrated to Australia to take up a grant of land, but once there had found the negotiations so long drawn out that he decided on a trip to New Zealand until they were settled. He started his travels from Tauranga, by no means the best place he could have chosen as the surrounding area was in the throes of tribal warfare. Only a short time before one raiding party had killed and eaten twenty or so of the local Maoris in sight of their own village, and the survivors were understandably shy of undertaking any trips into the interior. But Bidwill was not the man to let tribal customs stand in his way, and with the help of the missionaries he recruited a party and set off on what he called his "Rambles".[13]

They were fairly extensive rambles, from the hot springs at Rotorua, on to Lake Taupo, and finally breaking a Maori tabu by insisting on climbing the particularly sacred mountain, Tongariro, so forbidden that the Maoris when they came within sight of it were supposed to drape mats over their heads and even then avert their eyes. It was usually hidden by cloud, and when Bidwill finally reached the crest he discovered, rather to his consternation, that it was an active volcano even then rumbling up to a fresh eruption. He descended again rather more quickly than he had gone up, returned to Lake Taupo to find that the Maoris were outraged by his violation of the tabu and only extricated himself from that situation with some difficulty by arguing that no tabus ever applied to white men. It was near Tongariro that he discovered one of New Zealand's curiosities, the smallest conifer known, *Dacrydium laxifolium,* which yet belongs to a genus in which the other species will grow from eighty to one hundred feet. When Bidwill first saw it, at little more than two inches high, he took it to be a clump of moss.

It was a short visit, for he arrived in February and sailed again for Australia by April, but returned in August of the same year, and in 1848 visited South Island. He was the first botanist to make anything like a thorough investigation of New Zealand's diverse alpine flora, and from Australia he introduced the blue water lily *Nymphaea gigantea* and seeds of the Australian Monkey Puzzle Tree which bears his name, *Araucaria bidwillii.* There can be few men who have crowded so much into a short lifetime. He founded a fine garden of his own in Sydney and became widely known for his work on hybridization, was appointed director of the Sydney Botanic Garden in 1847, later became commissioner for Crown Lands and chairman of the Bench of Magistrates, and died in 1853 at the early age of thirty-eight, as a result of being lost for eight days in the Australian bush with one other companion but no compass and very little food.

Dieffenbach was relatively unimportant although he came out to

13 *Rambles in New Zealand* (London: Orr, 1841).

New Zealand as naturalist to the New Zealand Company and stayed
longer; from 1839 to '41. He travelled widely but Hooker found his
collections disappointing and he himself in his journals suffered from the
curious notion of "having a great disinclination to describe personal
incidents." He does observe, however, that he found the Maoris
friendly, cheerful and intelligent, but just as Richard Cunningham had
profited from his brother Allan's treatment of them so did Dieffenbach
suffer from Bidwill's high-handed ways; the natives were helpful enough
but they would not allow him to go anywhere near their sacred places.
He made a number of discoveries but no important introductions.

By 1841, before Dieffenbach left, there were several more botanists
in New Zealand. Captain Sir James Ross, on his Antarctic Expedition,
arrived at the Bay of Islands in August and with him came young Dr.
Joseph Hooker—son of Sir William Jackson Hooker, that year newly
appointed director of Kew Gardens, and himself later to become Sir
Joseph and director in turn—and Dr. Andrew Sinclair, a naval surgeon
who had already collected in Mexico. Before Colenso set off on the first
of his long missionary journeys in November 1841 the three men had
formed a personal and scientific friendship which through correspondence was to last for many years.

Colenso never failed in his mission works, but in all his writings—
chiefly papers later published in the *Transactions of the New Zealand
Institute*—he makes little reference to these activities and far more to
his botanical and natural history observations. Now with botany his
primary interest he penetrated to regions where not even the most
ardent missionaries had yet ventured, collecting, studying, and sending
large numbers of plants to Kew. He describes himself as often hungry
and thirsty, plodding through drenching rain, and occasionally pushing
through interminable New Zealand fern brakes, which seem to have
been among his worst trials since they gave him hay fever. One vivid
description comes from an expedition across the Ruahine Mountains in
1845—the first white man to accomplish this—after he had been
ordained a deacon the year before and moved to Waitangi near Napier.
Here he found an entirely new alpine flora and he says,

> When we emerged from the forest . . . on to the open dell-like land just
> before we gained the summit. . . . never did I behold at one time in New

Zealand such a profusion of Flora's stores. In one word I was overwhelmed with astonishment. . . . Here were plants of the well known genera of the bluebells and buttercups, gowans[14] and daisies, eyebrights and speedwells of one's native land, closely intermixed with the gentians of the European Alps and the rarer southern and little known novelties—*Drapetes, Ourisia, Cyathodes, Abrotanella,* and *Raoulia.* . . . But how was I to carry off specimens of these precious prizes, and had I time to gather them? . . . We had left our encampment that morning taking nothing with us so we were all empty handed. . . . However, as I had no time to lose, I first pulled off my jacket, a small travelling coat, and made a bag of that, and then, driven by necessity, I added thereto my shirt, and by tying the neck, &c., got an excellent bag; whilst some specimens I also stowed in the crown of my hat.[15]

In 1852 Colenso was removed from his office of deacon for having fathered an illegitimate child, and settled down on a farm. He continued to botanize to the end of his long life—dying at eighty-eight in 1899—and was still energetic enough to write a paper on some plants collected during a further journey made to the Ruahine Mountains in his eighty-fifth year. He became, rightly, the most celebrated of all New Zealand botanical explorers and many New Zealand species bear his name but, rather curiously, he contributed relatively few garden plants.

The two remaining important New Zealand collectors were Dr. Andrew Sinclair, already mentioned, and Julian von Haast. After his meeting with Colenso at the Bay of Islands Sinclair went on to Australia where he became friendly with Captain Robert Fitzroy, who had been commander of *H.M.S. Beagle* during Charles Darwin's voyage. Fitzroy was then on his way to take up the appointment of governor of New Zealand, and he invited Sinclair to go with him as his secretary in 1843. Sinclair became Colonial Secretary in the following year and thereafter botanized as far as his duties allowed, but to such effect that Joseph Hooker later considered him to be second only to Colenso. On the establishment of parliamentary government in 1856 he resigned this

[14] Also daisies; but by the derivation of the word golden daisies and therefore probably some species of senecio.

[15] Quoted in L. Cockayne, *New Zealand Plants and Their Story,* E. J. Godley, ed. 4th ed. (Wellington, New Zealand: Owen, 1967).

office and later joined Haast on explorations when Haast arrived in New Zealand in 1858. It was on one of these expeditions that he met his death, being drowned in an attempt to ford a branch of the Rangitata River. He was buried by his companions in the wild at the foot of the glaciers. Among his many other discoveries was *Veronica cupressoides*—now *Hebe cupressoides*—and he and Haast together found what is probably the most magnificent New Zealand perennial of all, the white flowered giant New Zealand buttercup or mountain lily, *Ranunculus lyallii*.

Julian von Haast was another traveller who appears to have been a man of many parts. Originally sent out by a German shipping firm who wished to investigate the suitability of New Zealand for German immigration, in 1861 he was appointed government geologist to Canterbury Province and thereafter spent the next ten years exploring the headwaters of all the rivers on the eastern side of the southern Alps. Little more is known about him and although he sent a number of plants to Kew few of them again are of any great garden interest.

By now, however, Australia and New Zealand were firmly established on the botanical maps.

(8)

The Last Great Years

To most gardeners the golden age of plant hunting will seem to have been the years from 1900 to the outbreak of the Second World War, when the famous explorer-collectors, working mostly in China, the Himalayas, and Tibet, became almost household names. Gardening was now a craft and recreation for all; new plants, particularly meconopsis, the blue poppy, captured public imagination and more than ever before were distributed quickly and easily by the growing number of nurserymen; the temperate and colder zones of the eastern countries produced a harvest of beautiful and hardy flowers; and not least, many of the plant hunters were themselves accomplished writers who could and did publish their own experiences and adventures for an ever widening audience. If I seem to do some of them less than justice here it is because their own works speak better for themselves.

It was again the nursery firm of Veitch that sent out Ernest Henry Wilson to China. He was their last collector. We have seen doctors, soldiers, missionaries, farmers, and printers turn to plant hunting, but Wilson was professionally trained for it from the start. At the age of fourteen he left school and went to work in a nursery, at sixteen moved on to the Birmingham Botanic Garden, attended classes at the Birmingham Technical College, and won the Queen's Prize for botany. By 1897 he was working at Kew, and a year later was considering taking a botanical teaching post when Veitch's applied for a collector, and Wilson was recommended. Thereafter he spent a further six months on the Veitch Nursery, and was finally sent to China by way of the United States and the Arnold Arboretum at Boston, where he was to learn the latest developments in plant collection and transport.

The Arnold Arboretum had been established in Boston as a branch of Harvard University by a bequest of James Arnold in 1872. It was by now the greatest center of arboricultural study in America—and probably in the world—and it had been planted with thousands of trees and shrubs by its director, Charles Sprague Sargent, who was at that time famous for his exhaustive analysis of the forest resources of the United States. It was this Professor Sargent we last met in Japan among the cherry trees (Chapter 5), and in the short five days Wilson spent in Boston the two men formed a friendship which ultimately was to bring Wilson permanently to the Arboretum.

He sailed from San Francisco to Hong Kong and first went to meet Dr. Augustine Henry. Henry (Chapter 5) had now been in various parts of China for eighteen years and few men knew more about local conditions; he had made some notable discoveries himself, was in regular correspondence with botanists and gardeners in America and Europe, and it was Henry's specimens which had decided Veitch's to send out a collector specifically to find the pocket handkerchief tree, the *Davidia involucrata* which Père David had described in 1866, but which had never been introduced. Indeed their instructions were to concentrate on that and not waste time and money looking for other things since by now, they thought, nearly everything worth having had already been found in China. Wilson was to surprise them there, for on his way back to the coast from meeting Henry he collected and sent back a number of valuable and unexpected plants. But to locate the single davidia that Augustine Henry himself had seen somewhere in a mountainous area of several thousand square miles twelve years before might not be quite so easy.

During his first season Wilson lived comfortably in a house boat on the Yang-tse at Ichang undisturbed by the Boxer Rebellion, which raged all around Peking and other provinces during the summer of 1900, and then set out in the following spring to reach the mountains when the tree should be in flower and recognizable by its festoons of paper-like bracts fluttering in the wind. Armed with a sketch map and taking some local Chinese collectors whom Henry himself had trained, he had less difficulty in finding the tree than Wilson had feared; or rather in finding where it had once stood, for it had been cut down to build a house. This was a disaster as the only other known specimens—even if they were still standing—were a thousand miles away to the west, where Father David had discovered them more than thirty-five years before. Wilson decided to search the local area, and, with the good fortune which was never entirely to desert him, within two weeks found first one more tree and then another twenty or so flowering profusely. He watched them all through the summer, and in the autumn gathered his first and last crop; after that although he saw many more fine davidias in the course of his travels he never found another carrying ripe seed.[1]

In the season of 1901 he went on to the mountains of Hupeh, a wild and inhospitable region but particularly rich in trees, shrubs, and other hardy plants. At the end of that trip alone, besides the consignments he had already sent, he reached England in April 1902 with thirty-five cases of roots and bulbs, seed of three hundred species and more than nine hundred herbarium specimens. They included acer and clematis, the climbing Chinese Gooseberry *Actinidia chinensis*, the handsome border perennial *Ligularia clivorum* (now *L. dentata*), and the wild garden plant *Rodgersia pinnata*.[2] That summer Wilson was twenty-six and just married, but by October he was off to China again. Apparently Veitch's had decided that there was still something to be found in China after all, for he was now instructed to concentrate on hardy herbaceous plants and in particular to look for seeds of the pale yellow *Meconopsis integrifolia*. This time he explored the province of Szechwan, where the mountains were covered with rhododendrons and other flowering shrubs. Working well above the tree line he found *Aconitum wilsonii*, and three of our best primulas, *P.P. cockburniana, polyneura* and *pulverulenta*, besides new species of berberis and rhododendron.

He returned to England in 1905 but did not remain for long. Professor Sargent now invited him to go to China again for Harvard University and private subscribers, and by this time the once great firm of Veitch was showing signs of decline—three members of the family had died tragically young and James H. Veitch himself was to die in 1907 leaving only Sir Harry who was then approaching his seventies. Wilson sailed for Boston at the end of 1906 and was back in China by

[1] The nut-like seeds may still be obtained, nowadays at a relatively modest price. They will germinate readily if planted in the autumn and exposed to normally wintry weather until the following spring.

[2] Named after Admiral John Rodgers, United States Navy, who commanded an expedition to China and Japan in the middle nineteenth century during which the first species, *Rodgersia podophylla*, was discovered.

Professor C. S. Sargent (Right) and E. H. Wilson (Left) standing in front of *Prunus salhirtella*. Courtesy The Arnold Arboretum of Harvard University.

the following year looking for the shrubs and trees which were Sargent's main interest, and exploring a wild and rugged area which was notorious for its bad weather; at one stage, on washed out tracks and by the edges of flooded streams, for seventy miles he never saw more than a few yards ahead owing to mist and torrential rain. But he brought back *Magnolia wilsonii, Hydrangea sargentiana,* and *Lonicera nitida,* the Chinese Honeysuckle, and *Paeonia veitchii; Ceratostigma willmottianum, Rosa willmottiae,* and *Lilium davidii* var. *wilmottiae* were later raised from his seeds.

In September 1909 he went to America to take up a permanent appointment with the Arnold Arboretum—where he ultimately became keeper—but by 1910 he was back in China once more looking for seeds of conifers and the bulbs of a beautiful new lily which he had seen before in the Min valley district of western Szechwan, north of Cheng-tu. These grew freely in masses of white and gold throughout the Min River gorges, alongside a main caravan route to Tibet and in an area of loose, shaley cliffs and sudden rock falls after heavy rain. Wilson and his party camped here safely enough while he arranged for six thousand bulbs to be lifted and shipped in October, but they had barely started on their return journey when an avalanche of mud and shale swept them off the track and down the hillside; and then, while he was struggling to get out of his sedan chair, one last boulder broke Wilson's leg in two places. His men got him back to the path and set about improvising a splint from one of the legs of his camera tripod, but while they were doing so a mule train came up. There was no room for it to pass, it could not stop on the still crumbling track, and there was nothing for it but to lie down and keep still while fifty animals one after another stepped over Wilson's body; and not a hoof touched him. By the time they reached Cheng-tu the leg was infected, and it was another three months before Wilson could leave on crutches for the long homeward voyage to America, where the bone was broken again and reset in a Boston hospital. He walked with a limp for the rest of his life, but the lily bulbs arrived safely and it is said to have been from this consignment that all of our stocks of *Lilium regale* are descended today.

He made several more journeys to the East, but never to China again.

His books are a mine of information on the plants he collected though even they do not mention all of them—as also they are vague about his exact travels—and the lowest estimate puts his introductions of garden plants at well over a thousand, of which a hundred or more received horticultural awards.[3] From the regions in which he worked they were nearly all hardy, and Professor Sargent himself made sure of their successful cultivation by distributing them generously to other botanic gardens and private gardeners all over the world. Wilson and his wife were both killed in a car accident in the United States in 1930.

Toward the end of Wilson's second Chinese expedition (1902 to 1905) another plant hunter, George Forrest, was just arriving in Yunnan. Forrest was a natural wanderer. Having started life as a pharmaceutical chemist he had spent several years in Australia, and at last returned to Edinburgh to work in the herbarium of the Edinburgh Royal Botanic Garden under Professor Isaac Bayley Balfour. A wealthy Liverpool cotton broker named A. K. Bulley was building a new house and laying out a garden and he asked Balfour to recommend a collector. He had already become interested in Chinese plants through correspondence with Augustine Henry, but attempts so far to get seeds from missionaries had been disappointing, resulting only, as Mrs. Bulley said, in "the best international collection of dandelions to be seen anywhere."

This was Forrest's introduction to plant hunting, and on his first journey to an experience which might well have induced him to remain in the peaceful quiet of a botanic garden for the rest of his life. He arrived in China in August 1904, when it was too late for any serious collecting, but the British consul at Teng-yueh, G. L. Litton, was interested and helpful and took Forrest on to a French mission station at Tsekou on the upper stretches of the Mekong River not far from the Tibetan frontier. Here the fathers showed him a collection of plants which decided Forrest to make this his base next season. It was not the best of places to choose, for the Tibetans were resentful of Sir Francis Younghusband's entry into Lhasa that year, and then still further

---

[3] *A Naturalist in Western China*, 2 vols. London: Methuen, 1913); and *Plant Hunting*, 2 vols. (Boston, Mass.: Stratford Company, 1927).

outraged by a Chinese attempt to take over the town of Batang. By
1905 the warlike border Lamas were slaughtering Chinese, missionaries,
and strangers indiscriminately wherever they could be found.

Forrest was at Tsekou early in July, when a frightened and exhausted
messenger came to warn the missionaries that a Chinese post less than
three days' march away had been overrun by the Tibetans and its entire
garrison massacred. It was then decided to retreat thirty miles down the
valley to where more Chinese troops were stationed, and about eighty
people set out at night; Forrest and his carriers and collectors, the two
elderly missionaries, and their Chinese converts and families. They
moved as silently as possible in the darkness, but in passing one
lamasery something gave them away, and although they stumbled on,
from that moment they had no chance of escape. The first early light
showed a cloud of smoke over Tsekou, one crowd of Tibetans coming
up behind the mission party, and another sent on ahead closing in on
them. They scattered in a panic, and all but fourteen were cut down as
they fled, one priest killed on the spot, the other captured after two
days in hiding and tortured to death. Forrest only escaped by accident,
happening to fall from the path and roll downhill into cover.

For more than a week he was hunted relentlessly, and on the second
day he threw away his boots to avoid leaving tracks. He still had his rifle
and revolver but no food except a little wheat and dried peas which
someone had dropped—he seems to have shown remarkable presence
of mind in scooping this up and still holding on to his weapons when he
pitched off the track—and by the end of the ninth day he was desperate
and decided to threaten the next village he found with his rifle to get
food. In fact the villagers were friendly, although it was only a
miserable place of half a dozen poor huts. Here Forrest lay hidden for
the next four days and was then hurried by secret tracks to the next
settlement, where the headman found guides to take him over the
mountains to the Mekong valley again. That too was a nightmare
journey. It rained incessantly and they dared not light fires, they had to
hack their way through dripping jungle and finally to climb through the
rocks and ice of a seventeen-thousand-foot ridge, Forrest without
European boots. They crossed this at last, and after a steep descent
began to reach cultivated fields. But here the villagers were in the habit

of protecting their crops against raiders by hiding sharpened slips of bamboo in the ground, and as a final misfortune Forrest stepped on one of these in the darkness and drove it right through his foot. It left a wound which took months to heal, but at least by then they were in an area where he was known, and the worst was over. Twenty-three days later, with one surviving French missionary from another station and an escort of Chinese troops, he joined up with Consul Litton once more and they were safely back in Teng-yueh by the end of September.

Eight days later he was off again with Litton for an exploration of the Salween River, actually closer to the Tibetan border than the Mekong but in a territory inhabited by people who, although they had a bad reputation and massacred a party of Germans a few months later, were genial compared with the border Tibetans. That trip passed off peacefully enough, though a month after they got back to Teng-yueh Litton died of blackwater fever and Forrest himself was infected with the virulent Salween malaria. The following March he was working new ground, the mountains in a loop of the Yang-tse north of Likiang. On the map it looks very small, but there are more than fifty miles of this range and Forrest afterward described it as one vast flower garden from the foothills to the limit of vegetation at 17,500 feet. He explored here until August 1906 when he was forced to give up by an attack of malaria, but by now he had a party of well-trained collectors and left them behind to work for him. He was so ill that he was advised to return to Europe at once, but fearing to lose the results of yet another season's work he made two other short trips to Delavay's country, the Tali mountains, before leaving. He got back to England by the end of the year bringing a vast collection of hardy shrubs and herbaceous plants, a number of new rhododendrons, and primulas including *P.P. bulleyana, beesiana, forrestii,* and *littonii.*

Forrest made many more journeys to China covering a total period of twenty-eight years, none of them quite so eventful as his first though with periodical revolutions, mutinies, and massacres, he said that living in China was like camping on the side of an active volcano. The second expedition, in 1910, was for a syndicate headed by J. C. Williams of Caerhays Castle, Cornwall. Now south Yunnan was in revolt and Forrest was ordered by the British consul to leave for Burma; he was allowed to return to Teng-yueh by the autumn, and in the following season recruited yet more staff and extended his working area looking mainly for primulas, camellias and rhododendrons, but also finding *Gentiana sino-ornata* and the striking evergreen on which the growing tip leaves are shining rose pink, *Pieris formosa* var. *forrestii*. By 1912–1914, his third trip, he was working on a wholesale scale with a staff of twenty Chinese collectors, and sent back two hundred pounds of seed in nearly six hundred different species.

Rhododendrons now were as fashionable as stove house plants had been fifty years before. The Rhododendron Society was formed in 1915 with J. C. Williams as one of its leading members, and Forrest's fourth and following journeys were all undertaken on their behalf, making more than five thousand gatherings of seeds and finding so many new species that the whole genus, with azaleas and intermediate forms, had to be revised.[4] During his fifth and sixth expeditions the American J. F. Rock, Frank Kingdon-Ward, and Reginald Farrer were all in China at the same time and Forrest was bitterly jealous of them invading what he considered to be his territories—in practice both the latter two carefully avoided them—although he had no hesitation whatever about working over theirs. By now he was nearing middle age and announcing every next journey as his last. He set off again in 1930 intending to revisit all of his best areas and to collect, in particular, seeds of species which had already been introduced but which had so far failed in cultivation. It was one of his best seasons, and he found nearly everything he wanted, seeds and bulbs in such quantity that he calculated he had at least two mule loads, each being about a hundred and fifty pounds. He had made, he thought, a glorious end to all his years of work. It was indeed; for on January 5, 1932, with all his collections packed and ready to return home, he was out with his gun when he suddenly called out, collapsed, and died of heart failure before anyone could reach him. He was buried at Teng-yueh close by his earlier companion and friend G. L. Litton.

One of the eccentrics about this period was Frank Meyer, a man who was fond of walking. Born in Amsterdam, he had been a gardener at the botanic garden there under the Dutch botanist Hugo de Vries before he

[4] There are now known to be some six hundred species ranging from prostrate alpine types to large trees.

went to America in 1900. He started work with the Department of Agriculture in Washington, but then with his incurable wanderlust drifted off again and was at the Missouri Botanic Garden, St. Louis, when Dr. David Fairchild of the Office of Foreign Seed and Plant Introduction was looking for a man to send out to China to search for economic plants. Meyer was the obvious choice; he was a natural traveller, a trained botanist and gardener, and also a Buddhist. This started him on a series of prodigious journeys of which the first between 1905 and 1908 took him from the Yangtze to Manchuria, more than eighteen hundred miles on foot, looking for varieties of millet, rice, and beans. The years 1909 to 1912 saw him tramping steadily from the Caucasus, through Persia to Turkestan and on to Tibet seeking forage plants, and in 1913 he started in Mongolia and walked south to Kansu Province, where Reginald Farrer was just coming to the end of his first season and was by no means wholeheartedly delighted to hear of the appearance of another collector—until he discovered that Meyer was only looking for peaches, almonds, and plums and not in the least interested in alpine plants.

Meyer was a man of curious contradictions. An entertaining conversationalist and good company when he chose, he could be excessively bad tempered, and sometimes suffered acute fits of nervous depression; though he could speak English, German, and Dutch fluently and make himself understood in French, Italian, Spanish, and Russian, he never made the slightest attempt to learn Chinese or to adapt himself to Eastern customs or habits of thought. On his third journey, when he met Farrer in Siku, he had taken an interpreter from Pekin with him and this man considered Kansu a barbarous wilderness and refused to go any farther, so enraging Meyer that he threw him and an unfortunate coolie downstairs. He had had similar trouble with his servants on other occasions, but this was serious. There was very nearly a riot, and only through Farrer's influence in Siku was he allowed to go on his way in safety.

His last journey was in 1916, searching about Jehol for the wild Pekin Pear, which will grow in almost pure sand. In the spring of 1917 he walked to Hankow and went on by boat to Ichang, intending to make it his base for that season. But China was again torn by revolution, with one local war lord fighting another, and Meyer was held up in near starvation, danger, and suspicion until May 1918, when he broke out through burned and looted villages to King-chow, picked up seeds and baggage left there for safety, and tramped on until he could get a river boat to Hankow. He disappeared from this steamer on the night of June 1. His body was later recovered, but it was never known whether he had fallen in the river, been murdered, or committed suicide in one of his attacks of nervous illness. He introduced more than two thousand species to America, most of them cereals, timber trees, and fruits, but including some garden subjects of which the Canary Bird Rose, *Rosa xanthina, Juniperus squamata* var. *meyeri*, the Beauty Bush, *Kolkwitzia amabilis*, and species of syringa were among the best.

Dr. Fairchild himself was a notable botanist, collector, and author who from 1898 was associated with W. T. Swingle and H. J. Webber in founding a Plant Introduction Garden at Biscayne Bay in Florida. He had joined the United States Department of Agriculture after study in Italy and Germany but his main interest was in tropical trees and economic plants, and though his travels took him all over the world his most important journeys were in Guatemala and more especially the East Indies, from which he introduced a number of exotic fruits to America. A man with a profound love of all nature, and plant life in particular, and with the gift to express it, he was the author of five books of which at least two are among the most charming and personalized reminiscences of plants, trees, people and places we have.[5]

Of the two other collectors in China at the same time as Forrest and Kingdon-Ward, Reginald Farrer was and remains well known while his companion, William Purdom, has almost vanished into obscurity, probably because once more one was an accomplished writer with several books already to his credit, while the other habitually said little about his plants and less about himself. Purdom was another of the trained and professional collectors who, after an early apprenticeship, worked in two famous London nurseries, and then with six years at Kew

[5] D. Fairchild (with Elizabeth and Alfred Kay), *The World Was My Garden* (New York and London: Charles Scribner's Sons, 1938); and Fairchild, *The World Grows Round My Door* (New York and London: Charles Scribner's Sons, 1947).

made his first journey in 1909–12 for Veitch's and the Arnold Arboretum. The Veitch nursery was broken up in 1914 and there appears to be nothing recorded of Purdom's first two or three seasons in China except by way of retrospective references in Farrer's own books, but it was this expedition which later made Farrer's much more ambitious exploration of the Kansu-Tibetan districts possible—he was to write that Purdom was an absolutely perfect friend and helper—and though they seem scarcely to have been noticed at the time Purdom brought back a number of important new plants. An uncommon dark red tree peony, and *Ligularia purdomii*, several rare (and difficult) primulas, the attractive and interesting yellow *Clematis tangutica*, and one of the parents of many of our modern large flowered hybrid clematis, *C. macropetala*.

Farrer had been an alpine plant enthusiast in the limestone area of Yorkshire from boyhood, and had published his first contribution to botanical literature at the age of fourteen with a note on *Arenaria anglica* in the *Journal of Botany*. As a delicate child with a hare lip he was educated at his home, Ingleborough House, and then went up to Balliol College, Oxford, came down in 1902, the following year set off for Japan and from this produced his first book, *The Garden of Asia*. In 1907 he visited Ceylon and became a Buddhist and that year also published *My Rock Garden*. He then spent several years exploring the European Alps for plants, about which he wrote *Among the Hills*, and in 1913 completed what was to be his best-known book although it was not published finally until 1919, *The English Rock Garden*, which he corrected for press during his first expedition, when he and Purdom were wintering at Lanchow, the capital of Kansu province, in 1914.[6]

When he met Purdom in London in 1913 Farrer had for a long time been thinking of exploring more northerly districts than those already being worked by Forrest and Kingdon-Ward, and Purdom's previous experience now made that possible. Farrer was to finance the expedition while Purdom was to manage it. The arrangements were very quickly made and, so different was plant hunting now becoming, at the end of February 1914 they travelled all the way to Peking by the

[6] *The English Rock Garden*, 2 vols. (London: Jack, 1919).

Trans-Siberian Railway—which had been open since 1904—and then on again by rail in China to the terminus in Honan. They planned to follow the Tibetan border from south to north, but in the district for which they were heading there was sporadic fighting between local chieftains, while in the south a rebellious army under a general who called himself the White Wolf was advancing northward. Farrer and Purdom were carrying with them enough silver in ingots to cover two years' expenses, which seems to have been one of the most hazardous aspects of the whole expedition. Nobody would hire out mules to go into such restless areas, but eventually they got three ox wagons to take them on to the next town, where they were held up again while waiting for permission to move farther west, and eventually they reached the foothills of Kansu in mid-April, only a little more than six weeks after leaving London. It was here that within a few days they made two of their most important finds—to Farrer the wild white tree peony, *Paeonia suffruticosa*, and to Purdom the scented *Viburnum farreri*.

Two days later they reached the Blackwater River and turned southward along its gorges before striking off again toward the west, and by so doing just escaped the White Wolf who soon after they left came sweeping up the valley burning and destroying everything in his path. By now Farrer and Purdom were crossing over into Tibetan territory where the border Lamas were still as warlike as ever. Farrer quite innocently rode along a track which for some reason of their own the lamas had declared closed. The entire party narrowly escaped being murdered in the uproar that followed, and retreated hurriedly to a Chinese village where the people were more friendly. Even here, however, the lamas had not yet finished with them. Another excursion they made happened to be followed by a violent storm which destroyed the local crops, and the lamas announced that the Celestial Powers who inhabited the mountain tops were enraged by the intrusion of the foreign devils, and raised the whole countryside against them. Once more they retreated, but now the only possible roads led even deeper into Tibet, or to the town of Siku, which was said to have been destroyed by the White Wolf. They decided that he was preferable to the lamas; and when they reached the town they found that it was still intact after all, though variously threatened by the White Wolf from one side and a tribe called the Black Tepos from the other.

In spite of these alarms they remained at Siku for some weeks, making short excursions as the country quieted down, and then moved on to the town of Cho-ni, which Purdom had made his headquarters in 1911. They were hospitably received by the resident missionary, who also had been reported killed but who had not even heard of the rumor himself, and here late in August they heard of the outbreak of the First World War, on 4 August 1914. There was a curious general impression at that time that the war would be over by the following Christmas at latest, so they decided to go on and in the autumn they separated to gather seeds, Purdom staying at Cho-ni and Farrer returning to Siku while their headman went back to a third district they had explored. It was a most successful harvest for when they returned together to winter at Lanchow—with the country now completely calm again—they had two mule loads to pack and dispatch, and among many other new species they had found *Buddleia alternifolia, Daphne tangutica, Gentiana hexaphylla*, and *Rosa farreri*. It was while in Siku at this time that Farrer met Frank Meyer, was relieved to find that he had no interest in alpine plants, and saved him from the consequences of his somewhat impetuous behavior with the interpreter.

Their second season was less eventful but, except for one final discovery, disappointing. Misled by over enthusiastic accounts of the earlier Russian explorers, Potanin and Przewalski, they decided in March 1915 to examine the Da-tung alps six days journey northwest from Lanchow. It was a frustrating summer, for these granite mountains were always too high and too inhospitable apparently to yield anything worth having, and finally it was decided that Purdom should make a quick trip to the south again while Farrer remained in this area for a further exploration of the heights. The only noticeable display at fourteen thousand feet was made by the common dandelion, impressive enough from a distance, no doubt, but hardly worth a costly and dangerous journey. Then Purdom returned with very little from the south and it was decided to make one last camp in the mountains before they left the district. And here the element of the unpredictable always inseparable from plant hunting appears. Their departure was delayed for one reason and another—bad weather and Farrer himself falling ill with influenza—and it was not until the end of August that they struck camp to return to their base. A week earlier and they would have missed it, but now just coming into flower the greatest find of the season showed itself: *Gentiana farreri*. Farrer himself considered this one plant alone to be worth all the danger and expense of the entire expedition, and in *The English Rock Garden* describes it lyrically as being by far the most beautiful of its race; it is a paler and clearer blue than *G. sino-ornata* with a white throat and darker markings on the exterior of the trumpets.

By now food was running short and the whole party tired; they still had to return to their base by September to prepare for the long homeward journey, and there was no hope of waiting in the mountains long enough to gather seed. Living specimens were lifted and set in biscuit tins to be carried hopefully, along with other plants, halfway across China. They reached Pekin at last in December after a further exhausting march through Szechwan and a hazardous stretch on the Yang-tse where brigands were reported to be operating, and where they were forced to keep a night and day watch with a rifle arranged on a camera tripod to look like a machine gun. Here all of their plants were put out to over-winter in the British legation garden and Purdom and Farrer parted, Farrer to return to England and join the Ministry of Information until the end of the war, and Purdom to take up a post with the Chinese forestry service, where he remained until his death in 1921 at the early age of forty-one.

In the following spring the precious plants were taken on the overheated trains of the Trans-Siberian Railway, transferred at Petrograd for another roundabout journey through Finland, Sweden, and Norway and finally shipped on the dangerous war-time crossing of the North Sea. Surprisingly some of them did survive, but not the gentians; no gentian will tolerate treatment like that. Farrer thought that *G. farreri* was lost, perhaps for ever. But then in the following season it appeared suddenly in Edinburgh Botanic Garden; apparently from seed collected unknowingly by Farrer's Chinese collectors with that of *G. hexaphylla* in the alps of the Min Shan range many miles from the

Da-Tung mountains where Farrer found the plants in flower. The introduction of *G. farreri* to our gardens—or rather to those gardens where it will condescend to grow—is one of the miracles of chance and good luck in plant hunting.

To come to another name as well known as that of Farrer, Frank Kingdon-Ward, we must go back to 1911 and the Liverpool cotton merchant, A. K. Bulley, who had first sent out George Forrest. Bulley said Forrest "had gone over" to J. C. Williams' syndicate, but remained as interested in seeds as ever, perhaps even more so as he founded the great firm of Bees Seeds Ltd. in 1905;[7] he applied again to Bayley Balfour (now Sir Isaac Bayley Balfour) for another collector and Kingdon-Ward was recommended. He was the son of H. M. Ward, F.R.S., professor of Botany at Cambridge, and in 1907 he had accepted the first post which offered any opportunity of travel, that of a teacher in Shanghai. Bulley wrote to him there in January 1911, and Kingdon-Ward found his offer so attractive that within three weeks of receiving the letter he was ready to set off for northwest Yunnan. That was the beginning of an active plant hunting career of forty-seven years, during which he made more than 23,000 collections of seeds and published 137 known papers on botanical and geographical subjects and twenty-three books.[8]

By March he was in Teng-Yueh, were he found the entire European population of six having tea with Litton's successor, the British Acting-Consul Archibald Rose. Scrupulously careful not to poach on Forrest's areas—who was now out on his second expedition—Kingdon-Ward asked for Rose's advice on a good center, and Rose suggested Atuntse, which lies near Tibet in the mountains which divide the upper

---

[7] The pioneers of cheap, attractively presented seeds in standardized packets. In the early 1920s "Bees Seeds that Grow" were still offered with their brilliantly colored illustrations at one penny per packet.

[8] A selection only. *The Land of the Blue Poppy* (London: Cambridge University Press, 1913); *The Mystery Rivers of Tibet* (London: Seeley Service, 1923); *The Riddle of the Tsang-po Gorges* (London: Arnold, 1926); *Plant Hunting on the Edge of the World* (London: Gollancz, 1930); *Plant Hunter's Paradise* Cape, (London: 1937); *Assam Adventure* (London: Cape, 1941); and *Pilgrimage for Plants*, W. T. Stearn, ed. (London: Harrap, 1960).

streams of the Yangtze and Mekong Rivers, and this proved to be so good that Kingdon-Ward returned here on his two subsequent expeditions to China in 1913 and 1921. In these three journeys he met all the delays, the brigandage, and rumors of war experienced by other travellers, and made large collections, mainly of rhododendrons, primulas and gentians, though nothing very new. His more important work was to come later in Assam, Burma, and Tibet.

During Kingdon-Ward's third expedition to China, and two years after Meyer died, one more of Dr. Fairchild's collectors arrived there: the Austrian of wide interests and abilities, Dr. Joseph Rock. Rock had gravitated to America as a young man and was professor both of Botany and Chinese at the University of Hawaii when, in 1920, Fairchild asked him to go out to Indo-China, Burma, and Siam to collect seeds of the chaulmoogra tree, the oil of which at that time was used in the treatment of leprosy. In 1922 he went on to China where, with only short intervals elsewhere, he remained for the next twenty-seven years. His various commissions included botanical and ornithological work for a number of American scientific societies, and his last fifteen years in China were spent living with and studying a curious tribe, the Na-Khis, in the neighborhood of Likiang.[9] So fascinating did he find these people that by the time he finally retired to Hawaii in 1949 he had published six papers and two books on them, and translated the key volumes of eight thousand books of Na-Khi literature.

In 1922-24 he worked mainly over Forrest's country—much to Forrest's disgust who was, as I've noted, always jealous of what he considered to be his own private territory—and before leaving for home moved on to an area which Kingdon-Ward had covered two years before. After a short stay in America he came back with fresh commissions from the Harvard Museum of Comparative Zoology and Professor Sargent of the Arnold Arboretum to explore the mountains of the Tibetan border, and early in 1925 established himself at Cho-ni, which Farrer and Purdom had used as one of their bases ten years before. Another of the happier stories of plant hunting hangs on this later, for he was soon on friendly terms with the monastery and the

---

[9] An aboriginal people of central China who appear to be ethnologically distinct from the Chinese themselves.

Prince of Cho-ni, who at that time provided him with escorts and permits to travel to unsettled areas farther north that had never been visited by strangers before. During this period he discovered the two exceptionally hardy conifers *Picea asperata* and *Picea likiangensis*, but in 1927 there were fresh political disturbances and he left for America again taking with him upwards of two thousand specimens and large collections of seeds, including those of a white tree peony growing in the garden of the monastery—the cultivated form of the *Paeonia suffruticosa* which Farrer had found growing wild but never introduced.

Rock made two further expeditions. The first in 1928–30, working for the National Geographical Society and gardeners in America and Britain, and the last in 1930–33, after which at the age of fifty he settled in Likiang for his ethnological study of the Na-Khi. In his four journeys he had made large collections of botanical and zoological specimens and seeds, but with the exception of the *picea* species very little that was new; possibly because by now there was little new left to discover in the areas he had explored. But the seeds of the Cho-ni peony he had found in the monastery years before were now to come back home again.

Professor Sargent had distributed these to growers in several countries of the West, where they had been cultivated successfully, and the shrub given the name of *Paeonia suffruticosa* Rock's Variety. In 1938 during one of the periodical revolutions or civil wars the monastery of Cho-ni was burned down, its monks slaughtered, and their garden rooted up and destroyed. But when it was rebuilt several years later Joseph Rock was able to send back to the new monks seeds of their own Cho-ni peony which was by now safely established on the other side of the world.

The eastern ranges of the Himalayas, where the frontiers of Bhutan, Assam, and Burma march with Tibet and China, were still unexplored. Its awesome mountains, wild rivers, and deep gorges, to say nothing of unpredictable tribes and a terrible climate, had so far kept the area closed. But it had the most magnificent flora in the world, of which rumors had been heard from time to time. The cotton broker turned seedsman, A. K. Bulley, sent Roland Edgar Cooper to Sikkim in 1913, but there is little record of that expedition except that Cooper himself considered the results were not worth the trouble. Cooper seems to have parted company with Bulley immediately afterward—perhaps for that reason—and in 1914–15 travelled in Bhutan, probably for the Botanical Survey of India. Neither were the results of that journey particularly interesting although Cooper covered a great deal of ground, often in regions where the native Bhutanese themselves never went, and rarely remaining more than a night or two in any single place. He found a few shrubs however, including *Ceratostigma griffithii*, *Cotoneaster cooperi*, and *Viburnum grandiflorum*, and then the plant which he considered to be the most exquisite of all the smaller Asiatic primulas; the pale blue *Primula bhutanica*.

The real exploration of these regions was made by Kingdon-Ward, Farrer, and Euan Cox and later by Ludlow and Sherriff. To Kingdon-Ward, as an explorer and plant hunter, and who preferred the Burmese and Tibetans to the Chinese, they held an irresistible fascination and they were to be his hunting ground for the next forty years. He made the first of his six expeditions to Burma in 1914—immediately after his second expedition to China—when he planned to follow the Chinese frontier northward and perhaps finally cross over into Assam, a journey which he afterwards described as disastrous.

He reached Fort Hpimaw—about a hundred and fifty miles north of the Burma Road built during the Second World War, where the Burma-Chinese frontier runs almost due north along the mountains which tower over the Salween River—in May and remained there three months for one of the worst seasons of his life. In all of his explorations out from the fort it rarely ceased raining, he was never dry nor free of fever, the forests of the lower levels were almost impenetrable and infested with a particularly bloodthirsty breed of leeches, and at higher altitudes the flies were intolerable. Several times on explorations out from Hpimaw he collapsed and had to be carried back to his camp, and at last was forced to give up. Leaving Hpimaw in August he turned south by a different route, discovering on the way an area that he described as a paradise of flowers—the Wu-law Pass into China—but still harassed by rain, intense cold and flies he could not stop to explore it. His carriers refused to be hurried and eventually he moved on ahead with a smaller party, reached the first outpost of civilization where there were two British officers toward the end of September and Fort Hertz, with four Europeans there, four days later. Here he collapsed and was ill for six weeks before he could attempt the final stage to the nearest town of any size in northern Burma, Myitkina, where he arrived on Christmas Eve.

That was the worst journey he ever made and the only one in which he was forced to retreat without gathering seeds. But it was of immense interest nevertheless, not only geographically but on account of the great number of flowers he had seen, particularly primulas and rhododendrons. He later claimed that as a result of his discoveries all the plant collectors in Asia went buzzing round the Htawgaw hills like flies looking for jam, and that Hpimaw in particular became one of the most collected areas on the frontier. There may be some doubt about that, and it was totally forgotten during the war years, but Farrer and Cox made Hpimaw their base in 1919, Kingdon-Ward himself returned in the same year, and Forrest searched it again in 1924.

Farrer and his friend Euan Cox went out there almost by chance. In November 1918 Farrer was in a nursing home recovering from an operation and Cox went to visit him. Within half an hour they had decided to go off plant hunting together, and by the following March they were in Rangoon. They had thought of the Tibet-Assam frontier but it was reported to be a region where there was neither food nor transport to be had and they decided to make for Hpimaw. Much had changed since Kingdon-Ward's journey now nearly six years ago; they travelled comfortably by train through Mandalay to the rail head at Myitkina, and then went on for most of the remaining distance by a fairly well-made road. As Kingdon-Ward had said, it was a good place, rich in dwarf rhododendron, berberis, cassiope, and willow, but with few herbaceous plants. These they found farther north in the flowery alpine meadows where they established a camp. There was company too; at one stage Farrer was annoyed by the appearance of a party of Forrest's native collectors, which he considered was poaching on his territory, though in fact they were working on the Chinese side of the pass and only visited Hpimaw to see the other English plant hunters. Then Kingdon-Ward, who was now exploring some distance to the

west, "strolled over" and spent four days with them, a meeting which
seems to have been much more festive. It was an enjoyable summer
with a comfortable base and company, but unfortunately very little in
the way of species adaptable enough to survive for long away from their
native mountains. "The sad truth," Cox wrote later, "is that these
Burmese hills do not breed species of Alpine that give any return for
care and kindness at the hands of the gardener."

They left Hpimaw in November and returned to Myitkina, where
Kingdon-Ward had arrived, and all three travelled back to Rangoon
together. Cox left for England, but Farrer made a fatal decision to stay
on for another year to follow up the exploration of the frontier
mountains farther north than the point they had already reached. He
passed the winter near Mandalay and in the spring of 1920 returned to
Myitkina, where all of his previous season's staff and his Gurkha orderly,
Jange Bhaju, were waiting for him. They set off following in a reverse
direction the difficult route which Kingdon-Ward had taken back to
Myitkina in 1914, and after some weeks reached Nyitadi, a "town" of
four huts placed at the confluence of two rivers and within reach of the
three passes Farrer intended to explore.

It was an even more than usually wet season and a very different
location from Hpimaw. There he had a comfortable bungalow, the
luxury of a telephone, and even a weekly postal delivery; here he had
only a leaky bamboo hut and flooded rivers with their bridges washed
away behind him. On the heights it was worse still, for there was mist as
well as rain and at one period for nearly a month he was never able to
see more than a few yards ahead. Nevertheless he made all the trips he
had planned and then by September settled down to wait for the seed
harvest. At the beginning of October he fell ill, and within two weeks
became so much worse that the devoted Jange Bhaju made an
incredible four-day, non-stop journey to the nearest military post at
Konglu to bring medical help. But it was then too late; Farrer died on
the morning of 17 October 1920, probably of pneumonia. His men
made a coffin and carried him to Konglu, where he was buried on the
hill overlooking the fort. They also brought back his possessions, but
unable to carry all of them and Farrer's body they saved only what

seemed to them most valuable, tents, stores and equipment. His papers and the collections he had already made were left behind.

The altogether more fortunate traveller Kingdon-Ward had now been twice to China and twice more to Burma, the second time while Farrer and Cox were there in 1919. The year after Farrer's death he was in China again until 1922 for his third and last visit, but then one of the most important and successful expeditions he ever made was his first to Tibet, to explore the Tsang-po gorges. Flowing eastward across the high Tibetan plateau the Tsang-po is a wide, slow river before it turns south and plunges into the Himalayas to reappear in Assam as the Brahmaputra, having carved its way through some of the most inaccessible valleys in the world and descended eleven thousand feet on the way. As long before as 1913 Colonel F. M. Bailey had followed part of its course, but in 1924 there still remained fifty unexplored miles of rapids, cataracts, and, according to rumor, great waterfalls.

The best approach was by way of the Sikkim ranges into Tibet, turning eastward and south of Lhasa, and then following the river downstream toward Assam. Permits from the Indian and Tibetan governments were arranged by Bailey—then political officer for Sikkim—and in March, 1924, Kingdon-Ward, the Earl of Cawdor, and their carriers and ponies crossed the Nathu La Pass, finding the high plateau still in winter and all ice, wind, and the dust of which most Tibetan travellers speak feelingly. Moving north and meeting the last six Europeans they were to see for ten months, they then took the Lhasa road to Lake Yamdok, worked along its fifty-mile southern shore, crossed the Shamda La Pass and reached the Tsang-po toward the end of April. Here they followed the river downstream, not very comfortably, for Cawdor was ill, a coolie was attacked by one of the savage Tibetan dogs, it rained every day, and their lodgings were filthy although the people themselves were generous and hospitable. But when they reached the village of Tumbatse which was to be their base for the next five months, they found themselves in a wonderland of flowers—a blazing sea of rhododendron broken by the handsome, straw-colored spires of *Rheum nobile, Primula florindae*[10] with its

[10] One of the few easy Himalayan primulas. Requiring only really moist soil it will grow from two to four feet high and is a striking plant placed beside a pool or stream.

drooping sulphur yellow bells, and the crumpled silk sky blue of
Meconopsis betonicifolia, the plant that captured the imagination of
gardeners all over the world when it was introduced.

M. *betonicifolia baileyi*—to give it its full style and title—had had a
curious history. It had been found and lost again, named and renamed,
but so far never successfully cultivated. Père Delavay first discovered it
in Yunnan in 1886 and sent herbarium specimens but no seeds to Paris,
where in 1889 it was classified as a new species by the botanist A. R.
Franchet and named M. *betonicifolia* on account of the basal leaves
having some resemblance to those of the betony. It appeared to be very
rare in China and George Forrest, who paid particular attention to
Meconopsis and found no less than twelve species in the course of his
travels, searched for it for some years without success until he
pinpointed Delavay's exact location. He then sent a small quantity of
seed back to England which, without exception, failed, as also did seed
collected by Joseph Rock and tried in America. M. *betonicifolia* was put
down as a beautiful and botanically interesting rarity which had little
horticultural interest because it seemed to be practically impossible in
cultivation.

It was 1913 when Bailey in exploring the Tsang-Po valleys, as already
mentioned, discovered it growing there too and sent an incomplete
specimen back to Kew, where it was regarded as another new species
by Sir David Prain, at that time director of the Royal Botanic Gardens
and an authority on *Meconopsis,* who named it M. *baileyi.* It still
remained only botanically interesting however until eleven years later
when Kingdon-Ward returned to Bailey's area, found it growing
strongly—although even there it was by no means common—and
brought back a substantial quantity of seed which was raised successfully in 1925 and the following year created a sensation at the Royal
Horticultural Society's Chelsea Flower Show. This time it proved not
only to be one of the most beautiful of the family, but also the easiest to
grow and it was subsequently distributed all over the world; it is quite
possible that by now there are more M. *betonicifolia* in cultivation than
there are in the wild. The remaining problem is why the Chinese forms
without exception failed while those from Tibet were successful, and it
is suggested now that there are certain minor differences that entitle

Bailey's more robust plant to the status of a variety within the species. Kingdon-Ward's own belief was that *M. betonicifolia* is not common anywhere, that it has a relatively small area of distribution in the wild, and that on the fringes of this area, particularly in China, it may actually be dying out.

Tibet was a land of surprises and sudden contrasts. From its gorges and wild rivers on one exploration north from Tumbatse they came upon a town, Gyamda, which boasted not only shops but also a post office; then at their next stage on this same journey they found themselves in a village where the monastery courtyard was ablaze with flowers like an English cottage garden; hollyhocks, asters, dahlias, pansies, stocks, and nasturtiums. The local governor had been on a trip to Calcutta and brought back with him a box of Messrs. Suttons' seeds. They were to find that this was by no means unusual; many of the Tibetans were enthusiastic gardeners and American and English flowers were much in demand, especially at the monasteries. By now some of these might even have escaped from the gardens and established themselves in the hills side by side with native plants.

After an autumn of carefully planned seed gathering they started on their exploration of the Tsang-po gorges in mid-November, when dry weather and low water in the rivers might be expected. Making a circuit to a point on the river south of that reached by Bailey they then worked upstream until they came to impassable cataracts, and here left the river for a further detour north to strike it again higher up and work downstream once more. The rumor of mighty falls somewhere on the Tsang-po proved to be a myth, and they only found two of thirty or forty feet each before coming to a last stretch of five miles racing down between high, sheer walls of rock that were impossible to negotiate. Then they turned back and reached Tumbatse late in December, having by now collected seeds of every rhododendron they could find, sometimes digging into three feet of snow to get at the bushes. This later was to produce at least ten new species, of which one, *R. pemakoense*, has never since been seen in the wild.

They started for home early in the new year, and their collection of seeds crossed Tibet in forty degrees of frost, India at temperatures of ninety, and was finally shipped to England in cold storage. Before the end of April they were all sown at Kew, Edinburgh, and other gardens, while shares were sent to the United States and South America, New Zealand, South Africa, and elsewhere. The extremes of their journey had not done them any harm, for out of two hundred and fifty species only twenty-five failed. Besides the blue poppy, rhododendrons, and *Primula florindae* there were many more such fine, hardy garden plants as *Lilium wardii, Primula cawdoriana* and *P. baileyana*, and *Berberis hookeri.*

Kingdon-Ward made many more journeys; in 1926 to the Seingkhu River in Burma, 1928 to the Mishmi Hills in northeastern Assam, back to Burma in 1930–31 accompanied once more by Lord Cawdor, and in 1933 his second visit to Tibet. He returned for the third time in 1935 for one of his longest journeys which, by a series of curious accidents, he made without a travel permit. At Shergoan he applied to the High Lama for permission to enter Tibet and was told to write to the Dzongpen of Tsona, the first important town over the border, and that a favorable reply could be expected in two weeks. He did not doubt he would receive this and he went on. The governor of Tsona's letter finally caught up with him while he was in a small and primitive village where nobody could read it; rather oddly neither could he nor any of his servants, and he decided to go on to a larger town to find an interpreter. But somehow the letter got lost in Kingdon-Ward's baggage on the way and did not appear again until he was back in India months later. It turned out to be a flat refusal. The incident caused a certain amount of diplomatic activity afterward, but during his journey none of the Tibetan authorities placed any difficulty in his way, except that they would not allow him to enter some regions inhabited by dangerous tribes not under their control.

There was one occasion however when the lost letter might have been translated all too readily. On Kingdon-Ward's first visit he and Lord Cawdor had glimpsed a vast range of snowy peaks fifty or sixty miles to the north, but though they seemed to have skirted the foot of these mountains they had never again seen them owing to cloudy weather. He now decided to look for them again and made for his old base at Tumbatse—where he was still remembered and given a great welcome—and then pushed on to a place called Tongkyuk Dzong. Here he was held up by a broken bridge; and here also he met a Colonel Yuri, chief of the Lhasa police, and had considerable difficulty in persuading him that he was not one Urush Marpo, a Bolshevik agent for whom Yuri was hunting. Travelling without a permit or not, Kingdon-Ward seems to have so completely convinced the colonel that he advised against travel in one particular direction and offered his personal escort to the Po-Ygrong where he was going himself in a few days, presumably still looking for the elusive Marpo. Kingdon-Ward decided to push on ahead to the river—and found himself in the lost range on the way, for one evening the clouds lifted for a few minutes to reveal magnificent snow peaks all around. But when he arrived at the Po-Ygrong he was taken for Colonel Yuri himself and given an awkwardly official reception before he explained and left to follow the river to its source. Marching westward for another eighteen days, and collecting a further one hundred species of plants, he reached the great glacier from which the Po-Ygrong springs, that itself an important geographical discovery, in late August. Satisfied then he turned back homeward by a different route through unmapped country, and arrived back at his starting point in the second week of October after nearly a thousand miles of exploration.

He was fifty by then, but during the four following years to the outbreak of the Second World War he made three more journeys, two in Burma and one in Assam. During the war he taught what few men could know better, jungle survival to troops in India, and later he was employed by the American military authorities to search for wrecked aircraft. In 1947 he married again—his first marriage having been dissolved in 1937—and his second wife accompanied him on five more expeditions including that of 1950 in which both narrowly escaped death in the Lohit Valley during one of the worst earthquakes ever known. During the greater part of one night they felt the ground drumming beneath them, heard the roar of boulder avalanches followed by a series of explosions—described by Kingdon-Ward as being like anti-aircraft shells bursting—and looked out next morning through a haze of dust to see that here and there even mountain crests had broken away. His last trip, in 1956–57, was to Ceylon, and he was planning a new expedition to the Caucasus or Northern Persia when he died suddenly in London in 1958 at the age of seventy-three. He was the greatest explorer of his time, whose single concession to comfort on his travels was to carry a hot water bottle.

The two remaining collectors of this period were Frank Ludlow and Major George Sherriff, both ornithologists as well as plant hunters and both deeply interested in Tibet. Ludlow had first gone out to India as a teacher and Sherriff was vice-consul to F. Williamson at Kashgar when they first met. On Williamson's appointment as political officer to Bhutan, Sikkim, and Tibet they made their first journey in 1933 in company with Williamson and his wife, and covered much of the ground already explored by Kingdon-Ward. In 1934 they planned an ambitious botanical and ornithological survey of the Himalayas, from Monyul eastward to the Tsang-po gorges, in a series of expeditions. Their first was unlucky; they were delayed by waiting for travel permits, the monsoon, and then malaria, and the results were generally disappointing. As if to make up for this, their next hunt, in 1936, was one of their most successful. They made their way to an area which Kingdon-Ward had visited the year before—the Tsari-chu valley, where all grazing and cultivation had been wisely forbidden by the Tibetan authorities—and found it another small paradise of flowers. From this journey they brought back two thousand specimens, boxes of living plants, and quantities of seeds which included thirteen new rhododendrons and fourteen new primulas.

In 1938 Sherriff travelled alone to central Bhutan, but in the following year he and Ludlow went back again to Tibet to take up their explorations where they had left off, and this time they were joined by Dr. George Taylor—later Sir George and another director of Kew. That season produced many more primula and rhododendron species, and probably what was their most important introduction, the tree Peony, *Paeonia lutea* var. *ludlowii*.[11] After the Second World War they made two further expeditions, in 1946–47 and 1949 and then both of them retired to England—Ludlow to Kew, and Sherriff to an estate in

---

[11] The easiest and most accommodating of the tree peonies, and among the best of garden shrubs. In my own garden near London it grows to eight feet high, carries flowers like giant buttercups in the terminal sprays of elegant, deeply cut leaves, and seeds itself around with almost reckless abandon.

Scotland where he grew almost entirely Himalayan plants with outstanding success; the climate, after all, is not dissimilar. Since that time the areas in which they and Kingdon-Ward worked with such distinction have become another world.

(9)
Today and Tomorrow

Kingdon-Ward and Ludlow and Sherriff in their specialized areas of the Himalayas and Tibet have brought us up to the nineteen-fifties, but in the earlier years there were other not so well known collectors working elsewhere. In 1925, H. F. Comber was making invaluable finds in the southern Andes, on the Chile-Argentine borders; an important and nearly hardy form of the showy Firebush with racemes of brilliant scarlet flowers, *Embothrium coccineum*, new species of berberis and varieties of alstroemeria. Two years later he was followed by Clarence Elliot, the nurseryman, and Dr. W. Balfour-Gourlay, who was collecting for Kew and Edinburgh botanic gardens. They introduced or re-introduced many more plants, bulbs of the beautiful blue and white Glory of the Sun, *Leucocoryne ixioides*—which in milder winter areas can be grown quite successfully in a sunny, sheltered spot facing south—and fresh seeds of *Alstroemeria violacea*. Then from a second expedition still farther south in 1929–30 they brought back the odd and gaily patterned but difficult little rock garden plant, *Calceolaria darwinii*, a new white form of *Fuchsia magellanica*, and yet more species of alstroemeria—the parents of most of our colorful modern hybrids of this so-called Lily of Peru. At about the same time Comber went on to Australia for a private syndicate of gardeners headed by Lionel de Rothschild and brought 130 new species of plants from Tasmania.

In 1927 also Collingwood Ingram, Dr. George Taylor—who eleven years later was to explore with Ludlow and Sherriff in Tibet—Laurence Johnstone, and Reginald Cory were in South Africa, though under rather different conditions from the early pioneering days, for where Masson, Thunberg, and Burchell travelled ponderously by ox wagon these sped on their way in automobiles and accomplished a six thousand mile round trip in three months, only making detours and stopping to collect where plant hunting seemed promising. Ingram was particularly interested in gladioli and found nearly a hundred species, several of them so far unknown and others already described but lost to cultivation. Among these was another of Africa's botanical oddities; the Brown Afrikander known to Thunberg, *Gladiolus liliaceus,* which has the extraordinary habit of changing the color of its flower from rusty brown by day to a pale faintly luminous blue at night and then turning back to brown again in the morning. Flowers that mature from one color to another, generally from pink to blue or from yellow to pink are by no means unusual, but one that can change in less than an hour and at the same time develop a strong nocturnal perfume is unique.[1]

Dr. Taylor later returned to Africa with Patrick M. Synge of the Royal Horticultural Society—who had previously explored in Borneo—on the second British Museum Expedition to Uganda in 1934–35. This was not primarily concerned with botany but Taylor and Synge accompanied it to make a survey of the flora of the Ruwenzori Range, the Mountains of the Moon, where it was hoped to find plants at such altitudes that they might prove reasonably hardy in cultivation. A number were introduced, including species of giant lobelia, hypericum, and impatiens but few if any seem to have survived though one at least in *Delphinium macrocentron* might pay for re-introduction. This is tantalizingly described as bearing large greenish blue florets on twenty-inch stems, flowers in October and is said to be easily raised from seed sown in gentle heat early in the year.

Since the war, with the devious politics of the new democracies, nearly one fifth of the world has become closed to us; in these wide, cool, and temperate areas still untouched by urban development and intensive cultivation we might reasonably expect as yet unknown hardy plants to exist. We do not know what remains in China, Tibet, the mountain fringes of Northern India, much of Central Asia, and Siberia. It is possible there is not very much, but something may still be hidden there. As long ago as 1927 E. H. Wilson considered that plant hunting was nearly finished and said in his book of that title that the world's

[1] Described by Collingwood Ingram in the *Journal of the Royal Horticultural Society,* vol. XCII, 9, September 1967. Not all forms of the species show this change. Thunberg named it *G. grandis,* it was later known as *G. versicolor,* and now seems to have settled at *G. liliaceus.*

flora was then almost an open book—yet many discoveries have been made since. Even much nearer home and as recently as 1966 a group of some sixty specimens of a new terrestrial orchid was discovered growing in Spain.[2]

Of recent years interest has turned again to southeastern Europe and the countries of the Middle East, Turkey, Persia, and Afghanistan extending eastward to India, some of the areas historically the gardens of the world, where Western horticulture found its earliest origins, and the natural home of the tulip and crocus, many of the most exotic species of iris, fritillaria, colchicum and the yellow *Delphinium zalil*. Some of the longest established plants in our gardens today found their way west from this area centuries before systematic plant hunting began, largely because its flora contains a higher proportion of bulbous and cormous plants than that of any other region of the world. As long ago as 1504 it was written "Tulips of many colours cover these hills. I once counted them up; it came out to thirty-two or thirty-three different sorts."

In these countries Admiral Paul Furse and Mrs. Furse have been the most regular travellers since their first journey in 1960, and have explored the tributaries of the River Oxus to the borders of Pakistan, bringing back thousands of plants and bulbs and quantities of seed from a terrain which at times must rival, even if it does not surpass, Tibet in richness and diversity. They speak, for instance, of the valley of Kashgar (1962) where they found banks of Judas trees covered in crimson purple flowers with kingfishers flying among them; or sheets of the yellow Fox Tail lily, eremurus, two to three feet high and as thick as a buttercup field (Afghanistan 1964), and along with many other irises a magnificent regelia with ash white flowers veined in blackish purple. More expeditions have followed since—their own and those of other collectors working generally for Kew and Edinburgh botanic gardens and the Royal Horticultural Society—and there is little doubt that these regions, which range from near desert and sun-baked plains to fertile river valleys and high peaks still have much to give—perhaps new species or

[2] A subspecies of Dactylorhiza. Described by A. J. Huxley and P. F. Hunt in the *Journal of the Royal Horticultural Society*, vol. XCII, 7, July 1967.

subspecies and varieties, and certainly plants that although known to botanists are still rare in cultivation.

The few remaining unexplored or incompletely explored regions lie mainly in the mountains and forests of the tropics, and here the enthusiastic amateur is now giving way to professional teams of highly trained specialists working for national bodies with a wide range of interests. In 1964 a party sponsored jointly by the British Museum and the University of Newcastle-upon-Tyne with assistance from the Australian government went to the Finisterre Mountains of New Guinea, a country which has the richest orchid flora in the world, consisting of some 130 genera with upwards of 2,600 distinct species. Two fresh journeys to Sir Hugh Low's old hunting ground in Borneo, Mount Kinabalu, were made for the Royal Society in 1961 and 1964 followed by another to the British Solomon Islands during the next year. There was an extended expedition in 1967–69 to Mato Grosso in Brazil—a vast area covering the southern tributaries of the Amazon— where the three botanists Philcox, Harley, and Ratter between them collected some 8,000 herbarium specimens including about 50 new species. At the same time (1968), farther to the north an American group from the New York Botanic Garden was making one more exploration in a series of surveys in the main area of the Amazon, and in 1971 another expedition went out for the Royal Society to the New Hebrides, the Anglo-French islands, with a localized flora, lying in the South Pacific roughly midway between Fiji and the west coast of Australia.

One of the most interesting of recent explorations was the expedition to Mount Roraima from July to September 1971. This was sponsored by the Scientific Exploration Society, the Royal Geographical Society, and the British Museum, and led by the zoologist Adrian Warren with David Philcox of the Royal Botanic Gardens, Kew, as botanist. Roraima is a curious plateau just over nine thousand feet high lying between Guyana, Venezuela, and Brazil on the watershed of the Mazuruni River and the Caroni, which flows out to the Orinoco. If it was known to Sir Arthur Conan Doyle sixty-three years ago he might almost have used it

A part of the Royal Botanic Gardens, Kew, London, showing the American Swamp Cypress, *Taxodium distichum*. Courtesy of the Controller, Her Majesty's Stationery Office, and the Director, Royal Botanic Gardens, Kew.

The home of the high alpines; in the Austrian Alps. Photo by the author.

as the setting for his novel, *The Lost World*. It is matched a few miles
away by the twin peak of Mount Kukenaam in Venezuela, and rises on
the eastern or Guyanan approach through tropical rain forest to finish
with practically unclimbable two thousand-foot precipices. Before 1971
it was totally unexplored from the Guyanan side. It also enjoys the
somewhat uneasy distinction of being the meeting place of three
frontiers on a few square miles of high, rocky plateau. As we have seen
elsewhere the possibilities for obstruction on any frontier are considerable; where three meet they are almost infinite, given a little diplomatic
ingenuity.

The party arrived in Georgetown in Guyana at the end of July and at
once the political difficulties began to develop. It had been intended to
move on to both mountains from the west, where the ascent though still
by no means easy was at least possible, but for some never to be
explained reason this apparently simple approach did not satisfy the
several authorities concerned. With a very expensive expedition and a
limited season it looked at one point as if the project would have to be
abandoned with nothing achieved. Philcox was kept busy negotiating in
Spanish, Portuguese and English, and eventually it was decided to make
an aerial reconnaissance of the Guyanan fringes of the mountain in the
hope of finding a practicable route from the east. From the air they saw
great waterfalls, previously unknown, plunging down from the heights
and a ridge breaking up through the clouds of the rain forest to the
precipices. This looked as difficult as it later turned out to be but it was
the only possible ascent, and it was better to attempt that than to turn
back.

Speed was now essential even for a limited survey of the plateau. An
advance group was sent out and landed by parachute to prepare
forward camps, probably for the first time in the history of plant
hunting; food and heavy equipment was dropped in free fall, while the
main party followed up by canoe from its base at Makuripai on the
Kako River. Then came a five week advance which could not have been
unlike some of Kingdon-Ward's early experiences in Burma. It rained
incessantly and steamy daytime temperatures varied only between 75°
and 85°F.; the first part of the journey was by flooded rivers against the
current, and the final ascent on foot began through a permanently

sodden moss forest with the added attractions of scorpions, poisonous snakes, and spiders. Fires were impossible, in the hot humidity clothes and boots rotted almost visibly, and in the last stages of the climb they passed through an area of permanent mist where everything, tree trunks, rocks and ground, was covered with thick, black slime.

At last, however, they broke through the cloud belt to get their first clear view of the massive cliffs of Roraima towering above them for a further two thousand feet. It was a magnificent sight but hardly an encouraging one, for when they got to within 1,800 feet of the summit it became quite clear that any further ascent was impossible, and at this point too one of the party went down with suspected appendicitis. They were forced to get back as fast as they could and, carrying their companion by relays in a hammock slung from poles, they made an incredible twenty-four hour non-stop night and day descent to their base camp on the river and the canoes; the difficulties of carrying a painfully sick man through those soaking and treacherous forests in darkness leave little to the imagination, but he did recover.

It might seem that the expedition had been a failure. But a new route to the mountain had been surveyed, the extent and altitude of several genera had been plotted for the first time, and Philcox had made nearly six hundred collections, mostly of orchids, bromeliads[3] and species of *Utricularia* or bladderwort,[4] including one which is unique to Roraima, an epiphytic giant form which grows from the leaf axils of a bromeliad and carries three or four inch flowers on three foot stems. These living

---

[3] The family Bromeliaceae—based on the type genus *Bromelia* which is named after the seventeenth-century Swedish botanist, Bromel—covers upwards of fifty genera, known at present, in more than a thousand species, nearly all natives of tropical America and the West Indies. It includes such diverse plants as the pineapple, the Brazilian *Billbergia iridifolia*, with showy bracts, and such popular house plants as *Vriesia tesselata, Aechmea rhodocyanea*, and *Neoregelia carolinae tricolor*. Most bromeliads produce a rosette of fleshy leaves around a cup-like depression used in nature to catch rainwater.

[4] The bladderworts are a much more interesting family than their common name suggests. They range from the simple aquatic species of North America and Europe to tropical terrestrial types and epiphytes—which grow on other plants without actually being parasitic. They are all insectivorous, and they trap and digest their food in the little sacs or bladders which give them their name, the Latin *utriculus*, a bag. Few families show such a diversity of form and habit and, as Philcox says of them, "You name it; they have it."

plants, like Farrer's gentians on the Trans-Siberian Railway nearly sixty years before, now had to endure the trials of the journey back—off loading from the canoes and reloading at every stage, changes in humidity, widely different temperatures from night to day and from the slopes of Roraima to the heat of Georgetown. Nevertheless losses were surprisingly light, and once they had been flown back to Kew and safely established in the propagating houses there the survival rate since has been nearly seventy per cent. These were the first plants ever to be collected and distributed from this area.

David Philcox is one of the new generation of specialized scientific botanists. Born in 1926 and trained at Leicester University, he worked for a time in the Department of Botany of Brighton Technical College, went to the Royal Botanic Gardens in 1959, and travelled on four other expeditions—mainly in Nigeria and Brazil—before going to Roraima. He firmly rejects the idea that plant hunting is finished and in his opinion there is still much to be found; perhaps new genera and certainly new species. But his work lies generally in the tropics and his botanical interest in three extraordinarily diverse families. Whether we shall ever see much more that is distinctively new in hardy garden plants might be open to doubt, but there is an Arabic proverb to the effect that under God all things are possible. We may be entitled to hope that even if the world's flora is now an open book there still may be some pages left to turn over.

General Index

203

Index of Plant Names

211

E₁